03/10/23
15/11/23 return to Desk

Voice

Chris

In order to avoid charges, please return or renew this item by the last date shown.

www.ealing.gov.uk

London Borough of Ealing
Library Service

Montage: thanks to the design department at Liverpool Hope University

VOICES FROM THE WEST BANK

Chris Jones
and
Michael Lavalette

Voices from the West Bank
Chris Jones and Michael Lavalette

First published in September 2011 by Bookmarks Publications
c/o 1 Bloomsbury Street, London WC1B 3QE
© Bookmarks Publications

Cover design by Constantinos Vakakis.
The cover includes the cartoon figure of Handala; his image can be
found all over the West Bank. This Palestinian boy, created by the
murdered Palestinian cartoonist Naji al-Ali, represents the poorest and
the most oppressed of Palestinians and has become one of the most
popular symbols of the Palestinian resistance.

Typeset by Bookmarks Publications
Printed by Halstan Printing Group

ISBN 978 1 90519 282 3

Contents

Acknowledgements

This book, more than most, is the product of many people's efforts and contributions. We have been moved and changed by the experience. Our debts range far and wide. But in the final analysis what has been included between these covers is our responsibility alone and while we hope that we have done justice to all those who contributed there can be no assumption that they would endorse all our points and conclusions.

First and foremost we would like to thank all the young people who gave up their time to talk to us – a number of them even agreed to speak to us more than once. Without them this book would not have been possible. We hope they agree with our decision to anonymise them by using alternative Arabic names. It was a decision we took with their safety in mind. A few lines at the start of the book seems an inadequate recompense for the hours of time they gave up and their enthusiasm and support.

Many families offered us their homes and provided us with drinks and food – even when they had little themselves. Palestinian hospitality is renowned and they are, without doubt, among the most generous and genuine people we have ever come across. This book has been enriched by the hours we spent in the company of new friends eating, drinking tea and chatting in Biet Leed, Tulkarm, Nablus, Jenin, Qalqilya, Ramallah, Aboud and East Jerusalem.

Although we have both had a longstanding interest in the Palestinian struggle, these became much more clearly focused after we organised a trip to the West Bank for anti-war activists in 2004. The trip consisted of trade unionists, local politicians, activists from the anti-war movement, Christian and Muslim activists and social justice campaigners. We would like to thank them all for their engagement on that first trip – and would especially like to thank Mukhtar Master for his help and support.

In Palestine our research has been helped by the immense time and support given by Ihsan Rajab and his wonderful family and by the extended Amara family in Tulkarm. Firas Helou and Joumana Joubran read, commented and encouraged us with the book and made us very welcome in their home in Nazareth. Ala Yousuf in Nablus provided access to the Palestinian National Photograph Archive and his media unit at An-Najah University met every request for help with generosity. We were also inspired and helped by the volunteer staff and members of the Yaffa Centre in the Balata refugee camp, at the Youth Centre in the Al-Amari refugee camp and by the activists with the Disability Project in the Jenin refugee camp who we met on a number of occasions.

Several people read the book, or parts of the book, and made a host of important suggestions to improve the text. We owe much to Tony Novak, who commented upon and proofread our script several times, Laura Penketh, who read chunks at various times during the book's germination, and at Bookmarks Sally Campbell, Colin Barker and Mark Harvey who did likewise. Vassilis Ioakimidis accompanied us on our penultimate research trip and his help is much appreciated.

Some of our students provided photographs from a field trip we organised to the West Bank. Thanks to Katie Pritchard, Andy Deaves, Nicki Mitchell and Katy Blease. And a very big efharisto to our talented cover designer, Costas Vakakis.

But this book would have been impossible without the particular help of Mohammed Amara. He organised our trips, sought out interviewees, translated the discussions we had, housed us, fed us, kept us safe and made us feel part of his family. His support for this project never wavered and was unconditional. For his help, support and solidarity we'd like to dedicate this book to him.

**For our dear friend and comrade
Mohammed Amara**

Thawra Hatta al Nas'r
(Revolution until victory)

Glossary

Spellings Those of you familiar with maps of Palestine will be aware that some place names vary in spelling depending on variations of the anglicised spelling of Arabic names. We have opted for the names which are closest to the Arabic, hence Tulkarm instead of Tulkarem and Qalqilya instead of Kalkilya and so on.

Areas A, B and C Following the 1993 Oslo Accords the West Bank was divided into three administrative areas. Area A is under PA control and administration and comprises 17 percent of the land and 55 percent of the population, including all the main Palestinian towns and cities. Area B remains under Israeli control but is administered by the PA and embraces 24 percent of the land and 41 percent of the population. Area C, which is 59 percent of the West Bank, remains under full Israeli control and includes all the settlements, the linking roads, all the Jordan Valley and the southern desert. Just 4 percent of the Palestinian population is in Area C.

Dunam A unit of land measure used widely in the region dating back to the Ottoman period. It has slightly varying values according to the country in question, but in Palestine since the 1920s a dunam has signified 1,000 square metres or 0.25 acres.

Fatah Fatah is a major Palestinian political party and the largest faction of the PLO. It was formed in 1959 mainly by Palestinians resident in Egypt, including Yasser Arafat. It rose to prominence following the Six-Day War in 1967 and is mainly nationalist, and not predominantly socialist. It dominated Palestinian politics until it lost the 2006 general election to Hamas. Fatah continues to control the West Bank and the PA, although it too is subject to fractures especially between the "old" guard dominated by

Mahmoud Abbas and the "young" guard in the Al Aqsa Martyrs Brigade and around Marwan Barghouti.

Green Line Refers to the 1949 armistice line that separated Israel from the West Bank (then under Jordanian control). After the 1967 war the "line" only nominally separated Israel from the West Bank as Israel controlled the entire area. After the Oslo Accord the Palestinian Authority gained some control over some areas within the West Bank. The Separation Wall is not being built along the Green Line (the 1967 border) but beyond the line, in effect absorbing a large part of the West Bank into Israel.

Hamas Founded in 1987 very much under the influence of the Muslim Brotherhood, this Islamist political party gained sufficient popular support to win the 2006 general election. Its popularity was rooted in its unwavering opposition to the Oslo Accords and the so-called peace process, in its reputation for being "clean" (unlike Fatah) and not least in its social welfare activities on which it spends over 90 percent of its overall income of $70 million a year. These welfare services have been a lifeline to many, especially in Gaza. Its Islamist outlook is much exaggerated in the Western media over its other characteristics.

IDF The Israeli Defence Forces, including army, navy and air force and formed in 1948. The IDF built on earlier Jewish militias fighting the British and the Arabs in Palestine during the Mandate period (1920-48). With some exceptions among orthodox fractions, all Israeli Jews are subject to conscription (men for longer than women) and compulsory reserve service. The IDF is a major institution of the Israeli state, actively involved in education, manufacturing industries, politics and government, which makes it distinct from other comparable societies where the military profile is low. Renowned for its arrogant claims to be the "most moral army in the world", and for its embeddedness in the US military industrial complex.

Incursions The name given to raids of IDF soldiers into West Bank towns and cities and above all refugee camps. These raids can vary from rapid hit-and-run raids involving one jeep and four soldiers to larger attacks with many soldiers in APCs (armoured personnel carriers) and Humvees, the all-purpose large jeep so popular with the IDF.

Nakba Nakba is an Arabic word meaning "grievous tragedy". It has been used in Arab countries since 1948 to describe the events surrounding the ethnic cleansing of Palestine that accompanied the creation of the state of Israel

OPT Occupied Palestinian Territories. Name used commonly by official bodies such as the United Nations for all the Palestinian lands occupied by Israel including the West Bank, Gaza and Jerusalem.

PA The Palestinian Authority, which was created in 1994 as part of the Oslo Accords and was to last initially for five years as the parties negotiated to a final settlement. Under these accords the West Bank and Gaza was subdivided (see Areas A, B and C, above) with the PA bearing the costs of sustaining the majority of the Palestinian population. Its power is severely curtailed and monitored by Israel, and its internal legitimacy has been challenged since the general election of 2006 and the subsequent schism which left Hamas in control in Gaza.

PFLP The Popular Front for the Liberation of Palestine, founded in 1967, is the second largest group within the PLO and is Marxist in orientation.

PLO The Palestine Liberation Organisation, founded in the mid-1960s. It is recognised as the "sole legitimate representative" of the Palestinian people by over 100 states with which it holds diplomatic relations, and has enjoyed observer status at the UN since 1974. It is an umbrella organisation currently including ten factions. Fatah is the largest and controlling group and has been since the PLO's inception.

Shekel Israeli currency used throughout the West Bank and Gaza. In 2011 one US dollar bought 3.5 shekels and one British pound bought around six shekels.

The Wall Also known as the Apartheid Wall and the Fence in the West Bank, or the Separation Barrier in Israel. In this book we refer to this affront to humanity as the Wall even though only about 10 percent of its length is built with 10 metre high concrete slabs, the rest being high-security wire fencing decorated with surveillance systems.

Prologue

The Amara family: a Palestinian story

Abu Mohammed Amara

My name is Abu Mohammed and I am 78 years old, but sometimes I feel as if I have only lived for 14 years.

I was born in a village near the Mediterranean called Messka. It had a population of about 1,000 in 1948. Messka is 15 kilometres south-west of Tulkarm, where I live with my family today. But though I live such a short distance from my home and land it feels like a different world.

In Messka I lived with my parents, grandparents and three

Abu Mohammed Amara (centre, with his wife and students from Liverpool Hope University) sisters. Everyone in our village was a farmer and even the smallest farm was over 100 acres in size. Our farm grew olives, oranges, apples, apricots, wheat and lots of vegetables. It had been in our family for generations, for thousands of years. But in April 1948 we were forced to leave our land and our village.

At first we moved to a small village near Tulkarm called Tira. Messka and Tira are both inside Israel today. The villagers were warned by the [Zionist] paramilitary forces not to give us and other refugees houses but, despite this, we were given accommodation in the village.

These photographs are courtesy of the Palestinian Photography Archive, An-Najah University

Above, original photos from the early days of the Balata refugee camp

Bottom right, by the late 1950s tents were replaced by prefab housing

But the conditions were very bad. It was like living under house arrest. We were told to stay inside the houses and this meant we couldn't work and the villagers had to provide us with food – we couldn't even go to the mosque in case we were spotted by the paramilitaries.

Life in the village was so bad that in 1950 our family decided to move to the newly established refugee camp in Tulkarm, one of the larger towns in the West Bank.

The new Israeli forces [as the paramilitaries had become] were happy to see the family and those like us move to the

camps, because they were outside of Israel. Tulkarm was then
under Jordanian control.

When we moved into the camp we lived in a tent, which
became our home for the next ten years. We had to get our
water from stand-pipes and the toilet facilities were very poor.
The pathways were just dirt roads which meant that, in the
winter, we were wading through knee-deep mud. In the summer the tents were baking hot; in the winter they were freezing
cold. Tents are no good in these sorts of conditions and this cli-
mate. There were six of us living like this, in one tent.

Eventually, after ten years, the tents were replaced by
small homes. This was better than a tent but it was still very
cramped.

Left and above, some
of the few remaining
"prefab" homes

The camp was not allowed to expand beyond its original
border. After ten years there were more children in the camp
and more people wanting to marry and have families of their
own. Myself, I have 13 children, 58 grandchildren and now I
have some great-grandchildren!

Top right, Tulkarm
camp today

As families have grown in size, houses have had to be built
up – now they run to two, three or sometimes four levels.

The houses have had to be packed in close to one another, with often less than a metre separating them. The connecting pathways are narrow and inaccessible to vehicles; everything has to be carried in on your back.

In 1967 the Jordanians were replaced by the Israelis. The people who had stolen our land now directly controlled our lives and movements around the Tulkarm camp. This led to great frustrations.

My son joined Fatah. He was arrested in 1985, and they then came and arrested me as well – just because my son was a

fighter. My first wife had her leg blown off by the Israelis, one of my sons was shot by undercover agents who entered our camp, two more of my sons have spent time in prison and now two of my grandsons are in prison because they joined the Al Aqsa Martyrs Brigade – this is what the Israeli occupation has done to my family.

Life for us is very hard. But we have our health, we have our family and with God's help we will soon have our land.

Abu Omar Amara
(son)

Abu Omar Amara

My name is Abu Omar. I was born in Tulkarm refugee camp in 1962. I am the oldest of my father's sons and was brought up with my mother, father and 12 brothers and sisters in a single-roomed hut.

When I was young the Israelis took over Tulkarm after the 1967 war. Life was very tough. All the time we were treated like second-class people in our own land. So when I was 21 I decided to go to Jordan and join the PLO.

I was trained and sent back to Palestine, but I was captured while carrying out my activities as a quartermaster.

I was sent to prison for four years on 9 June 1985. They let me out in June 1989, but in November 1989 I was arrested and placed in "administrative detention". I hadn't done any-thing – and never knew what charges were against me – but this is what they do and this is our life. I got out this time in June 1990, but not long after the first Gulf War started I was arrested again and imprisoned, again in administrative deten-tion, from February to August 1991.

During the five years of imprisonment they moved me from jail to jail. Sometimes I was in prison in the West Bank and sometimes I was in what they call Israel. The worst was the Negev prison, in the desert in the south of old Palestine. The conditions were terrible, with several of us living in tents. The days were very hot and the nights extremely cold.

But in prison I learned a great deal. I learned about the Palestinian struggle and our history, I read about politics and learned to speak English and Hebrew. We had regular classes, organised by the prisoners, which filled our days and deepened our understanding of our situation.

Most importantly I learned about solidarity and support – we prisoners were always very well organised, very disciplined and very supportive of each other. Inside the prisons we kept up our struggle and our resistance to the Israelis. On one occasion, in March 1987, I was involved in a hunger strike for 20 days to make sure we had our rights to food, televisions and visits.

In between prison terms I got married and I now have four children. I also came out of prison and joined in the activities during the First Intifada. I was in charge of building the Popular Committees for Education, Health and First Aid, and Socio-Economic Support across the northern West Bank region.

In 1990 I started to work within the PGFTU [Palestinian General Federation of Trade Unions]. I have spoken at many international gatherings of trade unionists where I tell fellow workers about our struggle and try to raise solidarity.

In 1995 I decided to go to university. It's difficult with the incursions and with the army – they disrupt our education in so many ways. I finished my BA in 2000 and my MA in 2009. I was studying for my MA right through the Second Intifada – on many days it was impossible to travel from Tulkarm to Nablus, so the degree took a long time.

I am the oldest son in a refugee family that now covers four generations. I have family responsibilities. I have to make sure that we are safe and strong as a family. I have nephews in prison and a brother who is disabled because of the Israelis. I have to make sure that their family is properly supported.

I am more confident today than ever before that we will one day return to our home and our land – there is no alternative. The Israelis want to destroy us. There is no peace process: for us, as refugees, we have to continue our struggle for dignity and our struggle for our rights.

My name is Mohammed. I live in the refugee camp, next door to my grandfather in a house that my family has built. It is a three storey house and I live there with my mother and father, two older brothers, two older sisters, three younger brothers and younger sister. I also have two brothers who are in prison – one due out soon and one who is serving 15 years for being a member of the Al Aqsa Martyrs Brigade.

Living all your life in a refugee camp is tough. There are always incursions into the camp. There are spies and undercover agents – all the time you have to be wary, and this is very stressful.

Mohammed Amara
(grandson)

School is overcrowded and the books are not very good. The schools in the camps are not as good as those elsewhere in the West Bank.

When I was younger I wanted to be a basketball player. I am over two metres in height and I am good at the game. We play all the time in the camp. I tried to get a contract in the Gulf and my uncle was trying to help me, but it didn't work out.

Three years ago I decided that I would go to look for work in Israel – there are no jobs for people like me in Tulkarm or in the West Bank.

I travel to work in Israel and go for up to three months at a time. I can earn money and I am saving up to get married and perhaps start a business back home. But it is not so great working like this. I have to be smuggled across the border, I work illegally and I have to hide away during the evenings and weekends.

I have been arrested several times by the Israeli police. I'm put in prison as an illegal worker. I am not with other Palestinians but with Russians and Israeli criminals – but what am I to do? How else can I earn money? What other future do I have?

Introduction

In September 2004 we were both part of an anti-war delegation that went to the Palestinian West Bank. For 13 days we moved between Jerusalem, Bethlehem, Ramallah and Nablus. Although we have both been politically active for a long time and both felt well-versed in the Palestinian struggle the experience was, nevertheless, shocking.

The reality of Palestine is hard to describe. Israeli checkpoints, armoured vehicles and young conscripts are everywhere. The refugee camps are wracked by poverty and the visible results of armed "incursions" (bullet holes, bombed out homes, destroyed infrastructure, etc). Everywhere you look there are posters of young Palestinians who have been killed by the Israeli armed forces or those who have been sent to Israeli jails.

On every street corner there are groups of people, old and young, hanging about, chatting and generally filling their time as best they can. The environment is strewn with rubbish and each evening skips full of refuse are set on fire – sending noxious fumes, ash and smoke across the towns and camps.

Schools and universities are overcrowded; the buildings are stark, with the signs of conflict visible in the play areas and on the walls.

The UN and their white cars are everywhere – as indeed are a range of international charities and non-governmental organisations, who announce their support for various welfare and infrastructural projects on large billboards in towns and cities across the region.

The Occupied Territories of the Palestinian West Bank feel very much part of the "Third World".

Making this situation even more strange is the fact that you are never very far away from "the Zionist entity" – Israel. Like most visitors we arrived in Tel Aviv at Ben Gurion airport, travelled along the motorways to Jerusalem (known to the Arabs as Al Quds) where we entered the western part of the city first.

West Jerusalem is very much like any west European city. It is full of designer shops, street cafes, bars and all the symbols of modern global capitalism. Israel is a European settler society. Just a short step away are the West Bank and Gaza: impoverished "Bantustans" like those in apartheid South Africa.

But while the reality of seeing and experiencing such things had an impact upon us – and enriched our knowledge of Palestine drawn from years of reading – it was our encounter with three generations of the Amara family that really brought home to us the plight of the Palestinians. The Amara family story is briefly summarised in our Prologue. It is a typical story, similar to many others we were to hear over subsequent years.

What struck us about the Amara family's stories were the expressions of pain, trauma and injustice that had carried on down the generations – but also their unswerving commitment to resistance and the struggle for Palestinian liberation.

As we talked with the family we started to wonder what ordinary life was like for Palestinians on the West Bank. Abu Mohammed's story reflects the pain of forced migration and a deep sense of loss that is sadly captured when an old man says he has "only lived for 14 years". There were hints in Abu Omar's story about the pressure of family responsibility in a life shaped by poverty and military occupation, of the struggle for education and about resistance. Young Mohammed's story reflects the frustration of a generation blighted at every turn by poverty, by the Wall and by a society offering few, if any, opportunities for any kind of stable life.

And so the Amara family's story got us thinking. Although we had read widely about the origins of what is euphemistically called the "Palestinian problem", about the Balfour Agreement and the role of British imperialism in the creation of the state of Israel, about colonial settlement and the ethnic cleansing of Arabs in the late 1940s and about Israel's continuing role as an imperial "watchdog state" in the Middle East, we were less clear about what Palestinians thought about all this today.[1]

We knew something about the Nakba and the history of Zionist settlement, but how did this impact on young Palestinians in the 21st century? We knew some things about the occupation, but what did it mean for Palestinians on a daily basis? We knew there were checkpoints everywhere in Palestine, but is it possible to get used to such monstrosities? Can checkpoints be "normalised"? We knew that there are large numbers of Palestinians under arrest at any given time, but how does imprisonment or the threat of imprisonment affect people? We knew that there were regular "incursions" by military forces into Palestinian areas and that this resulted in significant injury and death, but how did young people and their families cope with such constant mortal danger? We knew some things about the refugee camps, but what did second and third generation refugees think of their lives? What were their hopes, dreams and fears?

There were so many questions, to which we had many partial answers but what was missing most, we felt, was any sense of a Palestinian voice.

When we returned home we thought about these issues and decided that we wanted to go back to the West Bank and talk to young Palestinians about their daily experiences and the events that confront them. We wanted to explore their stories in their terms.

We focused on young people for a number of reasons. First Palestine, like much of the Arab world, has a very young demographic. The villages, towns, cities and camps are full of young people who play on the streets, hang around, laugh, shout – and, for some of the youngest, follow Westerners around with the constant refrain (in English): "Hello, what's your name?" (After a few trips visiting the same centres and camps this changed, as some of the young people would tell their friends that it was "Chrismichael" who was coming back – our names and identities seemingly merged into a single whole!) In this young society the young are the future and we wanted to explore their reality and their hopes and dreams.

Second, it was the young men (the "*Shabab*" – the lads) who were at the forefront of the struggles of the Second Intifada, who staffed the brigades, went on the marches, led the school and university protests and, as a result, found themselves shot at, arrested and harassed by the misnamed Israeli Defence Forces. This was a young society that was engaged in rebellion and subjected to trauma; we wanted to find out what young people thought of it all.

Finally we thought that young people might also be more open and critical about a range of aspects that have shaped Palestinian society. We wanted to explore divisions within Palestinian society. In the West people tend to homogenise the Palestinian experience. This is understandable, but even the shortest trip to the West Bank will quickly reveal that Palestine is subject to all sorts of social divisions and we wanted to explore these. We wanted to look at how young people felt about being excluded within Palestine, we wanted to explore

Map key
■ Full Palestinian control
Palestinian civil/Israeli security
□ Full Israeli control

This map shows some of the towns we visited. It also shows the stranglehold Israel has on the West Bank – even those areas controlled by the PA are separated off from each other

class and gender divisions, we wanted to look at schooling and education and we wanted to look at what is available for young people by way of leisure and pastimes.

But we were not rigid with our boundaries. Much modern academic social science is divided between "childhood" studies, "youth" studies and concerns with transitions across the life course. None of this really interested us here. We are both academics, but we despair at rigid academic boundaries – and in any case, we see ourselves as activists as much as researchers. Some of the people we spoke to were as young as eight, the majority were between 15 and 20, some were as old as 24. When it was relevant we talked to youth workers, some in their early and mid-twenties and some older; when we explored the working conditions in the "export zones" we talked to young workers, but also to older trade unionists from the Palestinian General Federation of Trade Unions (PGFTU). Our starting point was always an interview or a discussion with groups of young people, but once an issue had been raised we interviewed anyone who we thought could shed some light on what was happening.

Following our first excursion in September 2004 we planned a series of research trips that would take up chunks of the next six years. We returned to Palestine for periods of 11 to 14 days in September 2006, February 2008, June 2009, September 2009 March 2010 and more briefly in January 2011. A trip planned for 2007 had to be abandoned because of the sudden eruption of fighting between Fatah and Hamas and there were several other disruptions during the period because of work and political commitments.

One issue we had to address was our lack of language skills. Neither of us spoke Arabic (and even now we only have the most rudimentary vocabulary). Being able to order coffee, water and falafel is useful for a short time in the Arab world, but doesn't help much when the aim is to interview lots of young people. This was not a problem at the Friends School in Ramallah, which we were to visit several times, as all the students spoke excellent English. But elsewhere language was an important issue.

Luckily our friend Abu Omar was to become a vital member of our research team. He became our guide and translator. A trade unionist with the PGFTU and a Master's social science student he quickly understood what we wanted to do and who we wanted to speak to. His ability to arrange our interviews, wherever we requested, whether in refugee camps, youth centres, isolated villages or universities, was extraordinary. He was able to translate questions, concepts, themes and answers back and forth. He is a man of many talents all infused with humour which did so much to enrich our discussions with all those we met. Abu Omar is an ex-prisoner and a longstanding member of Fatah within the West Bank (there are important differences between the Fatah of the "interior" and the Fatah leaders who, historically, spent much time outside Palestine in Jordan, Lebanon, Tunisia, etc). Yet despite his party loyalty, he never flinched when we asked questions or entered into debates about Fatah corruption, about Hamas or about the enrichment of a layer of Fatah government officials. Without him the project would have flopped; with him everything seemed possible.

On the first trip back, in September 2006, we tried to talk to as many young people as possible. We worked 12 full exhausting days and by the end of the trip had spoken to close to 300 young people. We spoke to groups of varying sizes (something that wasn't always within our control). In Jenin, for example, it was an unusual event for a couple of Westerners to want to talk to children. So though we hoped to have groups of about 15, we ended up with a chaotic group of 36, all of them thirsty to tell us their experiences. But what this first trip did do was to raise and identify common issues that young people felt were important to them.

We heard repeated stories of incursions and night raids and the brutality meted out to young people by the Israeli forces. We heard how education was important, but constantly disrupted. We learned that the refugee camps suffered most – in terms of harassment, poverty and overcrowding. We were told about youth trips and activities that were blocked by the Israelis. And in Balata refugee camp we spent a few hours talking to a traumatised group who were agitated and grieving because the previous day a young child had picked up what he thought was a chocolate bar, only to have his hand severely burnt by an Israeli incendiary device.

Our initial feeling that the Israelis particularly targeted the young seemed to be vindicated.

But such traumatic stories were also punctuated by moments of humour. In Jenin, for example, two boys told us about their recent experience of being tear-gassed on their way to school. They laughed and joked with us when they realised that we knew nothing about how to counter the effects of tear gas – it was just common sense to carry an onion! In September 2006 the US, EU and Israeli blockade of the West Bank was in full swing after the Palestinians had voted for Hamas in their recent elections (January 2006). There were few savings, no salaries and, on the radio, the most popular song was a lament sung by a man about a broken relationship: he no longer spent any time with the cash dispenser machine and he missed it so very much!

We also heard about the importance of solidarity and "*sammoud*" (steadfastness). This was revealed, we were told, by acts of resistance (and what was meant by this was very broad), by carrying on in the face of Israeli oppression and, in a sense, by a collective sheer bloody-mindedness not to be ground down by the Israeli presence.

On the next two trips (February 2008 and June 2009) we moved to smaller group sessions. Our groups were made up of approximately six to ten young people and we spent a couple of hours with each group discussing topics and themes we had identified from the first visit: travel and negotiating checkpoints, schooling, university life, imprisonment, resistance, poverty and inequality, gender differences, environmental questions, and sport, leisure and cultural activities. These sessions afforded us the opportunity to explore these issues in depth. Where possible we saw the same young people on both trips. Our sessions were very open-ended and many times the young people took the discussions in directions that we had not expected. With those who we were meeting for the second and third time the sessions were often particularly rich as we debated and explored their experiences and opinions together.

On our last two trips (September 2009 and March 2010) we narrowed our focus even further. We undertook interviews with particular individuals whose stories we wanted to explore in greater depth. Many of these sessions form the basis of the stand-alone mini life stories that punctuate the chapters that follow.

There are two final points that we need to make. The first is fairly straightforward. The Palestinian West Bank is under Israeli occupation and the IDF target young people, especially those between the ages of 16 and 35. Therefore to protect the identities of those we spoke to we have changed all our interviewees' names. We have reproduced as many direct quotations from Palestinian young people as possible. After the quotation is a made-up Palestinian name, followed by the actual location and the actual month and year in which the interview took place.

We also need to make clear who we were talking with in

another sense. In the chapters that follow we draw on material that we gathered from young Palestinians in the West Bank. We have also spent considerable time talking with Palestinians in the refugee camps in Lebanon and from "1948 Palestine" (their term for Israel), but have not included any of that material here (although one photograph from Bourj el Bourajni, Lebanon is included). We did not speak to people in Gaza. The majority of our time has been in the central and northern zones of the West Bank – that is in the towns and villages around Nablus, Jenin, Tulkarm and Ramallah – with a smaller number of interviews with people from the southern sector (Bethlehem, Hebron).

When we first started we fully intended to include young people from Gaza but for large periods of our research Gaza was isolated and movement in and out near impossible. In the West Bank movement was difficult in 2004, 2006 and 2008 (though nothing like Gaza) but much easier in 2009 and 2010. This in turn highlights an important point about the period we cover. There is a cliché that suggests that a week is a long time in politics; in Palestine, sometimes a day can alter the situation dramatically.

When we first went to the West Bank the Second Intifada was still under way. We had to be literally smuggled into Nablus in the early hours of the morning via a circuitous route that involved crossing fields to meet a contact at the other side. The entire West Bank was "locked down" and people were just pleased and astonished to see Europeans coming to listen to their stories.

In 2006 we arrived in the immediate aftermath of Hezbollah's stunning victory over Israel in the 33-day war. There were posters of Hezbollah's leader Nasrallah everywhere and their television station was watched in most households. This trip took place nine months after Hamas's election victory and the West Bank was suffering from the US, EU and Israeli blockade. The levels of poverty were extreme.

Our planned trip for 2007 was cancelled at three days' notice because fighting broke out between Hamas and Fatah. When we returned to the West Bank there was a noticeable difference – one that became clearer in the visits in 2009 and 2010. When Fatah took control of the West Bank it was plain that they had come to some sort of accommodation with Israel. Investment had started to flow into the towns and cities. There were large rebuilding programmes taking place. Movement became much easier. Share and trading centres opened. The West Bank started to "develop". But this "development" highlighted and exacerbated inequalities in the region and fuelled grumbles about Fatah corruption. And on the streets the numbers of Palestinians in uniforms grew in number.

Thus we visited the West Bank over six years, spoke to many of the same people on these visits, established strong bonds of friendship and solidarity with our Palestinian comrades, and did this against a shifting social and political backdrop that raised new and different questions for our young interviewees and ourselves to grapple with.

In the chapters that follow we present the findings of our conversations with Palestinian young people. The first three chapters are much more descriptive and raise issues that the young people brought to the discussions using their voices to highlight the issues they raise.

Chapter 1, tries to capture the pain, the trauma, the humour and the resilience of West Bank life through the eyes of its young people.

Chapter 2 is devoted to young people's experiences of checkpoints. Checkpoints dominated the West Bank for much of this period. They disrupt life in myriad ways. And they become a point of conflict. This chapter explores these issues in some depth.

Chapter 3 looks at the whole issue of arrest, interrogation, punishment and imprisonment. The Palestinians are among the most incarcerated people in the world. Over 40 percent of Palestinian young men will be in prison at some point in their lives. This chapter draws on the testimony of prisoners to look at the whole process of arrest and imprisonment and the struggle within the jails.

The next three chapters are more analytical in that they draw on wider literature in an attempt to understand the young people's stories and the context within which they take place. We utilise the interviewees' responses to explore West Bank life (chapter 4), a range of internal Palestinian divisions (class and gender divisions, political divisions) and their impact on social life (chapter 5) and conceptualisations of resistance (chapter 6). The book concludes with a discussion of some of the current pressure points including the growing presence of settlements and settlers in the West Bank and the contradictions and tensions of a PA which increasingly manages the occupation as Israel's proxy (chapter 7).

In 2009 and 2010 many of the young people we spoke to were less confident, in some respects, about their immediate Palestinian futures. The Second Intifada had ended. Fatah was

running the West Bank with a tight grip and clearly adopting
a model of development that involved compromises with both
the Israelis and the imperial powers that left many Palestinians
in a state of uncertainty.

Some interviewees talked about the need for a "Third
Intifada", others looked back to the models of resistance developed in the First Intifada, others raised the possibility of
leaving Palestine altogether. What was missing was an alternative strategy, an alternative vision of how Palestinian freedom
could be achieved.

Yet as we finished writing this book the Arab world was
torn asunder by the Tunisian and Egyptian revolutions. The
great movements of the Arab masses removed local dicta-
tors and raised a series of social and political demands that
have changed the face of Middle East politics. They also hold
out the possibility of a different, alternative solution to the
"Palestine problem".

In a straightforward armed struggle between Palestinian
resisters and the Israeli state forces the odds are always going
to be with the Israelis. In any mass campaign based solely in
the Occupied Territories the conflict is likely to be confused
because Israel has effectively diverted decision making about
a range of issues to the PA – and social demands are as likely
to target the PA as the Israeli state. Of course these struggles
are likely to erupt, but if their focus is contained within the
Occupied Territories they are unlikely to seriously challenge
the Israeli state.

The great Arab revolutions of 2011, however, open up
another possibility: a pan-Arab "permanent revolution", led
by Egypt's massive, organised working class and embracing the
entire Middle East. Any such movement has to address both
social and political demands: to confront local, corrupt leaders
as well as the imperial presence in the region and its local proxy
Israel. The revolutionary socialist Tony Cliff once claimed
that the road to Palestinian freedom ran through Cairo. The
events of 2011 make it clear what this road might look like.
In the clamour for regime change the people's demands for
justice, dignity and a life free of fear, whether caused by state
oppression or by poverty, have rung clear. The hurt of the Arab
peoples has a history across the region and nowhere more so
than in the case of Palestine. This historic hurt and the ongoing suffering of the Palestinians have always lived deep in
wider Arab consciousness and now, as their governments are
either swept aside or forced to listen to the people, the current

political settlements are unlikely to survive. A new political terrain is opening up and it is one that offers a glimpse of an alternative future in Palestine. It raises the possibility of bringing an end to over 60 years of hurt and occupation, of establishing the right of return for the refugees and of creating a democratic, secular Palestine where Muslims, Christians, Jews and atheists can live together as one.

Note

1 For those who are less familiar with the broader political and social history see the "further reading" in the Resources section at the end of this book.

Chapter 1

Laughter and tears

Imagine yourself as a bird flying around. But there are hunters all around. You never know when you are going to be shot down. This is our life under occupation.

Hassan, aged 16, Nablus, 2006

Kids in the Balata camp,[2] left

In Al-Amari camp, right

Walk through any West Bank town or village and you will see hundreds of children and young people playing, laughing and having fun.

There are few fancy toys and bikes and even fewer play areas of any kind, but that is no deterrence. Sixty nine percent of the population of the West Bank are under 19 years old[1] and the youthfulness of the population is evident in the sight of so many children and young people in public – babies in prams and pushchairs, young people going to and from school or university, walking the streets and playing games. Their play and their presence and energy provide a sense of normality – at least during the daylight hours – in the most abnormal of circumstances.

Much of what follows in this chapter concerns children and young people's experiences of the diverse ways in which the Israeli occupation disrupts Palestinian lives and well-being.

It also looks at the ways in which their resistance has allowed them to endure without being defeated.

In any conversation it is almost inevitable that we are drawn to the brutalising aspects of the occupation. But amid the dangers of occupation, young people continue to laugh and joke and play:

> You know, despite all the hardships of our situation, we do live. We go out – we love, we live, we laugh and have fun. It's in that sense I meant that we are like any teenagers anywhere. We are not just the angry teenagers throwing rocks at the Israelis, which is how the international media present us.
>
> Mariam, Ramallah, June 2008

In the old city of Nablus

But we didn't need to be told this. Through all our travels and in all our meetings we met engaged and engaging young people who did not appear to be destroyed by their experiences of the occupation. Their jokes were some of the best we had heard in years and there is a high comedy quotient in daily West Bank life. But at the same time there is the never-ending tragedy of the occupation.

It is a combination that can be unsettling, as in the case when we were laughing and joking with Ibrahim, a postgraduate studying business studies in Nablus. Much of the banter was about Ibrahim's fascination with Western fashion trends or his diet, with him laughing about his mother's baking, before he changed tone completely and told us that his mother began serious biscuit-making only after his brother, three years his senior, had been shot and killed outside their home two years earlier by an IDF patrol. "But we can't cry all the time. We must live our lives," was how Ibrahim concluded that conversation (Tulkarm, 2009).

We had many similar conversations. It was common for us to discover, for example, that the people we were talking with often had close family members and friends in prison with all the attendant anxieties. Such personal catastrophes are commonplace and shared in the West Bank in such a way that it strengthens people to endure and survive. Walls in towns and villages are covered with poster-sized pictures of prisoners and martyrs; their names are painted on buildings; and of course in their family homes their photographs are always prominent. No one is forgotten.

The solidarity of the people is tangible, and we were by no means the first outsiders to be overwhelmed by the dignity and humanity of West Bank society. In our discussions with Rouwa in Tulkarm about her own prison experiences, she was very clear that you were never left alone with your anxiety and fears and that the bonds of solidarity and friendship helped keep her strong. Intangible as they may be, the quality of so many of the social relationships we witnessed in daily living in the West Bank was clearly a source of enormous strength and happiness. Jamal, a 16 year old boy from the Balata camp in Nablus, spoke for many when he told us in 2006 that he did not want to live anywhere else in the world other than in the camp. He had just returned from a visit to his brother in Cairo, who had been pressing him to stay and start a new life in Egypt. He returned because, he said, "it is the best place in the world. The friendships I have and the things we do together make me want to stay. I can imagine no other home." We were joined by some of his friends in the camp who all agreed with Jamal's view on the depth and quality of their friendships which had been forged through a common experience and a shared resistance to the occupation.

Martyr photographs of those imprisoned and killed, Bi'iln April 2009

Suha, a 15 year old girl in Nablus, was also clear that despite all the problems there was something special about life in the West Bank: "The people here make you want to stay and love the place," she said, although:

> It's like living in a prison. It is so difficult to get out and visit. But having said that I love living in Nablus and I can't imagine wanting to live anywhere else. I had the opportunity to go to Turkey for a holiday and I enjoyed it but I was so happy to return.
>
> *Suha, Nablus, September 2006*

Young Palestinians through films, TV, the internet and so forth are not isolated from global youth cultures, although the West Bank is free of the fast food chains and coffee shops which are ubiquitous throughout much of the world[3] (though there is a "Star and Bucks" cafe network across the West Bank!) You will hear rap alongside popular Arab music and see low-slung jeans as well as bare midriffs. Mobile phones are everywhere and we can't recall ever meeting a young Palestinian who did not have an email address. Many had

Facebook accounts. They had many reference points against which to assess their lives and recognise both the differences and similarities between themselves and other young people not living under occupation. A small number had also travelled to summer camps in Europe where they had met their peers from other countries. When we talked with Ali, a 16 year old boy active in the Jaffa Centre who had recently returned from a visit to Britain with his band, he told us how different his life was from those of the young people he had met abroad:

> But, [when Jamil aged 12 years was] asked what he wants to be when he grows up, he says he doesn't know... "It's because I don't know if I will be alive," he says. "The Israelis are always shooting at us."
>
> *Independent, 22 November 2007*[4]

I am a member of a dance band and was able to visit Britain recently with the band. I saw and met young people there and I saw some of the differences between the children of Britain and Palestine. I saw British children going to school in the morning with their friends. They did not have anxieties about checkpoints, about soldiers, killing and wounds. They went freely and happily. It was the same with the university students even when they had to travel far. They never were stopped. They could live freely out of the home. All of these things are not possible for us. When they met I saw that they had many things to say, about what was good in the cinema, where to swim, places to hang out and things like that. It was free talking about their free time and lives. And when we meet what do we talk about? Incursions, occupation, who has been arrested or wounded and how we might support people we know who are suffering. Our lives are so very different.

Ali, Nablus, June 2008

It was often more in anger than sadness that young people talked of how the occupation stole their childhood. They may have idealised what they were missing but they knew that many of their peers elsewhere had some fundamental freedoms which were completely denied to them.

Fear and uncertainty, in addition to direct threats of violence, were major themes of many of our discussions about daily life. The occupation fundamentally disrupts your life. You can never be sure from one day to the next the extent to which you can go about your usual routines of going to school, university, work, family visits or whatever. Ibrahim told us of some of the consequences:

We learn, as young people, that in the future we shouldn't expect good things because daily life has nothing. For example, today it is calm; tomorrow we could have an incursion, the day after a mix. So we can't plan, we don't think too far into the future. And if you are a student it is hard too. You have to travel about and the soldiers may let you get to university today, but tomorrow they might stop you. These issues affect us all, from the very young to the very old. Even workers who have to travel to their work – they face the same problems. As young people we make plans and have projects and then we find that part of our group is arrested, or the teacher or professor is arrested – all these things impact on all our lives and all our plans. These disruptions affect all the family. For example if a father is turned back at a checkpoint it means he has no job and no money that day. So what is all the family to do? Even psychologically we are affected. If you are a student and you study hard, you go to the exam to find it is postponed, or you can't get there. This is an immense frustration for young people. All these things push the Palestinian young people to look at life in this way: just live for the moment.

Ibrahim, Balata, February 2008

Nearly all of the young people told us the same thing: that the unpredictable character of the occupation made it impossible to think of, let alone plan, a future. They lived day to day or for the moment, as Ibrahim recalled. But of course they thought about the future and made plans such as going to university, marriage and so on. Their insistence that they only lived day to day seemed sometimes like a way of handling the constant dismay and disappointment that the occupation guarantees for the Palestinians: when they could not make planned visits to family, or go on school or club trips; when they saw their degree course double in length; when they had family members and friends arbitrarily arrested, jailed or shot; when they couldn't get to the olives because of the settlers. The list is endless before it even addresses the wider political context.

The individual and collective punishment of the people of the West Bank is largely kept hidden from Western gaze. In part this is due to the constant Israeli invocation of "security" as the one and only reason for its oppressive actions in the West Bank and Gaza. Refugee camps are daily invaded because they harbour those who are deemed a security threat; people going about their business are shot because they threaten the security of soldiers or settlers; checkpoints ensure security by making it difficult for suicide bombers to get through to Israel, and the Wall, we are expected to believe, is only about protecting the security of Israel and nothing else. The security exhortations are many and varied and all feed on a myth propagated by Israel that all Arabs want to see the Israeli Jews kicked into the sea and pose a real existential threat to the security of the country. Since its creation after the Second World War Israel has drawn on widespread revulsion and guilt over the Holocaust both to justify its presence in Palestine and to argue that it is entitled to secure, at whatever cost, a homeland that will be safe for all Jews, worldwide, who never again will be threatened with annihilation.[5] This Israeli perspective has been taken up and further honed, with only a few dissenting voices, by Israel's key allies in the West both in government and in all branches of the media.

Since the horrors of the Gaza War in 2008-09, Israel's moral authority is no longer Teflon-proofed by the Holocaust and, as we shall see later, this has significant implications for Israel's development. Nevertheless, even as Israel's own claim to have high ethical values is being daily eroded, the Palestinian perspective remains neglected, distorted and fragmented. The collective punishment of an entire group of people by another, as was the case with the Nazi extermination of six million European Jews during the Second World War, is now being experienced by Palestinians at the hands of Israeli colonisation. And yet again, now as then, the West does not want to know.[6]

While the Western media focus on episodic acts of violence, the more telling and fundamental story is the collective daily resistance of the Palestinians and their determination not to let the occupation destroy every aspect of their lives. The West Bank population starts each day determined to live its daily life which, in the case of many young people, involves negotiating checkpoints and barriers as they go to work, school or university (see chapter 2). They are not passive victims. The insistence on their right to everyday life and routines is expressed continually and, as Jamal told us:

> Despite all these provocations and all the difficulties of the checkpoints we insist that we must continue with our education and our lives. The Israelis want us to surrender. Never! They want to make our lives miserable so we will leave. Never!
> *Jamal, Jenin, September 2006*

Daily life is shaped by a relationship between occupation and resistance. For some Palestinians, as we shall see, it leads them to leave and seek their fortunes elsewhere. But for the majority, who not only stay but marry and have children, their dogged determination to secure education, work and family life confounds the occupation.[7]

Even where occupation fractures and destroys friends and families it so often leads not to defeat and despair but to renewed determination, as 18 year old Samira exemplified:

> When I was in my last year of secondary school the Israelis arrested four of my brothers. This made it very hard for me. I was upset and worried. I was really disturbed and anxious. I kept on thinking that they were going to come and take me. So as I was trying to study I was distracted by this fear. But I managed to sit my final exams and I was determined to get a good mark that would allow me to go to university. I thought if I can achieve this it will show the Israelis that they can't destroy our family. My education is part of my struggle.
>
> *Samira, Tulkarm, February 2008*

Between 2004 and 2006 many of the towns and villages we visited had been subjected to extensive periods of closure which included curfews extending to nearly a month at a time during which you weren't allowed to leave your home. There were many days when checkpoints were closed to isolate towns and villages and of course there were endless Israeli invasions and attacks. But, even during those difficult days, when the soldiers were in the towns and refugee camps, young Palestinians told us how they would check their radios every morning to see if their schools were open and if so would break the curfew to attend.

In 16 year old Mohammed's case, his school was on the other side of Nablus and as his area of town was completely sealed off he had no chance of getting to school. He told us that there were around 15 of them in this situation so the school decided to set up a "branch" in a nearby empty flat for the duration of the curfew (22 days in this case). Mohammed continued:

> We didn't even have chairs so we had to carry our own from home all the time avoiding the soldiers. The teacher lived close to the flat so it wasn't difficult for him to get there and we had three hours of classes every day. It was better than sitting at home and I didn't miss all my classes.
>
> *Mohammed, Nablus, September 2009*

Stories such as these are common in the West Bank and testify to the determination of the people not only to endure the occupation but to strive to counter its corrosive impact.

That the occupation seeks to demoralise, humiliate and harm well-being was well understood by the Palestinian young people we met and we were given countless examples. Najwa, for example, told us:

> The soldiers were in our house for 21 days. When we were allowed to return everything inside our home was destroyed and thrown outside. Why? For nothing. It is just to humiliate us and make us suffer.
> *Najwa, Jenin, September 2006*

Her friend from university, Ranya, told us that:

> At the time of the first big incursion in Nablus in 2002, soldiers came to our house. It was dark and it was raining. They told my father that we should all come out of the house. But he said it was raining and that he had young children. Out! he was told and we used some blankets to cover the young children. We stood outside for nearly two hours in the rain and in the dark. Then the officer came and said you can go back in, and "goodnight"!
> *Ranya, Jenin, September 2006*

In the same discussion, Fareeda recounted how:

> The soldiers came into my village late at night looking for the son of our neighbour. First they ordered the owner of the house to come out, naked. They made him stand under a water pipe which they then turned on. It was winter. Then when other family members came out of the house the soldiers used some as human shields as they approached the house to throw grenades. All the time the owner was naked and wet and cold. They didn't capture his son. The Israelis wanted to make us frightened. But when I saw all this I did not become more scared but more determined to fight and to resist the occupation.
> *Fareeda, Jenin, September 2006*

Periodic invasions of IDF soldiers into Palestinian homes are widely experienced, especially in the refugee camps. In the case of the Jenin camp many had been terrified by soldiers bursting through the walls of their homes during the massacre of 2002.

For those whose houses or apartments occupy strategic positions, military incursions are a more regular feature of their lives as their homes are turned into observation posts or sniper positions. Jumana lives with her family of six in such an apartment in Nablus. She is 16 years old and told us that the Israelis often use their flat as an observation post and they can have four or five soldiers there for days at a time. At these times, the family is moved into one room and made to sit on the floor in the dark. When they need to use the toilet they are escorted there and have to leave the door open. "My father gets so angry with the soldiers, especially when I or my sisters need the toilet. They deliberately humiliate us and my father can't protect me then" (Jumana, Nablus, September 2009).

Laughter and tears

During the period of our research in the West Bank the army's incursions into the camps, villages and towns were largely restricted to the early hours of the morning, often between 2am and 4am. This gave the night-time a heightened sense of anxiety as people knew with near certainty, especially in the camps, that the army would be coming – but for whom, when and in what numbers was never known. Although the Israeli military always argues that its incursions are driven by specific security needs, the reality is that many of the raids are not targeted but random. They shake the tree and see what falls; after all in the Israeli mindset all Palestinians are their enemies. The consequences are many and predictable. There is anxiety for everyone, as Usama, a teenage girl in Nablus, told us:

> At night there are many times when you are lying in bed waiting for sleep and then you hear the noise of an incursion, the jeeps, APCs, the random firing. Do children in Britain wake up to such noises frightened and scared by incursions? For us it is every night.
> *Usama, Nablus, September 2006*

Disturbed sleep, nightmares, bed wetting, aggression and muteness were all mentioned as being among the most prevalent consequences, especially for the young. It was common for us to hear brothers and sisters worrying about their younger siblings, as typified by 14 year old Rasha:

> My father is in prison. My younger brother is very young and he can't understand where our father is. He doesn't like to eat now and I am very worried.
> *Rasha, Jenin, September 2006*

The overwhelming reality of life in the West Bank is that it is dangerous and unpredictable for its entire people. As Kareem, a 17 year old student from Jenin told us, "I don't believe that young people are particular targets for the Israelis. The occupation affects everyone here without exception" (Kareem, Jenin, September 2006).

While it is true that the occupation is universalising, it is also differential in its impact, as we came to discover. The most obvious example is those crowded into the refugee camps who, as we shall see, are hardest hit by all aspects of the occupation, from the psychological to the social and economic.

Vulnerability because of either age, gender or illness provides no protection from the occupation. Thus in the case of children we found that not even their play areas are safe:

> Last Friday night the Israelis spread "chocolates" around some of our playgrounds near the school, for the kids to pick up. My eight year old brother found one and picked it up. It was shining in silver foil and he thought it might be a toy or a sweet. It exploded in his hands as he opened it and he got seriously burnt. This is how the Israelis target the kids. Why is this never reported?
> *Kareem, Balata, September 2006*

That so many young people are injured, killed and traumatised by the Israeli occupation is in large measure due to their sheer numbers in the West Bank coupled with their greater public exposure either going to and from school or university or simply being out on the streets. Between 2000 and 2007 a total of 974 children were killed in Gaza and the West Bank, with the second most common cause of death being "random Israeli gunfire".[8] Or, to put it more bluntly, being in the wrong place at the wrong time.

For younger people this exposure to random violence is heightened by the shifting boundaries of physical space due principally to the construction of the Wall and the expansion of settlements and their interconnecting road systems. We heard many stories of children in particular being caught up in these boundary changes where a once favourite hillside for playing becomes a forbidden place because of its proximity to a settlement or the Wall or because settlers have fenced off the water hole on their family's land. In all such cases, the children entering these areas become liable to being shot at or arrested or both. We too experienced roads that we had previously travelled on now being closed to all Palestinian traffic, either by checkpoints, concrete blocks and piles of earth and rubble, or by being redesignated as roads reserved for Israelis.

These are not minor shifts. Even in the five years of our visits the landscape of the West Bank has changed significantly as Israel writes its "facts on the ground" with military areas, "nature reserves", settlements, roads, checkpoints and the Wall, which all devour Palestinian land and push the Palestinians into smaller and smaller urban enclaves around the major towns and cities of the West Bank. Some sense of the scale of these changes is provided by Raja Shehadeh in his evocative book *Palestinian Walks: Notes on a Vanishing Landscape*:

> When Israel began establishing settlements, opening roads through the hills, flattening hilltops and connecting far-flung places with water and electricity I was filled with awe. And fear. The countryside I grew up in was being transformed so rapidly I could hardly keep up… Vast areas of my beloved country were being fenced to become off-limits to us.[9]

These issues were among the principal concerns of the young people we spoke with, and often motivated their involvement as volunteers in the many youth centres across the West Bank. Sami's comments, informed by his experience as a youth worker in the Balata refugee camp, reflected the views of many we met:

Salim's story

Salim: There were five of us [teenage boys] and we were together walking home at about 9pm in the evening. It was dark. There were undercover forces in the area but we didn't know that at the time. They were hiding behind a wall and there were no street lights. We had started to cross the street when they started to fire at us and I got shot. The bullet went through me and then hit my friend as well. They then shot my friend with another bullet.

CJ: There was no warning or shouting?

Salim: No, nothing. No shouting, there were no lights, we didn't see them – they just shot at us.

ML: Then what happened?

Salim: I didn't feel anything at first. But the bullet that went through me broke my friend's leg and he couldn't move. I then felt the blood and I couldn't move.

We were puzzled, scared and confused. We didn't know what had happened. Who had shot us? Where were they?

The neighbours around the area started to shout and there were volunteers who came to help us.

Then a taxi came and we were dragged in. All the ambulances were busy, so they sent a taxi.

I was off school for two months. But my friend who was shot twice was in bed for three months, and missed taking his final school exams.

Qalqilya, February 2008

All the youth workers in the Centre were brought up in the refugee camp and still live here. We know what it is like and we know what difficulties the children face. You know the children

66

here are brought up in such strange and difficult circumstances. They have all seen dead bodies and body parts. They have all witnessed shootings, bombings and attacks from the Israeli forces. They all have brothers, cousins, uncles or fathers who are martyrs or prisoners. Many of them have been hurt – if not physically, then at least mentally and emotionally. As a result, we have a lot of angry children. We have a lot of aggressive children. We have a lot of depressed children. We have a lot who behave in a crazy way because they have no way of releasing their anger and anxieties. Sometimes it is difficult to talk to them, they are often nervous.

Sami, Yaffa Centre, Balata, June 2008

The youth centre in Balata, like those elsewhere in the West Bank, is explicit that its purpose is to minimise the Israeli theft of Palestinian childhood through its occupation.

As Jamal told us:

We have to find a way to give our young people a glimpse of a better life. To run classes and groups which take them, even for a short while, away from the horrors of our lives in the camps.

Jamal, volunteer, Yaffa Centre, Balata, February 2008

The centres we visited were impressive, not in terms of their facilities which were always overused and under-resourced, but with respect to their achievements. They were able to create oases of childhood which were not dominated by the occupation and which soothe some of its frustrations and anxieties. We didn't see rocket science but children drawing and painting, playing sport, dancing and making music together. We met those who had literally found their voice again after muteness and many told us that the activities helped relieve their frustrations. During the course of our research we witnessed a growing concern to help those children with profound individual psychological reactions to the occupation, whether it was bed wetting or nightmares. Youth workers and social workers told us that parents' growing trust in their work meant that more and more were turning to the centres for help with problems that had previously remained firmly closed within the family.

According to one Palestinian writer:

Palestinians are hard and they work hard. They have faced many problems but they keep rebuilding their lives, they don't give in... Palestinians have huge strength (*mubaadira aasimiya*)... Although walking on thorns, he maintained his image in front of the world that he is very strong, that he can beat anything.[10]

Such values and beliefs were evident amongst all the people we met. It was a source of great pride that they were able to withstand all the brutalities of the occupation, and keep going in the face of extraordinary hardships and violence. But in turn this can also have negative consequences for that behaviour which may be perceived as weakness but which includes a range of psycho-social responses to trauma and stress. We were told by social workers in Nablus that this led to such problems often being "hidden" within families with adults who from shame were reluctant to seek help for either themselves or their children. But the social workers we met were unequivocal in seeing the psychologically related reactions to persistent fear as wounds of occupation as much as the wounds and injuries caused by firearms:

Laughter and tears

> Today I have seen a young boy and his sister. Both can't control their peeing. These two are both casualties of the daily incursions of the Israeli army. We will work with them now.
> *Ahmed, social worker, Nablus, September 2006*

These are difficult and sensitive issues in a society where hope and courage are so central to its very survival. We were unable to probe as deeply as we would have hoped, for in common with many societies, psycho-social difficulties are still widely considered in West Bank society to be "private" matters for the individual and their family. Nevertheless, the number of activities we witnessed that involved art and music work with young children suggested an awareness of the importance of such activities in combating high levels of stress and anxiety amongst children and young people. In 2002 one West Bank survey showed that "at least half of the school children showed psychological symptoms such as crying and fear from loneliness, darkness and loud noises. About a third showed symptoms of sleep disorder, nervousness, decrease in eating and weight, feelings of hopelessness and frustration, and abnormal thoughts of death. About half of the children showed deterioration in their schoolwork and one-third were unable to concentrate".[11]

We talk in more detail later in the book about the multi-layered resistance and solidarities that characterise life in the

West Bank. The concern with young children is but one example of that solidarity and extends from social work projects with individuals to the youth work of the many community centres and organisations. There are not the same inter-generational divisions that are visible in some Western European societies. Young people spend time with their elders whether from the family or from the neighbourhood. Many told us how much they learned of their history from older relatives and family friends. The Yaffa Centre in Balata was not alone amongst West Bank youth centres in positively valuing the testimonies of older people and set about recording them in print and on video and using them as a basis for youth work activities. Likewise students at An-Najah University in Nablus have for many years been collecting stories and testimonies from older people, especially those with personal experience of the Nakba and its immediate aftermath.[12] These people's histories take on further significance given the sanitised nature of the Palestinian school curriculum.

For slightly different reasons, the two main providers of schooling – UNRWA for the refugees and the PA for the rest – steer clear of recent Palestinian history and politics. The UN on account of its avowed "neutrality" and the PA because Israel monitors the curriculum and course content.[13] Much of what we heard from young people about the Palestinian struggle and its background, some in close detail going back to the British Mandate and the Balfour Declaration, was learnt in the family. This was a history that was personal, and for those in the camps accounted for why they were there and had been for over 60 years. It is a history as important as the ancient land ownership documents and keys they retain of their lost properties in Israel. And it is a history which would seem to bind generations closely together.

Such close relationships and friendships combine to form solidarities that mitigate some of the worst excesses of the Israeli regime and provide young people with the sort of perspectives and broader political understandings that help them understand what is happening and how to manage. What it cannot do is shield children and young people from the occupation.

This was particularly evident when young people talked about their concerns for their younger siblings and those other youngsters around them. Again and again we heard Palestinian youth express their anxiety that the occupation was leading to a generation of boys obsessed with guns and war.

When we run a workshop for children between five and 16 years old I normally ask them to draw a picture. But they don't draw trees or flowers or an amusement park. Instead they draw pictures of jeeps, APCs, guns, and battles. This is one of the difficulties that we face – how do we break this psychological barrier? Their lives lead them to thinking this way – we cannot change this in a few hours of a course.
Hamed, volunteer, Balata, September 2006

I don't think our children play like other children in the world. All their games involve war, weapons and blood. This is not a normal life, it is a disaster life.
Suha, aged 16, Nablus, February 2006

We hear similar talk in the West with some commentators suggesting that violent computer games and movies are having a similar impact on their youth. But rarely in the West will you meet, as a matter of course, so many young boys who appeared (to us at least) to have a comprehensive knowledge of the main guns and armaments of the Israeli forces. Many young people can recognise a military vehicle by its engine noise alone. Planes and helicopters are readily identified. But this knowledge is not just part of a "boys with toys" syndrome but useful survival knowledge. We had a fascinating discussion with five cousins, all boys from Qalqilya and Tulkarm who tried to explain how we could recognise a rifle that fired plastic bullets as against one shooting live ammunition, what action to take in the event of a tear gas attack, and the calibre of shells from this or that tank or APC. Similarly during an evening in Beit Leed, an agricultural village, the children of one large family fetched down the shell that had landed on their roof but had not exploded. It was a magnificent trophy for them.

Paradoxes of life in the West Bank abound. For some Palestinian children and young people there are moments of acute excitement and adventure alongside the fears and depression of occupation, as 17 year old Tariq from the Friends School told us:

For me the 21-day curfew [2002] was kind of fun. I was lucky in that my house has a back garden and it was possible to get outside of the house and friends and neighbours would visit. Sometimes me and my friends would go out onto the streets, get shot at and then rush home. Then there were times when jeeps would chase us bunch of boys. It was exciting. I know we missed school and all that but for me I had some fun too in the curfew. I was caught and beaten three times by the soldiers during the curfew but it didn't stop me. But in 2002 we were kids. Riding our bikes and looking for fun. Our parents weren't happy but that's how I was as a young kid.

Tariq, Ramallah, June 2008

We heard many similar stories. It wasn't just stone throwing or dodging the military which exhilarated but many less conspicuous everyday activities such as visiting friends or getting

Left, children in Beit Leed with an unexploded shell

Right, Balata camp[14]

to school which under curfew carried considerable dangers. Mohammed, for example, was excited by getting to his "ad hoc" school in Nablus during one of the long curfews, while the two sisters Rima and Manal were excited by crawling through their bedroom window and over the narrow divide to visit their friends in the next building (Nablus, September 2009). Such events take on greater significance as they dramatically puncture the monotony of much daily life in the West Bank where restrictions on movement combined with extreme poverty for many youngsters entail long periods "knocking about" in or near to the home.

People spend most of their time just around the home, perhaps in the street but never far away. And this makes the pressures of home life very great.

Firas, Tulkarm, June 2008

In the already overcrowded refugee camps such pressures are amplified:

The Balata camp is very over-crowded. We have 22,000 people

living in one kilometre square. In the camp we have mosques,

schools, some shops, and we also have the Social and Cultural
Centres like ours. All these are important, but they eat into
the space of the camp. So each house is now reduced to 60-70
square metres where you often find a family of 10 people living
there. Some of the houses in the middle of the camp are built so
close together – and they are all two or three storeys high – that
there is no natural light, no sun and little ventilation.

People in the camp live in these circumstances because they
have no choice. They are too poor to move out of the camp.
Many of the families in the camps don't
even go out of the camp for even one
day. They don't go to the nearby park
even, because they think about the cost
of a drink or an ice-cream their children
will want and they'll have no money for
– they simply don't have the money. So
the result is that the kids just spend all
their time running around the streets
and near their homes.

Sami, Yaffa Centre, Balata, June 2008

But it is not only young people who
now spend most of their time in the
streets or at home when they are not at
school or university. It now applies to
large numbers of adults who have no
work. As Firas said, "if you don't work,
life will be miserable – but where can you work?" (Tulkarm,
June 2008). Mohammad thought that as a result of unemployment the people of the West Bank spent more hours watching
(satellite) TV than anywhere else in the world.[16] For men
there are also the ubiquitous coffee shops where they can pass
the time at very little cost in the company of other men. For
women there are no such opportunities for socialising in public without appropriate chaperones. Although we came across
variations from town to town and certainly between the villages
with respect to gender conservatism, the general rule was that
the space for young women at least was much more domesti-
cally confined than was the case for boys. The variations within
a small geographical area such as the West Bank are marked;
hence, Qalqilya is much more conservative than Tulkarm,
which in turn is less liberal than Nablus and certainly does
not compare with Ramallah for the freedoms it affords young

"Life here has a lot of pressure –
economic, social and personal,"
explains Nooreddin Amara, 14. "The
economy is usually very bad. There is a
lot of unemployment." And, he said
explaining how overcrowded the camps
were, "here is the club, and here is a
house. If I make any noise at all, they
can hear it."

"The camp is small," says
Muhammad Libdeh, 15, a youth
representative of the management
committee at the Tulkarm after-school
programme. "Your life is limited by
what is here".

UNICEF, May 2009[15]

women to go out with their friends – both male and female. In common with many societies, villages and rural areas tend to be more conservative on a wide range of issues including gender freedoms than the urban areas and larger towns.

When not at school or visiting family, girls and young women spend their time in the home, helping with the household – cleaning, cooking, caring for younger siblings – as well as watching TV. When we met a group of four femail friends in Tulkarm in September 2009 who had just graduated from university, they gave no sense of being locked into domestic drudgery. Rather for them it was a matter of making their contribution to the household which also allowed them time to socialise and meet one another – which they did on a daily basis by visiting each other's homes. Their friendship was intense and they told us that they often spent their time laughing and giggling over the sort of husbands they hoped to marry and discussing what was going on in their lives.

The home is also the place where many hours are filled by women embroidering intricate and decorative tapestries – the most common being the map of historic Palestine, Handala the cartoon character symbolising Palestinian resistance and the Al Aqsa Mosque – which decorate their homes in addition to other handicraft arts such as beaded flowers. Such activities consume hours of time and from our observations are often social events involving female neighbours and relatives working alongside one another. They are also one more example of the inter-generational solidarity which is a characteristic of West Bank society, often with three generations of women and girls working and talking together. As ever, we discovered that occupation brings new twists to even these activities such as when we spent an evening with Rasha and her two teenaged daughters, Minel and Nisreen. They were expert paper folders and in a few minutes were producing birds with flapping wings and frogs that could be made to jump! This, they told us, was the consequence of curfew when they filled the hours making toys from paper. We subsequently came across a range of other quirky skills all learnt either in prison or under curfew and requiring little or no space or resources. These included elaborate finger contortions and animal sculptures from the foil of cigarette packets!

Mobile phones and the internet, both widely used by young people,[17] do allow for some of the acute physical barriers to travel and communication imposed by the occupation to be circumvented. Through mobiles and emails, friends can stay in touch even during the curfews and closedowns. In some cases, they allowed families to have contact with friends and relatives in prison. We also learned that mobiles allowed some young women to breach some of the traditional conventions that limited their contact with boy friends. Even if they couldn't meet easily they could at least text.

In the minority of homes which had an internet connection we suspect that our limited observations of heavy and continual use would hold true more generally. When we stayed in the Tulkarm refugee camp in 2006 not only was the internet in continual use but a tight rota allocating times had to be operated to ensure that all of the family's six siblings (and their friends) could have some time, to either play games, download music or email.

It is, in our view, remarkable the extent to which everyday life is sustained in such adverse circumstances. The sheer density of population in the camps alone, for example, would strain any social system, but add the haunting uncertainties created by occupation and its damage to people and communities then it is even more remarkable that so much of daily life is characterised by good humour and grace.

Examples of the tapestries made by Palestinian women

Yet there can be no getting away from the dark shadow of occupation. As Reem, who in June 2008 had just completed her secondary education at the Friends School in Ramallah, told us, "Everything we do is affected by the occupation from the smallest to the biggest thing."

That the occupation is uncompromising and universal gives it a particularly brutal character and, hardly surprisingly, unifies rather than divides the West Bank population. There are no subtleties to the Israeli strategy: no attempt to win hearts and minds; no deployment of softer strategies of control and containment in an attempt to divide one section against another. The result for the Palestinians at least, over the years, has been the development of a common understanding of the Israeli position which was articulated by Mustapha, a young social worker we met with in Nablus in February 2008:

The Israeli occupation is calculated fully to destroy – or to try and destroy – our psychological well-being as well as our physical well-being. It is clear in all their behaviour and in all their activities that they want to degrade and humiliate us. They want to de-motivate us. To make us give up.

Mustapha, social worker, Nablus, February 2008.

As Noam Chomsky argued in his characterisation of the Israeli occupation:

> The point [of occupation] is to teach the Palestinians that every aspect of their life is controlled by the authorities, and the master will do what he likes with impunity. They must be taught not to "raise their heads".[19]

According to a survey undertaken by Sharek Youth Forum and funded by UNDP, over half of 1,220 respondents between 16 and 25 years old [in the West Bank and Gaza] said they did not feel secure. The great majority described themselves as either extremely depressed or depressed; more than half said they spend their spare time at home, with friends or relatives; and a limited proportion said they attended youth centres and clubs. Low morale was especially pronounced among Gaza refugee camp residents.

UNICEF, April 2009[18]

But after over 60 years of occupation it is becoming clearer that the strategy of making the life of the Palestinians as miserable as possible, in the belief that it will lead to their defeat and departure from the West Bank, is not working. The West Bank is dangerous but it is not a miserable place. The hardships are extreme but the Israelis have not destroyed totally the ability of people to make a life for themselves. The population of the West Bank has not diminished but grown since 1948. The occupation ironically has solidified the population despite all their suffering. Popular consciousness is clear – the more they want us to go, the more determined we are to stay; the more they try to destroy and distort our lives, the more determined we are to laugh and play.

It is a ubiquitous resilience played out at many levels from the students who strive to travel daily to university and arrive at checkpoints not knowing whether they will be allowed to pass. It is expressed in the formation of sports teams and cultural clubs in a context where travelling to the next village for a match can never be assured. It is about the myriad ways and means that Palestinians live their daily lives.

It is a durable resistance too, because there is collective understanding. Palestinians know what the Israelis want – their land without their presence. And they know how they are seeking to achieve this goal. As a result, the Palestinian pre-occupation with all aspects of trying to live as much a "normal" life as possible is consciously understood as part of their resistance and hence survival. This was exemplified for us by Ali, a 15year old school boy in Jenin, who in 2006 told us:

> Naturally all our parents are nervous for us when we leave the home in the morning and go out to school or the university. But my parents never show me their nerves even though I know this is how they feel. Instead they want us to be calm and relaxed. They so much want us to have a normal life so we can move forward. It is like a culture of survival.
>
> *Ali, Jenin, September 2006*

His insight helped us make better sense of what we saw and witnessed: the laughter as well as the tears; the many-layered solidarities, the determination to go to school, to play games, to visit family and friends, to go out with the family for a walk or a picnic, to harvest the olives, all of which are so mundane in other countries but so perilous and difficult there.

Notes

1 *Palestine Monitor* "Children" factsheet, updated 18 December 2008.

2 B Utela, "The Children Of Balata: Putting Faces To Statistics", *Palestine Monitor*, 18 October 2010, www.palestinemonitor.org/spip/spip.php?article1571

3 There are many examples of the ways in which cross-national youth cultures interact. See, for example, "Refugee Camp Kids And Rappers", *Palestine Monitor*, 19 July 2009, www.palestinemonitor.org/spip/spip.php?article1015

4 Quoted in R Walker, "Another brick in the wall: saving schools in the West Bank", *Independent*, 22 November 2007, pp4-5.

5 See A Shlaim, *The Iron Wall: Israel and the Arab World* (Penguin, 2000). In the case of former prime minister Menachem Begin, for example, Shlaim observed that because of the Holocaust, Begin "saw the world as a profoundly anti-Semitic, extremely hostile and highly dangerous environment. He perceived Arab hostility as an extension of the anti-semiticism that had resulted in the annihilation of European Jewry." (p553)

6 Within the mainstream English press there are some exceptions such as Robert Fisk and Patrick Coburn of the *Independent*.

7 According to the UNRWA Population Census of 2007 the West Bank population grew by 25.47 percent between 1997 and 2007, from 1,873,476 to 2,350,583 people, not including Palestinians living in Jerusalem. UNRWA Briefing Paper, January 2010, p9, http://www.unrwa.org/userfiles/2010012035949.pdf

8 *Palestine Monitor* "Children" factsheet, updated 18 December 2008.

9 R Shehadeh, *Palestinan Walks: Notes on a Vanishing Landscape* (Profile Books, 2008), p114.

10 N Al Rais, "Suicide in the Time of Ashes", Al Hayat, March 1998, quoted in N T Dabagh, *Suicide in Palestine* (Hurst, 2005), p80.

11 S Halileh, "The effects of Israel's 'Operation

Defensive Shield' on Palestinian children living in the West Bank", Spotlight, 29 June 2002, www.redress.btinternet.co.uk/shalileh.htm

12 For example, L Morgan and L Morris (eds), *Nakba Eyewitnesses: Narrations of the Palestinian 1948 Catastrophe* (An-Najah University, 2007).

13 UNRWA schools are continuously monitored for anti-Israeli bias by Israeli right-wing groups and pro-Israelis in the US Congress. The consistent message is that UNRWA is pro-Palestinian and promotes terror. For a typical example see "Israeli refugee program a 'stack of lies'", *Palestine Note*, 11 August 2010, palestinenote.com/cs/blogs/news/archive/2010/08/11/unrwa-israeli-tv-s-depiction-of-palestinian-refugees-a-quot-stack-of-lies-quot.aspx

14 B Utela, "The Children Of Balata: Putting Faces To Statistics", *Palestine Monitor*, 18 October 2010, www.palestinemonitor.org/spip/spip.php?article1571

15 UNICEF oPt Monthly Update, 15 May 2009, p5.

16 95.3 percent of households had a TV set and 80.4 percent had a satellite dish in 2006. *This Week in Palestine*, Issue 121 (May 2008), p82.

17 In 2006, 81 percent of households had a mobile phone whereas only 15.9 percent had access to the internet at home. *This Week in Palestine*, Issue 121 (May 2008), p82. As we note elsewhere, however, access to the internet through cafes and shared multiple use is widespread.

18 UNICEF oPt Monthly Update, 15 April 2009, p4.

19 N Chomsky, *The Fateful Triangle* (Pluto Press, 1999), p480.

Chapter 2

Checkpoints

The right to freedom of movement provides that people are entitled to move freely within the borders of the state, to leave any country and to return to their country.
Article 13 of the Universal Declaration of Human Rights and article 12 of the International Covenant on Civil and Political Rights, 10 December 1948

Moving around in the West Bank has some similarities to travelling in London or any other large congested city. You never talk about distance when calculating the time it takes to meet friends; traffic and transport is such that time is the unit of distance. But there is a big difference: in the West Bank it is impossible to give anything but a rough guess as to when you hope to arrive. You set out on your journey never sure whether you will arrive and with no idea of how long it will take.

Samira is 19 years old and attends university. She travels about 12 kilometres daily from her village to attend An-Najah University in Nablus:

I need to be in the university by 8am, as that's when classes start. Without any checkpoints it would take about 25 minutes to get to Nablus, but it now takes me almost two hours. I have to get up at 5.45am and then I leave home and get a taxi. I used to get a bus but that meant leaving even earlier, just after 5am. But then the buses stopped because they were targeted by the Israelis. They would stop every bus at the checkpoint and the soldiers would make us all get off to check each of us, our ID, our bags, and then they would check the bus. So the buses took a long time.
Samira, Tulkarm, 2008

This is the daily reality for thousands of young people. And it's a twice daily routine if they don't stay in rooms or student hostels during the week near their university. Hours of wasted and frustrated time is spent at checkpoints, waiting to be processed while going about your daily business. Some sense of this frustration was conveyed by Abdel when he told us of his journey into school in Ramallah from a nearby village on the morning of our meeting:

> Today was very typical for me. At the first checkpoint they asked all the same questions as always: Where are you going? Where are you from? The name of your school and the street? What villages have you passed through? It just pisses me off. Then we come to the next checkpoint. This is not fixed – just an army jeep and three soldiers sitting on the front of the jeep doing nothing. There must have been 300 cars waiting and we just had to sit it out.
>
> *Abdel, Ramallah, September 2006*

Illegal Israeli military checkpoints in the West Bank, 2002.[2] The map gives some impression of the spread of checkpoints across the West Bank (though to highlight the extent of checkpoint areas this map inadvertently exaggerates the size of the West Bank compared to Israel)

The checkpoints come in various shapes and guises, from the border-crossing style of the recently revamped and refurbished Qalandiya checkpoint that separates Jerusalem from Ramallah to the smaller and more run-down affairs on the roads between Tulkarm and Nablus which seem more militarised with their tall, round concrete watchtowers and a collection of huts for the soldiers. In addition to these fixed checkpoints there are the ever-present mobile checkpoints which control all travellers' movements. These are often, as Abdel noted, no more than a handful of soldiers in a jeep or Humvee who control the traffic with a stinger across the road. We found these mobile checkpoints scary, especially at night on fairly remote side roads deep in the countryside. We always had to stop about 50 metres before the three or four soldiers and switch the car's internal lights on so they could see who was inside. More often than not the driver was summoned – the wait can seem endless – to take all our IDs to the soldiers. The soldiers themselves, though they had guns, seemed both very young and nervous.

According to the *Palestine Monitor* in September 2008 there were 699 "closure obstacles" in the West Bank. Approximately 130 of these had been added after the Annapolis Conference began in November 2007. Somewhere in the region of 74 percent of the main routes in the West Bank are controlled by checkpoints or are blocked entirely. In addition, during the period from April to September 2008 there was an average of 89 weekly temporary or random checkpoints. Due to their unpredictable nature and more intensive search procedures, the random checkpoints are usually even more problematic for the Palestinians than the regular ones.

Table 1 presents a breakdown of 630 of the "closure obstacles" in place in September 2008.

Table 1: Checkpoints and closure obstacles (percent)

Trenches	3
Partial checkpoints	3
Earth walls	7
Roadblocks	11
Road barriers	12
Checkpoints	12
Road gates	16
Earth mounds	36

If you are one of the lucky few to be travelling in a private car then driving in the West Bank is like going from one traffic jam to the next. If you are on public transport or in one of the ubiquitous yellow taxi minibuses it is even more frustrating, as you are compelled to get on and off to be processed at the checkpoints. And, irrespective of the type of checkpoint, there is a common cardinal rule you soon discover: the pace and the character of the processing is completely dependent on the whims and attitudes of the soldiers at the checkpoints. It has nothing to do with the time of day, the weather, the extent of the queues, or whether you are young, old, sick or well. We shall return to this cardinal rule later.

Stealing time

Checkpoints steal time from the lives of the Palestinians: great chunks of time, every day. From our conversations with university students it is this and the uncertainty of getting through the checkpoints that result in so many

What is a checkpoint?

Let me give you a brief description. Usually it's some cement blocks in the road that you have to stop at. Soldiers with big guns motion for you to come forward when they want; sometimes they'll keep cars for hours while they stand around and joke with each other. Usually there's maybe one soldier checking a long line of idling cars and one checking a long line of tired pedestrians, and about five sitting in the shade, doing no apparent "work". Sometimes they let you through with a cursory ID check, sometimes they make you unload all of your gear, they check under the vehicle, they question you about irrelevant facts, and they turn you back. At checkpoints near Jewish settlements, there is a separate way, without a stop, for settlers, who are distinguished by yellow Israeli licence plates as opposed to green Palestinian ones. Allegedly set up for Israeli "security", their effect…is to slowly strangle Palestinian life and freedom.
Jews Against the Occupation[3]

How the checkpoints evolved

1967 General entry permit conferred on Palestinians wishing to enter Israel. Entry restrictions loosely applied.

1991 Continuous general closure imposed on the [occupied] territories with outbreak of first Gulf War; a personal permit is now required for individuals wishing to enter Israel. Military checkpoints are erected at key points to monitor the system.

1991-93 The checkpoint system is tightened. Passage between the northern and southern West Bank, between Gaza and the West Bank and East Jerusalem is subject to a permit from the Civil Administration. Paradoxically, the Oslo Accords signed in September 1993 result in further ramifications to the system.

1996 A first internal closure is imposed on the [occupied] territories; restrictions on movement between Palestinian towns, villages and areas are accompanied by severe limitations on entry into Israel. The system is implemented by an ever more elaborate checkpoint system.

2000-04 [During the Second Intifada] checkpoint policy is intensified and systematised by means of reinforcing all the measures outlined below: general closure, internal closure, curfew and, of course, proliferating and expanding checkpoints. At the same time the permit system is rigorously implemented and since May 2002 extended to cover any and all movement of Palestinians within as well as outside the West Bank.

2005 Some checkpoints, mostly between Israel and the West Bank [are upgraded]. Metal detectors and revolving gates have been introduced. The upgraded checkpoints are strategically located to close off access to and within the West Bank at will.

Checkpoint Watch: Testimonies from Occupied Palestine [4]

of them having to prolong their studies. Very few students are able to complete their courses in the allotted time and often have to extend their courses by one to two years to catch up on the classes or exams they have missed through being delayed or refused passage. It became abundantly clear that the disruption of university education was a deliberate aspect of checkpoint practice both daily and at especially sensitive times. Here is what Jamal told us:

> The soldiers want to disrupt our education – make us late for classes and miss examinations. I think that they recognise our education as one of our weapons in this fight and they want to weaken us. And education is one of the main ways we can resist as young people.
>
> *Jamal, Jenin, September 2006*

We met two young women in Tulkarm and Qalqilya whose higher education choices had been restricted by the checkpoints. Their parents would not permit them to go to the university in Nablus where the girls wanted to study because they were not prepared for their daughters to stay unaccompanied overnight in Nablus. In both cases, their home towns were no more than 40 minutes from Nablus, but because of the checkpoints there could be no guarantee that the girls would be able to get home in the evenings. Both have ended up studying degrees they wouldn't have chosen simply because they had to study in the higher education programmes in their home towns.

It is impossible to anticipate what might happen at a checkpoint on any given day. This is what Amal, another student from Nablus, told us about her experience of going for an examination in Ramallah during 2006:

Checkpoints

Last winter I had to take an English exam in Ramallah. It was not possible to do the exam in Nablus so I had to travel. When I got to the Huwarra checkpoint [near Nablus] I heard that the soldiers weren't allowing girls through who had a Nablus ID. Each day, you never know what the soldiers are going to say. Sometimes they put an age limit, like no girls under 20 can pass, or only girls and no boys, or 50 years is the limit. Sometimes they use IDs so that Jenin and Tulkarm IDs are not allowed today, only a Nablus ID or whatever. We never know in advance.

Because I had this exam I thought I might be able to persuade the soldiers to let me through. For half an hour I tried to convince three soldiers – two women and one man. Eventually it seemed that the male soldier was going to let me through when the two women soldiers intervened and said we will only let you through when you stop bombing yourselves! I said I was no bomber just a student trying to get to my exam. Oh well they said, you are not passing through here.

It was now raining so I went to a taxi that could take me around the checkpoint. It was a 45-minute trip on rough country roads in the rain and it brought me out onto the road directly the other side of the checkpoint. Forty-five minutes to go 20 metres! So I got to my exam. This is a common experience. How do you have a normal day at the university or even do an exam when you arrive after all this tension and frustration?

Amal, Tulkarm, February 2008

So much for the pressing security imperatives of Israel that it is possible to take a taxi to bypass the checkpoint! But as these Israeli soldiers recognised, security was not their "business":

> The only function of…[the] checkpoint is to put pressure on the Palestinian population. Officers explicitly told me that the checkpoint has no security value and was meant to harass the population. [Another soldier agrees.] The idea is to make life hard for the Palestinian citizenry. There is no operational objective to the checkpoint.[5]

Destroyed road between Tulkarm and Nablus, September 2006

This is well known in the West Bank. But Amal's taxi ride around the checkpoint also reveals an equally commonplace feature of the occupation and the checkpoints whereby a kind of "cat and mouse" game is played out between the Israeli military and the Palestinians. Bypass routes and paths are developed around the checkpoints. The rough terrain or circuitousness of the routes often make them inaccessible to the old or very young and taxis rule out many through expense. But younger people will use them as they attempt to go about their lives. The Israelis are aware of these routes and they will shoot at those they see, but we became aware that not all routes are closely monitored.

It struck us the one time we trekked through fields to bypass a checkpoint that the Israelis had still won by messing up our travel plans and making us struggle over farmland and walls.

This was also typified by another journey to Nablus from Tulkarm in 2006 when the Israeli army closed the main road with a metal gate. Just before the gate our minibus turned left onto a dirt road which we then drove up for about 10 kilometres into the nearby hills and then back down the track to the main road, this time on the Nablus side of the gate. However, just to make the final part more frustrating the Israeli army had bulldozed the final end of the track so it was impossible to drive back up onto the road. We got out of the minibus with tens of others and walked the remaining 50 metres to the road where another line of taxis was waiting to taking us on to Nablus. The Israelis are simply messing you about and stealing your time.

Between September 2000 and October 2003, 83 patients died at checkpoints, 57 women were forced to give birth at the checkpoints and of these 32 resulted in the death of an infant.[6]

All of this is deadly serious, as Ali reminded us. He was at university in Nablus when we met him in 2006 and he talked of his and his friends' frustration at the checkpoints and how they would look for ways to get around them. But, he continued:

It is dangerous to try and get around as the soldiers will shoot you if they see you. My friend was shot and killed when he tried to get round the checkpoint. But what can we do? We need to get to the university.
Ali, Nablus, September 2008

Checkpoints

We rarely had a conversation with young people on the West Bank that didn't remind us that checkpoints were dangerous places. They were places where ambulances had no priority, where patients on the way to hospital died, where babies were born without proper facilities.

It was the unpredictability of the soldiers – young con-scripts including women – which was a major cause of stress for many. These soldiers exercise total control. As 19 year old Mohammed told us, how you got through was:

entirely up to the mood of the soldier. There are no standards or criteria. One day they can let you through and the next they say all those from Nablus have to go back. We can never ques-tion the soldiers or they put us in the jura. The soldiers have guns and we have books. What can we do?
Mohammed, Nablus, September 2006

Every checkpoint has a jura, a detention area, for holding people at the checkpoint. We quickly discovered that being detained in a jura was commonplace, especially for young men over 16 years old. Ibrahim is 21 and lives in a village about 20 kms from Nablus. He told us about his experiences:

I am now in the fourth year at the university. I haven't got a hostel room so I travel in every day from the village. I get up at 5am to get to classes for 9am. In the evening it is the same,

Checkpoint births

Checkpoints restrict Palestinian freedom of movement and this has a serious impact on the ability of many Palestinians to access medical care, including emergency medical treatment. The UN Population Fund, UNFPA, claim that travel restrictions mean Palestinians often cannot reach and use essential medical facilities. They argue, "As a result of the increased security procedures at checkpoints...access of the Palestinian people to hospitals and medical facilities has been significantly impaired".[7]

According to the UN between September 2000 and September 2005 more than 60 women gave birth at checkpoints. These women endured labour in unsanitary and inhumane conditions that brought significant risks to both mother and baby. During the same period it was estimated that 36 of the newborn children died, as did five of the women.[8] Israeli journalist Gideon Levy, who writes for the *Ha'aretz* newspaper, has covered a number of checkpoint birth stories.[9] Here is a summary of Rula's story:

"We took a taxi and got off before the checkpoint because cars are not allowed near... I was in pain. At the checkpoint there were several soldiers; they...ignored us... I was lying on the ground and I crawled behind a concrete block...and gave birth there... I held the baby in my arms and she moved a little but after a few minutes she died in my arms".[10]

According to Article 38(5) the Fourth Geneva Convention, "...pregnant women...shall benefit by any preferential treatment to the same extent as the nationals of the State concerned".

three to four hours. Sometimes I am lucky to get a minibus, more times not. I have been stopped and handcuffed at the barriers so many times. It is humiliating. I am innocent, simply a student trying to go home.

When I am held in the jura I am so frustrated that although I love life I would prefer to explode myself. It is because of the humiliation. The daily humiliation.

Ibrahim, Beit Leed, September 2006

We saw numerous jura. They are crude open-sided shelters with a tin roof. They are about 5m by 4m. There are no seats, no water and no toilets. In the summer you cook and in the winter you freeze. They are near to the checkpoints and can be easily seen as the surrounding wall is rarely higher than two feet. If you are in the jura you are on public display – like a modern-day version of the stocks.

In all the cases we heard about, the young men were released after some hours. None of them were charged with anything; none had irregular papers. The detention could be anything from two to 12 hours, then an officer would appear, hand them back their ID and tell them to go. In a few cases one or two were questioned, especially when they had family members either in prison or known to the Israelis, but again they were usually released. As we were to learn time and again, you don't have to do anything to be picked up and detained by the Israelis. So time in the jura was yet another means whereby the power of the occupier can be wielded – where they can show who is boss.

Humiliation

The key feature of the occupation has always been humiliation: they [the Palestinians] must not be allowed to raise their heads. *Noam Chomsky*[11]

It is the humiliation which the young people talk about most:

The checkpoints are places where they try to humiliate and insult us. Many times they get us to strip naked, or to make the noises of dogs or donkeys. This is on top of the many delays, making us stand out in the sun.
Ibrahim, aged 16, Jenin, September 2006

The major problem at the checkpoints is the humiliation. The soldiers treat us badly. I hate it so much. They treat us like sheep. We have to line up and wait for them to look at our papers – they keep us so long, they talk to us so badly, it's humiliating. It never ends.
Usman, Tulkarm, February 2008

Usman is a female student from Tulkarm. Her friend Amal, also a student, poignantly reflected on the way the checkpoints can dominate the lives of the young on the West Bank:

As a young person these are supposed to be some of our best years but for us here in Palestine they are not. We don't think about what activities we are going to do this week. Instead we are thinking about how we are going to manage the checkpoints. Will they let me through? Are the soldiers going to tease me and humiliate me? Things like this.
For example, when I went last year to visit my grandfather in Ramallah I came to this checkpoint where the soldiers were

very bored. So to have fun they said to all the girls that we had to make two queues: one for the beautiful girls and one for the ugly girls. Then this soldier walked down and he stopped at one girl and said you are not beautiful, move to the other queue. Then he came to a beautiful girl who was wearing a scarf. He told her to take it off so he could see her hair. I didn't wait my turn. I didn't want to face this so I turned round and came back to Nablus. Another time at the Huwarra checkpoint [on the outskirts of Nablus] I was in the turnstile when they stopped it. It is very narrow and you are stuck in like a cage and I was with my bags and books. I kept saying to the soldiers let me through but it was like talking to a wall. After 30 minutes they let me through and as I came through the soldiers were joking and being sarcastic.

When you are in these situations you feel as though you can't say or do anything. The soldiers have guns and they might shoot you or at least hurt you. So you hold all feelings inside and I feel that we hurt our friends and families when we release our anger from inside. Many of the students have nightmares. The checkpoints are a major cause of anxiety for us.
Amal, Tulkarm, February 2008

Routine insults are a common part of the humiliation. Many times we were told of soldiers having a laugh at older men who they forced to make donkey noises, or dance with loads on their backs. The young Palestinian women, whether they wore the hijab or not, felt constantly at threat from the young male Israeli soldiers. Sexual innuendo was rampant. The constant fear of being strip-searched is heightened in a culture which is deeply modest with respect to the body. This the young Israeli soldiers know only too well. We heard many accounts of youths and older men being stripped to their underwear at checkpoints. The sexual harassment of women and girls is rarely so explicit in terms of making them strip in public. It would be a provocation the Israelis would find hard to contain, such would be the outraged reaction. However, inappropriate touching at checkpoints is commonplace for young women, as are offensive sexual remarks.

Dividing people up at checkpoints is also common. Young people described how they are often divided by age, gender and place of residence. We heard from young people in the largely Christian village of Aboud near Ramallah that soldiers sometimes divided them by religion – Christian from Muslim. As this teenage girl from Aboud explained to us:

We live in the same situation as the Muslims. There is no difference. We are one people, Palestinian, and it makes no difference if you are Christian or Muslim. But the Israelis try to make a difference, for example at the checkpoints they will announce in a loud voice that only Christians will be allowed through and the Muslims have to go back. Yet at night the soldiers will come to Aboud knowing it is a mainly Christian village and ransack our homes and disturb our lives. We know what the Israelis are trying to do and it doesn't work.

Aboud, September 2006

Power at the checkpoints

These crude efforts at divide and rule had no purchase on the young people we met, but each of these efforts was also an exercise in power with no sanction or accountability. Soldiers could and did act with impunity when messing around with the lives of Palestinians. This is what frightens and disturbs and makes every checkpoint experience one of tension and anxiety. As Saree Makdisi relates in his compelling book on the occupation, many IDF soldiers get a kick out of having such unrestrained power:

> You can't help but enjoy it. People do what you tell them. You know it's because you carry a weapon. Knowing that if you didn't have it, and if your fellow soldiers weren't beside you, they would jump on you, beat the shit out of you, and stab you to death – you begin to enjoy it. Not merely enjoy it, you need it…it makes you feel good. I remember a very specific situation. I was at a checkpoint, a temporary one,

Noor – are you strong?

This was the question put to Noor by the Israeli officer who questioned him. He had been "pulled" and put in the jura at the Enab checkpoint. He comes from a large family some of whom are in prison, others who are politically active. It was, he thought, on account of his family name that he was stopped for questioning.

He was on his way home to Tulkarm from the university in Nablus where he had just completed the first year of his law degree. He was questioned after a two-hour wait. His answer was that sometimes he feels strong and sometimes not. The officer promised him that he could make him strong all the time – give him a car, a house in Israel and even a wife! In return he would have to work for them as an informer, especially with respect to his family in Tulkarm and supply information about students at the university. Noor flatly rejected this offer and told the officer he was being ridiculous to expect such a thing from him.

He was then released and told he could go, but not before the officer told him that he managed many informers at the university and that they would be keeping an eye on him. As far as Noor was concerned this was an empty threat. The students all know that there are collaborators among them and they take care.

As it happens, Noor has not enjoyed his law course and is going to transfer to Finance and Accounting. He can study this subject in Tulkarm so he will no longer have to make the long, uncertain daily journey to Nablus.

a so-called strangulation checkpoint, it was a very small check-point, very intimate, four soldiers, no commanding officer, no protection worthy of the name, a true moonlighting job, blocking the entrance to a village. From one side a line of cars wanting to get out, and from the other side another line of cars wanting to pass, a huge line, and suddenly you have a mighty force at the tip of your fingers, as if playing a computer game. I stand there like this, pointing at someone, gesturing to you to do this or that, and you do this or that, the car starts, moves towards me, halts besides me. You come here, you go there, like this. You barely move, you make them obey the tip of your finger. It's a mighty feeling. It's something you don't experience elsewhere. You know it's because you have a weapon, you know it's because you're a soldier, you know all this, but it's addictive.[12]

As we were told so many times, the decisive factor governing all interactions at the checkpoints is that the soldiers have weapons and the Palestinians don't. Moreover, everyone knows that the soldiers use them. As the young male student at the Friends School in Ramallah told us ironically, "It's a Bush thing – shoot first and talk later" (Ramallah, September 2006).

We did not hear many stories of overt resistance at checkpoints, although we did hear that people in the queues will shout at soldiers who are being especially brutal or unreasonable. We also heard a story about a delayed crowd at a checkpoint near Nablus which advanced on the checkpoint singing patriotic Palestinian songs and pressed the soldiers to open the checkpoint. However, such stories were rare and we met no young people who had been personally involved in any open form of collective resistance at a checkpoint. People want to get through and to get on with their lives and they know that the Israelis will close a checkpoint at the first sign of trouble and delay reopening as a form of collective punishment. Of no less importance is the knowledge, either through personal experience or from other sources, that checkpoints are notorious for arbitrary and random acts of violence on the part of the soldiers. This is what happened to Wafa, a young woman from a village about 20km from Ramallah:

In 2004 when we had many closures I went to Birzeit University with two friends. When we got to the checkpoint at the entrance to the university it was packed with people as the checkpoint was closed. After a two-hour wait the soldiers announced through the loudspeakers that only girls and women would be allowed through. There were very many of us but as we began to move towards the checkpoint the soldiers fired tear gas without any warning. We turned shouting and screaming and ran. People fell over and were hurt in the panic, and as we ran the soldiers began to fire their guns and wounded some of the women.

Wafa, Ramallah, September 2006

A Palestinian at a checkpoint can never be sure when one soldier or more will "kick off", especially if the checkpoint is crowded and discontented. As one teenage volunteer explained:

A friend said to me that the soldiers are playing a game with us. But you know it's not like a game. In a game there are rules and logic. But there is no logic in how they operate, they know they can do what they want, they can fire their guns – we don't know when, where or why they will do this. There is no logic and no rules.

Nayef, Balata, June 2008

One evening we were with crowds of students trying to get through the checkpoint out of Nablus before it closed at 7pm in order to get back to Tulkarm. As we shuffled forward the young Israeli soldier who had been patrolling the queue suddenly rifle-butted a young male student in the face. He was standing only a few metres in front of us and from what we saw the attack was completely unprovoked. The student was taken away. We said nothing even though as "internationals" we were at minimal risk of any reprisals from the soldiers. No one around us said anything. We just kept moving forward. It was an awful feeling which left us troubled. Later we came across Raja Shehadeh's account of his

Nayef's story

Nayef is one of the young volunteers at the Yaffa Centre, Balata and a student in graphic design at the An-Najah University in Nablus. As we were talking about his work he happened to mention in passing that he had been delayed in his studies through being shot by the Israelis while at the Huwarra checkpoint near Nablus. He was 17 years old. He was luckier than many. The bullet passed through his lower arm and missed the bone and main arteries and nerves. With physiotherapy he has now got about 80 percent usage of his right hand and it has not stopped him from continuing with his art.

As with so many of the young people injured and shot by the Israeli army he was simply in the wrong place at the wrong time. He was in the queue and suddenly some soldiers started shooting and he was hit. He still does not know why they started firing live ammunition. There had been no disturbances or hassle. Nayef was not arrested; indeed the soldiers near him gave him immediate first aid and put him in the Red Crescent ambulance to take him to hospital.

But this story, which can be repeated endlessly by young people in the West Bank, is not simply about random shooting. The young here know full well they are being deliberately targeted by the army. It is their gender and youth that endangers them, regardless of what they do.

experience when he was with a friend who had been humiliated at a checkpoint:

> After we passed the checkpoint I realised that I was seething with anger. Not at the soldier, but at myself. I a lawyer, for many years a human rights activist, stood silently by and allowed this travesty to take place. More than any of the others, who also stood by in silence, I should have spoken up. What had happened to make me so passive that I made no attempt to stop the soldier from humiliating my friend?… We all stood meekly by, without so much as a whimper of protest and ended up feeling grateful just to have been allowed to pass.[13]

We should have intervened even though we were taken by surprise and were frightened by the soldiers and aware that we would no doubt be deported from Israel. But it was a salutary, disheartening and disturbing experience and a stark reminder of the power of those with guns and the profound vulnerability of the Palestinians.

Every aspect of a checkpoint confirms this unequal power relationship – the drab surroundings, the absence of facilities, the level of surveillance, the holding pens and queues, and the turnstiles. What better demonstrates the banality of evil than the Israeli government's request that the manufacturer of their turnstiles should reduce the standard length of the arms of between 75cm and 90cm (as used commonly in swimming pools and libraries) to a mere 55cm for those destined for checkpoints. The tighter squeeze, it was argued, was needed to disclose bombs or weapons hidden under clothes, although in practice it hurts and humiliates those who are overweight, parents with young children, women with shopping and so forth.[15]

We laughed with the retired primary school teacher from Beit Leed who refused to go through the new narrow gates on his way to school. He argued with the soldiers that it would tear

---

Checkpoint incident

The barricade is coming up! We run back to our cars. But shots suddenly ring out and the order is shouted into a megaphone – "Back! Back!" Terrified, people move back and take shelter behind the vehicles.

"They usually fire blanks," the engineer reassures me, "but you never know. People have been wounded even killed. The soldiers then say that the crowd threatened them! They are almost untouchable – the army never tries them, unless foreign witnesses report a blatant case…"

"But why did they shoot just now? People were going back to their cars. It doesn't make any sense!"

"No it doesn't make any sense," he agrees gravely, "It never makes any sense… It is that inconsistency and injustice which, minute by minute and day by day, eats away at us, perhaps more than the real tragedies…"

France-based journalist Mourad[14]

his suit and as a teacher he needed to set an example to the chil-

dren. After much banter the soldiers relented and from that day until he retired shortly after he never went through the gate.

However, checkpoints are not places for laughter. As Amal related checkpoints are a cause of nightmares and phobias. We heard older children describe how their younger brothers and sisters had been frightened at the checkpoints by the behaviour of the soldiers. It was especially difficult to hear how upset and shocked they had been when they had seen their parents humiliated by the soldiers. As Najwa (16 years old) related to us in the Balata refugee camp in Nablus:

> Look into the eyes of the young kids at the checkpoint and barriers. You can see that they are nervous and are humiliated. It is a very terrible thing to see your elders, your parents treated so badly by the Israeli soldiers many of whom are only a few years older than us. We look up to our parents and respect them and to see them treated as though they are nothing is very hard for us.
>
> Young children often hate to go to the checkpoints because of their bad expectations about what might happen to them or their parents. That is why so many of them don't want to visit relatives if it means going through a checkpoint.
>
> *Najwa, Balata, September 2006*

Checkpoint turnstiles. Photo: Reality Check Point, draykcab. wordpress.com

For Najwa, reaching the age of 16 was a cause of sadness because of what it meant for her at the checkpoints:

> I am now 16 years old and I have to get an ID. I don't want it. I hate the idea. I don't want to be on my own at the checkpoints being questioned by a soldier with my own ID. I want to be with my parents and on their ID. Not on my own.
>
> *Najwa, Balata, September 2006*

It was a sentiment echoed by Abid, a male university student at the same meeting:

> I would like to say that I am now 20 years old and I want to be 35 because then I can move through the barriers with no trouble. Here we are, the youth, in what should be times when we

can give much of ourselves and yet we hope to be younger than 16 or older than 35!

Abid, Balata, September 2006

Targeting education

Many young people told us that they were convinced that the occupying forces targeted schools and universities and were intent upon disrupting their attempts to develop themselves through education. Young children told us how they are frightened when soldiers stop and search them on the way to school; older children told us that the army always increased its patrols and incursions into their towns, villages and refugee camps during important school examination periods. Then there were the incursions into the schools themselves with soldiers firing tear gas and rubber bullets. All the primary school aged children we met knew about tear gas and some had even been gassed but all knew what to do in the event of a gas attack – using cut onions to alleviate the effect and avoiding all use of water around the eyes. We were also told many times and in many different places of army patrols at or around their schools as they went or left for home – a time when there was the maximum number of young people on the streets. Lina from Nablus was very clear about what she saw happening during 2006:

> In the past year the soldiers have been deliberately provocative. For example, I noticed that soldiers in jeeps would concentrate around the schools between 7am and 9am when all the students were going to school. I saw this every day in an area where there are two boys' schools. The students aged from seven to 18 would be passing these soldiers every morning and some of them got into groups and threw stones and shouted at the soldiers. The soldiers would then shoot. This is how my friend's cousin aged 15 was killed. Going to school and killed by the random shooting of the soldiers. None of this is an accident. The soldiers by going to the schools at this time know they will provoke a response which leads to shootings. It's been a terrible year for our right to education.
>
> *Lina, Nablus, September 2006*

As we have already noted, Palestine is a young society and during term times it is moving to see literally thousands of young people making their way to schools and universities. For many of them dealing with the checkpoints is a daily experience rarely without long delays and, at the mere whim of the soldiers on duty, they are either refused passage or delayed so long that their day is ruined. And the next day they try again. It is one of the clearest examples of *sammoud* – steadfastness and resoluteness – which, as we discuss later, is at the core of the Palestinian resistance to the occupation.

Knowing your country

At the Balata camp we were told in early 2008 that 50 percent of the picnics and summer camps organised by the cultural centre fail, because they cannot get through the checkpoints. On one occasion Hassan, another Yaffa Centre volunteer, told us about going on a day trip for a picnic:

Checkpoints

> We had to go through the Huwarra checkpoint. This time they got us all out, they checked all our bags then they even inspected the bus. Then the Israelis insisted that it wasn't enough that we had birth certificates for all those under 16 years old, they said these were insufficient. They said each child should have one of their parents come to the checkpoint and prove who they were. After hard negotiation and a lot of time they left us and they agreed we could go on, but it took so much time that we couldn't get to our picnic and they had ruined our day.
>
> *Hassan, Balata, February 2008*

And from the Al-Amari camp in Ramallah we heard:

> Last year we tried to take a trip to Jericho. We got them on the bus. They were seven to 14 years old. They were so excited and happy. But then the Israelis turned them back. You can't imagine their frustration, their hurt.
>
> *Mohammed, volunteer worker, Al-Amari, February 2008*

These words can only capture part of the hurt and upset experienced by young people. A picnic outing might sound small to many in the West, but for young Palestinians who spend virtually all of their time in overcrowded refugee camps where the world outside the camp is a great mystery, the few chances to leave the camp are filled with immense excitement. But so many of these trips fail.

As a result of the checkpoints many on the West Bank, not only from the refugee camps, travel little and have little knowledge or sense of the West Bank as a whole, even in its fractured state. Unless one has close family elsewhere in the West Bank there is little movement even though the distances between the major Palestinian cities are small. Of course the major yearning for nearly all those in the West Bank and Gaza is to have access to Jerusalem. Since the 1967 war this has been denied to most Palestinians other than those with clear documentary proof of their historic Jerusalem residency.

Travel is further restricted by a complex system of permits which determine movement between "governates" in the West Bank and between Gaza and the West Bank. Some cities such as Nablus have been subjected to periodic general closures since 2002 and the start of the Second Intifada. The checkpoints compound all of these difficulties.

As our guide Mohammed told us, it is easier to travel from Tulkarm to London than it is to travel to Hebron or to Jericho or Bethlehem in the West Bank. These are cities of great historical and cultural significance for Palestinians and never further than 150 kilometres apart, and yet largely unknown except to those who live there. This is why schools and youth organisations make such efforts to travel to other towns and cities in the West Bank to give young people a chance to meet and share experiences. All of these groups would much prefer to visit nearby Jerusalem or take the children to the yearned-after sea, but such choices have been virtually impossible since the mid-1990s.

Nablus

Nablus itself, a city of over 130,000 people, used to provide specialised health care and higher education facilities to a further 350,000 residents of the northern West Bank. If they have the right permits, they can now enter the city in one of the handful of buses and taxis that are allowed through the local checkpoints. Otherwise, access to Nablus is on foot – and Nablus, the largest city in the West Bank, has been under this siege for years. All entrances and exits are regulated by Israeli army checkpoints, where identity papers and permits are checked. There was a day of total closure for every three of "normal" movement in 2006, and one day of closure for every two "normal" days in 2005. On such days 3 million Palestinians go nowhere.

Palestine Inside Out:
An Everyday Occupation [16]

Of course some succeed and we did meet youngsters who had travelled around the West Bank (and further afield), but it always involved enormous effort and uncertainty and too many failures. The more time you spend discussing the checkpoints the more destructive effects you discover. In 2008 for example the football league was unable to complete its fixture list because so many matches had been disrupted and postponed as a result of teams being stopped and detained at checkpoints.

Football

Football is one of the most popular sports in the West Bank. In the refugee camps and on bits of waste ground you often see young boys kicking a ball around. Satellite channels cover football from around the world.Mohamed Iraqi is a librarian in Tulkarm, a sports journalist for the local press and a coach for the Tulkarm under-15s football team.Mohamed told us that, like everything else here, football has been disrupted by the occupation. Before 2000, for example, Tulkarm used to play in front of crowds of 3,000 to 5,000. The league was competitive and the standard okay. Palestinian players had been picked from the

league and made some progress in other Middle Eastern leagues and even in Europe. But then came the occupation.

Nablus used to have a good team – but not any more. They find it hard to train, their pitch has been destroyed, the spaces to play football have been closed down and many of the youngsters who would normally take up the games have been arrested.Tulkarm are now sitting at the top of the league. We asked Mohamed when the league would finish and got an astonishing answer: it doesn't! It is often impossible to travel to matches, the Israelis stop supporters and team members at checkpoints when they travel, pitches are destroyed, and games cannot be planned ahead because it will never be known when towns, cities and roads will be cut off. Teams play who they can, when they can.

Checkpoints and occupation

Checkpoints are a formidable weapon in the armoury of occupation. They are enormously destructive of economic, social, political and personal relationships. They cause anxiety and fear and above all humiliate and frustrate. The checkpoints that now scatter the landscape of the West Bank have the capacity to lock down the cities, towns and villages of the West Bank.

They are so invasive and destructive that human rights groups routinely refer to Israel's checkpoint policies as collective, and hence illegal, punishment.[17]

They have been one of the most obvious factors destroying Palestinian economic life. How is it possible to trade, to build or to manufacture when there is such uncertainty over moving people and goods around? This was exemplified by the three young male farmers we met in Qalqilya who were not only having to cope with the trauma of losing land to the Wall but were facing destruction of their market due to the checkpoints. The barriers had made it impossible for them to reach such important markets as that in Hebron, which meant that fruit and vegetables were left to spoil or sold locally at below cost price. The consequences have been widespread and damaging, as we discuss in more detail later, with unprecedented numbers of Palestinians without work and aid-dependent.

August bodies such as the World Bank, the UN and the EU have routinely identified checkpoints as a major obstacle to the economic development of the West Bank. According to a World Bank report published in May 2007, economic recovery and sustainable growth within the West Bank would "require a fundamental reassessment of closure practices, a restoration of the presumption of movement, and review of Israeli control of the population registry and other means of dictating the residency of Palestinians".[19]

This is important criticism, for acute poverty is widespread and deepening both in the West Bank and Gaza. In May 2008 the Palestinian Central Bureau of Statistics published data showing that 67 percent of the population needed assistance with their basic living costs in 2007. That figure is rising. However, the case against checkpoints is not one-dimensional. It is not simply a matter of weighing the economic development of Palestine against the presumed security of Israel.

The young people we met had a clear and multi-faceted understanding of checkpoints and Israeli policies in the West Bank. They recognise that checkpoints have emerged as a key tool of the occupation for management of the people of the

---

Transporting goods

The driver of a van carrying fruit and vegetables tells me that the previous week he had waited for 48 hours, sleeping there for two nights; when he finally reached his destination on the other side, almost all his cargo had rotted…

"I have seen entire loads of chickens die from dehydration," a lorry driver tells me. "So we don't often risk transporting them now. It's the same for fruit and vegetables, which rot very quickly. The only solution is to sell what you can on the spot".

Our Sacred Land[18]

West Bank and that this control is their purpose – they do not
exist to prevent suicide attackers from getting through to Israel.
Indeed Israeli human rights organisations such as Checkpoint
Watch have long argued that checkpoints increase the security
threat to Israeli by radicalising Palestinians.[20]

The daily Israeli provocation of the Palestinian population
in the West Bank is beyond most of our imaginings. Just how
they deal with these pressures – sometimes well and sometimes
not – we discuss later. But something needs to be noted here.
Whatever else they are, checkpoints are generators of immense
frustration. The young people we met were aware that the ultimate purpose of the occupation and with it the checkpoints
was to defeat their resolve to claim their rights to their land
and country by provoking such levels of frustration that they
would leave the West Bank. As Nancy Hollander observed in
her account of resistance in Latin America during the 1970s
and 1980s,[21] it was the realisation that the state and its military
could act with almost total impunity that weakened resistance and morale. These features of power are all too evident
at the checkpoints. The soldiers can do pretty much as they
want. What is more, this goes on daily and has been going
on for years with no sign of any relief. Yet, unlike Hollander,
what we witnessed in the West Bank were young people who,
in the main, simply refuse to be defeated or provoked by this
behaviour, which is routinely racist and extends from insults
to bullets and tear gas. They may rage inside, but at the checkpoints you would never know. The levels of self-discipline
evident here are extraordinary.

Checkpoints are one of the few places in the West Bank
where large numbers of Palestinians come face to face with
their occupiers and, notwithstanding the violence of the IDF,
are possible sites for acts of mass civil disobedience and protest.
That has not happened, or if so only rarely. We were given a
number of explanations for this, not the least the evident reality that the soldiers had guns, gas and batons and they did not.
This made checkpoints dangerous places especially when everyone knew that the soldiers used tear gas and shot live rounds
or rubber bullets at the slightest provocation. Moreover, whenever any sort of incident occurred at a checkpoint the Israelis
immediately retaliated, often through closing the checkpoint
for days at a time.

Also such collective action, throughout the years of our visits, has not been encouraged by the PA. From before Oslo,
under the tutelage of Arafat, the PLO had set a course that

only through negotiation and collaboration with Israel and the US would the Palestinians achieve national liberation. One result of this strategy was the preparedness of the PA to take on the policing of its own people on behalf of Israel. Indeed, the Israelis made it a condition that progress in "peace" negotiations is dependent on the ability of the PA to control its militants, especially those in Hamas and other radical left or Islamist groups, including some within Fatah.[22] The consequences have been far-reaching, as we will show, but it has meant that for much of the post-Oslo period a decisive element of the historic leadership of the Palestinian people has been opposed to initiating or organising any sustained collective resistance. The PA's insistence to Israel that it had no role in sparking the Second Intifada in the autumn of 2000 is but one stark example of this position, and there are many more which demonstrate the PA's distrust of popular protest and mass mobilisations.

In 2009 the Israelis reduced the number of checkpoints within the West Bank, although they simultaneously upgraded all the major checkpoints such as at Qalandiya and Qalqilya which give direct access to Israel. This policy shift was not merely a reflection of Israeli sensitivities to international protest about the crippling consequences of the checkpoints but also an indication of Israel's growing confidence in the PA's security forces to do their work for them.

Although there is much relief that the car journey from Tulkarm to Nablus is now 30 minutes rather than two hours, and involves none of the hazards and hassles of checkpoints, our Palestinian friends pointed out that the checkpoint infrastructure has not been dismantled or removed. Despite the then Israeli government making much of the new prosperity supposedly accruing to the West Bank following the opening of some checkpoints, especially around Jenin and Nablus,[24] as of August 2010 there were still 59 permanent checkpoints in the West Bank, 18 of which are in and around Hebron. Flying checkpoints had increased to 310 per month by March 2010, compared with 89 a month in 2008. In spring 2010 there were

Collaboration at the checkpoints

Officers in the IDF's Judea and Samaria division told *Ha'aretz* that the increasing cooperation with the Palestinian security forces, along with the Shin Bet security service's intelligence capabilities in the West Bank, meant the IDF could handle such a change. "The security organisations control the cities well," one officer said, "and a terrorist who escapes into one of the cities will find it difficult to hide there." The IDF has removed many of the West Bank checkpoints over the past year, but still has troops stationed at the entrances and exits of Palestinian cities.

Ha'aretz, 25 October 2010[23]

still 418 obstacles – rocks, earth mounds, pre-cast blocks and the like – blocking access for Palestinian travellers.[25] In addition, many of the more strategic checkpoints such as those near settlements and the Green Line with Israel have been significantly refurbished with sophisticated surveillance systems. These seemingly empty checkpoints are still operational. In April 2009 we were told about three Palestinian men from Nablus who had been involved in an attack on settlers near one of the now empty checkpoints, and they were caught and executed in or near their homes by Israeli forces within a few hours of the attack. The swiftness of the response suggested they had been identified on CCTV evidence gathered at the checkpoint. The students from Nablus who recounted this story were very clear that as long as checkpoints were still standing then whatever ease they now enjoyed in some of their travels could only ever be considered temporary.

Notes

1 *Palestine Monitor*, December 2008, "Checkpoints", www.palestinemonitor.org/spip/spip.php?article8 (accessed 1 April 2009).

2 Israel-Palestine in Maps, 31 August 2006, www.hweb.org.uk/content/view/69/3/ (accessed 17 April 2011).

3 Jews Against the Occupation, "Israeli Checkpoints in West Bank", www.jatonyc.org/checkpoint.html (accessed 20 March 2009).

4 Y Keshet, *Checkpoint Watch: Testimonies from Occupied Palestine* (Zed Books, 2006), pp13-14.

5 S Makdisi, *Palestine Inside Out: An Everyday Occupation* (WW Norton, 2008), p52.

6 Y Keshet, as above, p20.

7 UN Population Fund quoted in BBC News, "UN fears over checkpoint births", 23 September 2005, news.bbc.co.uk/1/hi/world/middle_east/4274400.stm (accessed 1 April 2009).

8 UN High Commissioner for Human Rights quoted in BBC News, "UN fears over checkpoint births", as above.

9 See G Levy, "Twilight Zone: Born in the shadow of a checkpoint", *Ha'aretz*, 24 January 2008, www.haaretz.com/hasen/pages/ShArt.jhtml?itemNo=947917 (accessed 1 April 2009).

10 G Levy, "Twilight Zone: Birth and death at the checkpoint", *Ha'aretz*, 12 September 2003, www.haaretz.com/hasen/pages/ShArt.jhtml?itemNo=338937 (accessed 1 April 2009).

11 N Chomsky, *The Fateful Triangle* (Pluto Press, 1999), p489.

12 S Makdisi, as above, pp53-54.

13 R Shehadeh, *Palestinian Walks: Notes on a Vanishing Landscape* (Profile Books, 2008), pp133-134.

14 K Mourad, *Our Sacred Land* (One World, 2004), p153.

15 E Weizman, *Hollow Land: Israel's Architecture of Occupation* (Verso, 2007), p151.

16 S Makdisi, as above, pp57-58.

17 Such groups include some significant

organisations formed by Israeli Jews who oppose the occupation, such as the Israeli women's group Machsom Watch (www.machsomwatch.org/en) and B'tselem (www.btselem.org/English/index.asp) which since 1989 has monitored and published reports on many aspects of human rights abuses in the Occupied Territories.

18 K Mourad, as above, pp152-153.

19 World Bank, *Investing in Palestinian Economic Reform and Development* (2007), siteresources.worldbank.org/ INTWESTBANKGAZA/ Resources/294264-1166525851073/ ParisconferencepaperDec17.pdf (accessed 24 March 2011).

20 See, for example, Y Keshet, as above.

21 N C Hollander, *Love in a Time of Hate: Liberation Psychology in Latin America* (Rutgers University Press, 1997).

22 See M Rabbani, "A Smorgasbord of Failure: Oslo and the Al-Aqsa Intifada" in R Carey (ed), *The New Intifada* (Verso, 2001), pp79-81.

23 www.haaretz.com/print-edition/news/idf-planning-for-potential-pa-ban-on-west-bank-raids-1.320977 (accessed 25 October 2010).

24 Summed up clearly in the article by then Israeli US ambassador, Michael Oren, in his extraordinarily titled comment piece in the *Wall Street Journal*, "West Bank Success Story: The Palestinians are flourishing economically. Unless they live in Gaza", 13 August 2009.

25 B'Tselem, "Restrictions on Movement" (2010), www.btselem.org/English/ Freedom_of_Movement/Statistics.asp (accessed 24 March 2011).

Chapter 3

Imprisonment and arrest

A recurring theme in our discussions with young people across the West Bank, whether it was in isolated villages, in the camps, or in the larger cities and towns, was imprisonment and arrest. In every group we met there were always some young people who had been arrested at one time or another and there were very few indeed who did not have a close relative – a brother, an uncle, a father, more rarely a sister, aunt or mother – who was either in prison or had been in prison. Saed, a 15 year old boy living in the Jenin camp told us it was a matter of when rather than if he or his friends would be arrested:

> We live in fear always of arrest. We know they will catch us one day. It is inevitable but we don't know when. It is incredible.
> *Saed, Jenin, September 2006*

There are over 1,500 military regulations governing the Palestinian population in the West Bank.[1] These regulations cover all manner of "infringements" and hundreds of thousands of Palestinians have been detained by Israel during the occupation and colonisation of Palestine. Indeed, "Often Israeli military commanders in particular regions issue military orders which remain unknown by the Palestinian population subject to them, who in turn only find out about them once they are implemented or 'broken'".[2]

The military regulations include, for example, Military Order 101 which forbids taking part in a political march or a meeting of more than ten people without the prior approval of the Military Commander. The same order prohibits the distribution of political pictures, articles or newspapers, while Military Order 938 prohibits holding the flag of "a hostile organisation" (such as Fatah, Hamas or the PFLP) and makes it clear that singing or listening to a nationalist song can be considered a "hostile action".[3]

Only a minority of the young people we met had been arrested and imprisoned for direct political activity, but this does not mean young Palestinians are defeated or cowed into submission by the occupation of their land: resistance at many levels, rarely within organised political parties, is part of their daily life. It takes many forms, from throwing stones at soldiers, tanks and jeeps, or defacing the Wall or other Israeli installations, to looking into the eyes of the soldiers who question them as they pass through the checkpoints. For the Israelis all these actions are sufficient reason to detain Palestinians and to categorise them as a threat to the security of Israel. For the Palestinians resistance is not an option but a necessity for their very survival and humanity. This resistance is enshrined in international law and conventions, as article 51 of the UN Charter makes clear: "A state which forcibly subjugates a people to colonial or alien domination is committing an unlawful act as defined by international law, and the subject people, in the exercise of its inherent right of self-defence, may fight to defend and attain its right to self-determination." Likewise, in the 1977 article 1(4) of the First Additional Protocol (IAP) to the Geneva Conventions international humanitarian law was expanded to include "armed conflicts in which peoples are fighting against colonial domination and alien occupation and against racist regimes in the exercise of their right of self-determination".[4] Israel is not a signatory to this protocol, but as we shall see, being a signatory or not to a swathe of international conventions and laws has never been a hindrance to the Israeli occupation of the West Bank and Gaza.

The Palestinian prisoners' organisation Addameer suggests that since the end of the 1967 war, over 650,000 Palestinians have been detained by Israel. This equates to approximately 20 percent of the total Palestinian population in the OPT. The majority of prisoners are male and this means that somewhere in the region of 40 percent of the total male population of the OPT have been imprisoned at some point,[5] making Palestinians one of the most imprisoned peoples in the world.

For Ibrahim, a 16 year old boy in the Al-Amari refugee camp, the daily incursions of the Israeli army made the prospect of prison almost inevitable and very much shaped his immediate outlook on life:

My brother is in prison, he is 18 years old. He was a worker and he tried to save money to build a flat over the family home and get married. This was his dream and his expectation for the future. But then they came and arrested him – now all his dreams have disappeared.

Why should I study, and train to get a good job and money because there are no jobs and anyway the Israelis are going to come for us and put us in prison? Many of my friends in Amari think the same.

Ibrahim, Al-Amari, February 2008

As in many cases there was no evident reason for his brother's arrest other than that he was deemed a "security threat" – which in his case appears to be because he was a member of the youth centre's sword fencing team!

Arrest

In most cases…arrests happen during house raids, often conducted after midnight, and in which no reason is given for the detention. The soldiers frequently open fire against the building before entering, raid the family home, beat the family members or use them as human shields during the arrests. Arrests are often carried out in a humiliating way; …the person is…beaten or forced to strip in public, before being taken away to a location undisclosed to either the detainee or their family.[6]

Arrests are often random. Young people can be picked up on a series of pretexts, but often their only crime is to be in the wrong place at the wrong time. Hassan told us what happened to him:

There was no reason for my arrest. The soldiers came to my house at night and turned the place over, breaking many things including doors and cupboards. They never spoke or said what they were looking for. I was sure they had made a mistake and had come for the wrong people. Neither my father nor my brothers had ever been arrested and I had done nothing. At first I thought they were looking for my cousin who was "wanted" at the time. But when they finished the search they arrested me. I was cuffed behind my back and blindfolded and taken to a centre for interrogation. They questioned me about whether I had guns or whether I had ever been involved on an attack on Israel – I had done nothing! When I came to the Military Court they asked me similar questions and then said I'd been throwing Molotov cocktails. It was ridiculous! I thought it was a joke! But the judge gave me six months in administrative detention.

Hassan, Qalqilya, February 2008

Another was arrested because he went out without his ID:

I came to the checkpoint and the soldier asked me my name. I gave it and he then asked me for my ID but I told him that I had left it by mistake at home. With this he and three other soldiers started hitting me and then shouting at me to make the noises of donkeys. I was then arrested, put in the jura and later taken away. I got six months administrative detention.

Ibrahim, Jenin, September 2006

The smallest act of defiance can be enough to get you arrested:

At the Hawara checkpoint when we were going on a trip an officer and three soldiers were provoking us. They stood very close and pushed their faces towards ours. As soon as my friend looked back into the officer's eyes the soldiers grabbed him, handcuffed his hands behind his back and took him.

Maman, Nablus, September 2006

Amal was a member of a youth theatre group in Balata refugee camp. In 2005 the group got permits to leave Palestine and tour Britain over the summer. But:

One of our members of the dance band was arrested at the Bridge [Allenby Bridge] as we were on our way. He was 16 years old and they refused to let him leave. He got seven years in prison. It's a long sentence…and we all knew…he had done nothing. This is how it is. Whenever you are arrested you never know what they are going to say or do.

Amal, Balata, September 2006

Hassan, Ibrahim, Maman and Amal all cite cases where young people have been arrested without any obvious cause – a defiant look or the minor infringement of forgetting an ID card represent the full extent of the young men's crimes.

Some find themselves arrested because of their involvement in political campaigning – this marks them out as "suspect". Adeeb is a young community activist who had spent one year in administrative detention. He spoke to us at the Jenin Disability Project offices:

Mahmoud's story

Mahmoud comes from the Jenin refugee camp. He was arrested by the IDF in Jenin in April 2002, as part of the events now known as the Jenin Massacre.

In April 2002 the Israelis launched a fierce attack against the camp. Tanks, Humvees, bulldozers and troops descended on the camp from all angles. People retreated to their homes in panic – yet that was to prove an insignificant barrier to the troops as they implemented a policy called "walking through walls": the troops would enter a home, kick out, arrest or kill the inhabitants before blowing a hole in the wall adjoining their neighbours' home, where they would start the process again. The troops pushed on relentlessly forcing people into the central camp area.

The defenders (affectionately known as the Shabab) tried everything to protect the women, children and elders of the camp. They often deliberately drew fire upon themselves to divert attacks from the homes of the defenceless – and they paid a huge price in terms of arrest and loss of life.

After two days of fierce fighting the Israelis announced over tannoys that there would be a brief ceasefire. Mahmoud and his family left their home and were immediately arrested. Men were separated from women and children. The men were forced to take their clothes off, down to their underpants, and then had their hands cuffed behind their back and their eyes blindfolded.

In this state Mahmoud was marched off to a field at the edge of Jenin, about 2 kilometres away. From there he was put on a military bus and taken to prison. After a few days of interrogation he and a few of his mates were let out. But they were now just over 15km away from Jenin and had to walk back to their homes, dressed in only their underwear. But as they got closer to home they realised that Jenin was still "locked down" and there would be no way into the city or the camp for them.

Luckily at a neighbouring village they were taken to the local school and given a blanket to cover themselves and, later, tracksuits sent in from a Palestinian village within Israel.

I have just spent one year in administrative detention, though I am innocent and I am not a fighter. They came for me during the night. I was living in a flat in the old city because our house had been destroyed during the incursion in April 2002. About 20 vehicles turned up – APCs, jeeps, and tanks – and about 250 soldiers… The soldiers shouted for everyone to come out of the building without any delay. They then started to break the windows and doors and let off explosives against the walls. I came out with others, we had our hands up. One of the soldiers asked me for my ID and he just said, "You're wanted." I was blindfolded and had my hands fastened behind my back and I was pushed onto the floor of an APC. There were a few of us in the APC. I had no idea of where we were going and we must have driven for about two to three hours, but later I found out we were held at Salem military base, not far from Jenin. They had driven around to confuse us.

Adeeb, Jenin, February 2008

As we were to discover, not only are many of the arrests arbitrary and random, but as in Adeeb's case involve disproportionate force. Such large mobilisations can only have one purpose: to terrify not only the targeted victim but their family and neighbours.

Thirteen year old Omar had a lucky escape. When there was an incursion into his village he joined his friends, throwing stones at the soldiers – a common response from young men defending their homes, villages and towns from IDF incursion.

I was with three of my friends in my village when some soldiers came in a jeep. We threw stones and the soldiers chased us. I got away but my friend was arrested.

Omar, Beit Leed, September 2006

Some of the young people we met were arrested because they had decided to get more directly involved in the liberation campaign. Jamal was 16 when he undertook a mission with the Al Aqsa Brigades, the main Fatah paramilitary force of the Second Intifada. He lived in Nablus and had been radicalised by the occupation and lock-down of the Old City – including the death and injury of friends, some family members and neighbours. He had been prepared by the Brigade for his mission – one that he was not expected to return from – but at the last minute it was called off.

After it was cancelled I returned home. Later that night, at 1am, the Israeli soldiers came to my home. There were many soldiers in jeeps and when they arrived they began to shoot towards our home. The soldiers grabbed one of our neighbours and used him as a human shield – and then they came into my home. When my brother opened our door the soldiers smashed a rifle butt into his face. They arrested me and took me into the yard where an army captain began to interrogate me and beat me on the spot. My hands were tied behind my back and my feet were also bound... After a while I was put on the floor of a jeep with the soldiers resting their feet and legs on my body. I was taken to the Huwarra interrogation centre.[7]

Jamal, Nablus, September 2006

Two young people we spoke to were arrested as a result of isolated, unplanned episodes that were out of character. Classified by the Israelis as "terrorists" and a threat to the state, the reality is that they were driven to an act of despair, which can only be understood within the context of the occupation. Both Riham and Rouwa were "normal" students, performing well at school, until they witnessed horrific events that triggered the acts that led to their arrest. As a result of mental anguish and torment, both took a small knife and went to the local checkpoint to confront numbers of heavily armed Israeli soldiers.

Riham is from Tulkarm, which witnessed a major incursion and much fighting in 2003. She was 16 years old at the time. Here is what she had to say:

It was a Thursday in February 2003. It was cold and wet. Nobody knew what I planned. I put a small vegetable knife in my bag. I left home at 6pm and walked to the checkpoint. I arrived at about 7pm. I got to the checkpoint – I was a 10th grader and they didn't suspect me. But when I got to the checkpoint I became afraid. I felt confused – I was a child but I had big dreams of helping my country. I hesitated, felt afraid and was surrounded by soldiers. The soldiers didn't have any protection vests, but I hesitated, and started to look at them... I was frightened. They told me to get back from them – I heard but I didn't obey.

Riham at home, February 2008

They surrounded me and started to shoot. I remember many bullets going all around me. I was injured – I took two bullets in my stomach and one in the leg. I fell down on the ground – I was still conscious – they left me bleeding for 30 to 45 minutes as they searched the area. It was raining and I was lying there.

Riham, Tulkarm, February 2008

Rouwa was arrested in 2005. Her story has some similarities:

Sometimes you have emotions that are difficult to control. The atmosphere, what is happening to us, what has happened to my family, our community, our friends – everything just presses on you.

Our camp was under curfew. I was going to school, but this was very difficult because of the soldiers. One day I ended my classes for the day and was coming home when we came under attack from the soldiers. They were just firing randomly. A small boy next to me got shot in the head. I got a taxi and took him to the hospital. They took him for emergency treatment.

But I was deeply affected by the events of the day. I had blood all over my clothes and all over my hands. So I went to the checkpoint at Netania.

The checkpoint was frightening. The soldiers started to shout at me and encircled me and they took my bag – inside I had a knife – and so they arrested me, handcuffed me behind my back and put me in the jura at the checkpoint... I got sentenced to two years and nine months in prison.

Rouwa, Tulkarm, February 2008

For Rouwa and Riham the horror of occupation – death, injury, arrest, humiliation – provoked an unthinking moment of retaliation that was doomed to failure and led to several years of imprisonment for both and, for Riham, a lifetime of disability.

Interrogation

After arrest most Palestinian young people will face some form of interrogation. Interrogation is normally conducted in one of seven centres: Huwarra (near Nablus), Etzion (near Bethlehem), Salem (near Jenin), Askelon (within Israel, near Gaza), Jalama (in Israel, near Haifa), Mascobiyya (known as "the Russian compound" in Jerusalem) and Petah Tikva (in central Israel). It is worth noting that the removal of prisoners to another country (from the Occupied Territories to Israel) is a breach of international law.

Interrogation normally lasts for many days. A Palestinian child can be detained by the IDF for up to eight days before being brought before a military judge; during this period interrogation will have taken place.

> The interrogation takes place in the absence of a lawyer and, according to Military Order 378, a military judge can prohibit a child from seeing a lawyer for 15 to 90 days.
>
> After eight days the military judge will normally extend the child's detention until the end of the court process. Under military orders, a Palestinian child can be detained for up to 188 days before being charged with an offence and can be held for up to two years between being charged and brought to trial.[9]

It is now well documented that Israel routinely uses torture and other cruel methods when interrogating its prisoners.[10] Firas told us:

I was arrested when I was 19 and taken to the Jenin interrogation centre where they charged me with killing a collaborator. I spent 48 hours in interrogation. I was very scared and intimidated. I was alone and couldn't talk to anyone. They were shouting and roughing me up. I thought many times that I should just admit it, but admit what? I thought to say okay I killed him with a knife even though I hadn't. Then they started to say I'd killed him with a gun, but I don't have a gun.

Firas, Balata, September 2006

Mohammed's story was similar:

The Israelis put a lot of pressure on you when they catch you. They want to scare you, to make you very afraid. They threaten your mother, your sisters, they say they will demolish your house – and this is hard when you are young. You are alone and isolated when they have you. You don't know how your family is and have no contact with anyone. People react in different ways and not everyone can be strong. The Israelis try to trick you when you are frightened. They tell you, "If you sign the confession you will be free or receive only a short sentence." They give you statements that are in Hebrew and so you don't know what you are signing – it could have all sorts of charges.

Mohammed, Balata, September 2006

Razik's story

"I was beaten very badly when I was arrested by Israeli Defence Forces soldiers. I was kept in the back of a jeep for over four hours in the freezing cold. During detention my head was covered with a foul-smelling dirty sack as I was shackled to a chair with my hands handcuffed behind my back in a stressful position. Periodically, between punches and slaps, the interrogator would suddenly pull me forward causing extreme pain to my wrists and back."

Razik was eventually sentenced to four years for being a member of the Al Aqsa Martyrs Brigades.

The Electronic Intifada[8]

Jamal was 16 when he was arrested. He was taken to the Huwarra interrogation centre and held there for ten days:

Although I was not interrogated at Huwarra I found it very tough. I was young, I was scared of the soldiers and I knew what they did to prisoners. I was kept in isolation the whole time. There were no windows in my cell and so I didn't see the sun and was confused about the time. The guards were always insulting me and my family – saying awful things about them. And when I did manage to get some sleep they would come in and shout and kick my legs.

Jamal, Nablus Old City, September 2006

But this was just the start of Jamal's ordeal. After ten days he was sent to an interrogation centre inside Israel. He was there for a further 40 days.

When I first arrived they sent me to a clinic for a medical check-up. Alongside other new prisoners I was taken to a room full of prison guards and we were made to take all our clothes off. They then made us stand and crouch, up and down, many times. After some time they made us dress again and then I was taken away to start my interrogation.

In the first session the interrogators behaved in a good way. They took off my handcuffs, they asked me to relax, they talked in a friendly way and they offered me tea, coffee and cigarettes. But when I didn't respond they turned nasty. They cuffed my hands behind my back and pushed my arms over the back of the chair – so it was painful to sit… A new interrogator came who was much tougher. He came with a really big guard and they started to shout at me and created a frightening atmosphere. I was interviewed from 12 noon until about 6pm. After that I had to go back to my cell, strip and try to get some sleep. At 2am I was woken with shouts and kicks.

The next day was the same. This time they put black glasses on me, so I couldn't see anything or really know who was in the room. They strapped me to a lie detector. And they questioned me again and again wanting to know the names of people I knew. All this psychological pressure – the isolation, no sleep, the awful food, the shouting, the insults and the humiliation.

After 40 days I told them I had been planning a mission. After that they sent me to prison inside Israel, but the interrogation stopped. I got a four-year sentence.

Jamal, Nablus Old City, September 2006

Ahmed was arrested at the Allenby Bridge. He was part of a student delegation on it s way to an Arab Youth Congress in Sudan. He told us:

The Israelis arrested me and said that I was wanted for being an activist in the military wing of Fatah. I was held at the Bridge for 12 hours before being transferred to the Qadim custody centre. I was there for five days before being taken to a military court. At the court they told me they had secret files and secret papers about me and that I was to go back to the interrogation centre.

On the day I went back to Qadim they came for me at night and took me for interview. For the first two days they didn't ask me a question! But there were plenty of questions after that – they kept me 45 days at the interrogation centre.

When you are being held in interrogation you cannot

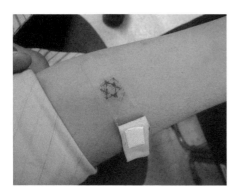
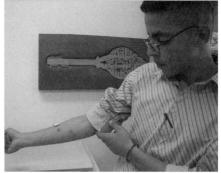

shower. I never saw the sun. I had no chance to shave. We had five really poor cigarettes a day. We had little time to eat the food which was always too little and bad. I had no shower for 45 days.

The interrogation sessions lasted seven hours a day. At the beginning they made all sorts of allegations about what groups I was in and what I had done… They said unless we get a result we will keep you for 90 days and then for another 90 days… This was the pressure, not direct violence.

Ahmed, Balata, February 2008

Above, Ahmed, from Balata, shows us his right arm where interrogators made cuts as part of the "questioning" process. Left is a close up of the arm

A few of the young men also told us about their experiences with the "canaries". These are "prisoners" sent inside the cells by the Israelis to try to win the confidence of the young people and get them to talk. Ahmed told us about his experience:

After some days the guards bring some other prisoners into your cell. It is a real psychological pressure because you know that these "prisoners" are really spies. We call them canaries. But you may have been isolated for three or five days, spoken to nobody. You want some contact. They say the same. They say they have been isolated too. They start to make contact, to speak. They always come over as heroes. "We've been here before," "We were let out last time and we'd said nothing," "Don't admit anything," they say. "Don't confess." Then, when they have built up your spirits, they try and get you to talk about why you are inside, what you did, and so on. But I knew about this trap beforehand so I was very careful about what I said.

Ahmed, Balata, February 2008

Zeeb's story

I was in my third trimester when I was arrested and they wanted to perform an abortion on me. I did not let them. They took me to Majdal prison and did an ultrasound to check the gender of the baby. When they knew that the baby was a boy, they started screaming at me, "You are going to bring a Fedae" (freedom fighter). They put me in a cell that was one and a half by two meters. They kicked my stomach with their huge military boots, spitting and cursing at me. They left me there for four days with no food or water. They did not allow me to use the bathroom for one week. I was very weak, my feet were swollen, and my entire body was aching.

Global Lockdown: Race Gender and the Prison-Industrial Complex[11]

Fear, isolation, sensory deprivation and psychological torture; these become the staple methods of Israeli interrogation of the young. But it is also the case that sometimes they just resort to downright brutality, as Zeeb's story reveals.

Between 2001 and 2008 the Israeli State Attorney's Office received over 500 complaints of ill-treatment on the part of Shin Bet (ie Israeli state security) interrogators. Not a single criminal investigation was carried out – the decisions against investigation being based on the findings of an initial review of conduct carried out by an inspector who was himself a member of the Shin Bet.[12]

Once the interrogation phase is completed, Palestinian detainees from the West Bank are processed for trial, sentencing and imprisonment in one of the two Israeli military courts currently in operation in the West Bank. The period of time between the issuing of charges and the actual trial is often prolonged, with detainees sometimes waiting for months before being tried before a military court. The military tribunals are presided over by a panel of three judges appointed by the military. Most of the judges do not have long term judicial training and as such the court procedures rarely fall within the required international standards for a "fair trial". When we visited the Ramallah offices of Defence for Children International-Palestine Section (DCI-Pal) in September 2009 we were given a number of examples where in the absence of the requisite "judge", military officers were simply brought in to sit on the bench – even though they had no legal training or experience.

Such a cavalier approach to the law and due process characterises the occupation of the West Bank where there is a blatant disregard of international law and conventions – even when the Israeli state is a signatory. Nowhere is this more evident than with the 1989 United Nations Convention on the Rights of the Child, which is the first legally binding international instrument to incorporate the full range of human rights – civil, cultural, economic, political and social. Despite being a signatory, Israel flouts virtually all its principles. Thus whereas the Convention defines children as all those below 18 years, in the West Bank a different series of thresholds prevail.

Imprisonment
and arrest

The Israeli Military Order No 132 contravenes the internationally accepted definition of a child as anyone below the age of 18. The Israeli domestic law defines a child as anyone under 18, which is in accordance with the international standard. The Military Order No 132 is a discrimination against Palestinian children. This Military Order defines a Palestinian child as follows:

A child is a person under 12 years [of age].
A teenager is a person above 12 years and under 14 years.
An adolescent is a person above 14 years and under 16 years.
An adult is a person 16 years and above.[13]

From the standpoint of the Palestinians, the Convention is little more than waste paper with virtually every legally binding principle disregarded, from the rights of children to security, to legal representation, to protection from torture, to separate courts and so on. Moreover, whereas many young people across the world might be unaware of the Convention and the protections it is supposed to afford them, this is not the case in much of the West Bank. Young people here know of the Convention, just as they know that Israel is blatantly in breach, as it is with so many other resolutions and rulings whether from the UN or the World Court. So many times we were asked why and how it was possible for Israel to behave so criminally and with such impunity, although they knew the answer well enough. As long as Israel enjoyed the unconditional support of the US, a state which also has a distinguished track record of ignoring international law when it suits its interests, it could and would continue to be above and beyond the law.

Administrative detention is a procedure under which detainees are held without charge or trial. In the occupied Palestinian West Bank, the Israeli army carries out administrative detention on the basis of Military Order 1226. This order empowers military commanders to detain an individual for up to six months if they have "reasonable grounds to presume that the security of the area or public security require the detention". On or just before the expiry date, the detention order is frequently renewed. This process can be continued indefinitely.[14]

Administrative detention is arrest and imprisonment without charge or trial. It is authorised by administrative order rather than judicial decree. Although incarceration under these circumstances is allowed under international law, the conditions of its use are, in theory, restricted by tight controls. Essentially states have to show that the internment process is required for state security. Israel regularly uses administrative detention, yet it has not defined the criteria of the "threat to state security" that might justify its use. The relevant section from Military Order 1226 states:

> If a Military Commander deems the detention of a person necessary for security reasons he may do so for a period not in excess of six months, after which he has the right to extend the detention period for a further six months according to the original order. The detention order can be passed without the presence of the detainee.

According to DCI-Pal:

> Administrative detention is permitted under international law in strictly limited circumstances and only if "the security of the state…makes it absolutely necessary" and only in accordance with "regular procedure". Further, international law to which Israel is bound provides that "No child should be deprived of his or her liberty arbitrarily and detention should only be used as a measure of last resort for the shortest appropriate period of time." Administrative detention should never be used as a substitute for criminal prosecution where there is insufficient evidence to obtain a conviction.[15]

The possibility of becoming an administrative detainee is

an ever-present threat in the daily life of all Palestinians and severely impacts on the lives of Palestinians living in the West Bank. Omar told us about his experience:

> I was taken to the military court which is also inside Offa. I had no lawyer. Here I heard the charges for the first time and they were completely random and unknown to me. Indeed it was crazy as they said I had been involved in the assassination of Sadat! You see how they don't care about any truth. There was no evidence given. The only questions I had been asked before the court were simple personal details, name, age, etc. The case against me was all in the secret file. I can never see that, nor my lawyer if I had one. The judge said that I was a danger to Israeli security that I had to serve six months' administrative detention.
>
> *Omar, Jenin, June 2008*

Administrative detention orders are often based on "secret evidence" collected by the Israeli Security Agency (ISA). Neither the detainee nor the detainee's lawyer is given access to the evidence, and therefore they have no effective means of challenging the detention – as is required under international law.[16] So Omar didn't know that he was accused of being involved in the assassination of President Sadat of Egypt – an event which took place in 1981, before Omar was born – until he appeared before the military judges. The confidential materials determine the period of detention and its extension thereafter. As Table 2 shows many are detained for relatively short periods, but detention orders can be repeatedly extended.

Table 2: Length of time Palestinians held in administrative detention (April 2009)[17]

Duration	Number of detainees
Under 6 months	176
6 mths-1 year	154
1-1.5 years	120
1.5-2 years	56
2-2.5 years	19
2.5-3 years	18
3-3.5 years	2
3.5-4 years	0
4-4.5 years	1
Over 4.5 years	2
Total	548

Imprisonment and arrest

Hamdi Tamri

Date of birth:	20 August 1992
Age at arrest:	16
Place of residence:	Bethlehem
Occupation:	11th grade student
Date of arrest:	18 December 2008
Place of detention:	Ofer Prison

At 2am on 18 December 2008, Hamdi was woken up by a loud banging on the family home's front door. The Israeli soldiers had come to arrest him again, just one month after his release from prison. Hamdi was only 16.

Hamdi was tied and blindfolded by a group of five soldiers, and was taken to Etzion detention centre in a military jeep. On 21 December 2008, three days after his arrest, he was transferred to Ofer for interrogation. While under interrogation, he was questioned about the display of flags on the family house roof, the people he had encountered since the moment of his release and his political activities. Hamdi maintained that he was not involved in any activities and had only met with relatives and neighbours.

On 28 December 2008, at the Administrative Detainees Court in Ofer, Hamdi was informed that a four-month administrative detention order was issued against him based on "secret evidence" and that he would be held without charge or trial. Hamdi was accompanied neither by a lawyer, nor by his family, whose presence is banned in the Administrative Detainees Court. The administrative detention order was confirmed at the judicial review for a period lasting until 15 April 2009. An appeal hearing also confirmed the order. On 15 April, however, Hamdi was not released. Instead, a second administrative detention order was issued against him for a period of four months, and was set to expire on 14 August 2009. Again, however, on 14 August 2009, a third administrative detention order was issued against Hamdi. The order was confirmed six days later, on 20 August 2009 at the Administrative Detainees Court in Ofer. It was the date of his 17th birthday.

Background
On 12 March 2008, Hamdi's family learned of the killing of Hamdi's father by the Israeli Occupying Forces along with three other people in what seems to have been an extra-judicial execution, also known as targeted assassination. Only a few months later, on 6 June 2008, the Tamri home was demolished in Bethlehem as a punitive measure against Hamdi's father's alleged activities. The soldiers gave the family only one hour to gather some of their belongings before they executed the demolition order. Both events had a huge impact on the mental well-being of all the children in the family and were reflected in the subsequent deterioration of their educational achievements. Hamdi's mother relates that, before the murder of his father and the loss of their family home,

Hamdi had been an outstanding student, and was very active in extra-curricular activities, especially musical activities. He volunteered with the school's radio station as a host and used to sing at school events and parties. The family had a number of recordings of his performances, but these were all destroyed during the house demolition.

Following these devastating events, his grades dropped, and he became noticeably more introverted.

When Hamdi was first arrested in July 2008, one of the soldiers told him that his father was killed because "he was a terrorist and that they were going to kill all terrorists".

Addameer [18]

Hassam talked to us about the renewal of detention orders.

With administrative detention you can never be sure if or when you are going to be released. There appears to be no logic to it. You can get right to the end, have no trouble and then you are told it is being extended – no reasons given. There was a guy inside with me who was released after three years on administrative detention. He had had six consecutive terms. They let him out and he got to Jericho when he was phoned by a prisoner, who had an illegal mobile, who told him that his detention had been renewed yet again but the order arrived after he had been released. The poor guy was picked up at the checkpoint and brought back. When you hear these things you have no expectations about your release.

Hassam, Jenin, June 2008

Administrative detention is an especially nasty form of oppression as its terms are so arbitrary and, in true Kafka fashion, the victims rarely get to know the grounds of their incarceration. For many of those we interviewed who had been in administrative detention this was completely consistent with many other aspects of the occupation. Curfews, lockdowns, closure of check-points, removal of permits to work or access olive trees and lands were all characterised by the same features – arbitrary acts with little or no warning and all legitimised in the name of "security". But notwithstanding their collective brutality and the distress, hurt and misery caused, we got no sense that these methods were successful in undermining resistance. If the Israelis were intent on raising the cost of resistance, it seemed that they had sorely underestimated the Palestinian people for whom it was never a matter of cost but of their inalienable rights.

In January 2006 a report by the United Nations Special Rapporteur found:

> Prison conditions [for Palestinian prisoners] are harsh: prisoners live in overcrowded and poorly ventilated cells which they generally leave for only two hours a day. Allegations of torture and inhuman treatment of detainees and prisoners continue. Such treatment includes beatings, shackling in painful positions, kicking, prolonged blindfolding, denial of access to medical care, exposure to extreme temperatures and inadequate provision of food and water.[20]

Prisoners are held in one of approximately 30 detention centres (21 prisons, five detention centres, four interrogation centres, and at least one secret interrogation facility) located within the 1967 borders of Israel.
Palestine Monitor [19]

The claims made in the UN report were supported by the young people we spoke to: inadequate and overcrowded conditions, brutality from the guards, and the poor quality and inadequate quantity of food were constant themes in our discussions with young ex-prisoners. Mohammed described what the overcrowded cells were like:

> My cell was 2 metres square. There were three of us inside. It had two small beds and the third slept on the floor between the beds. There was also a shower in the cell. We were very crowded.
> We were in our cells 21 hours out of 24. We only saw the sun in the three hours we spent outside of our cells. Our cell was so small that it was only possible for one of us to stand and move. The three of us could never stand at the same time. We would take it in turns when we did our exercises. We took our meals in the cell.
> *Mohammed, Jenin, September 2006*

Mealtimes were a problem:

> We had two meals a day, one at 12 noon, the other at 6pm. The food was very little and very bad. Rice and beans, which were the main food, was very little, just one plate for three of us. We only had one piece of bread a day. It was just enough to keep you alive. I lost weight. When I was arrested I was 90 kilogrammes; when I was released I was 63 kilogrammes.
> *Mohammed, Jenin, September 2006*

More recently the Israelis have tried to push the costs of feeding their Palestinian prison population back onto Palestinian families and the PA. As Hassam told us:

> We now pay for our food in prisons. The Israelis did not want to pay all the costs of imprisonment so they reduced the quality and quantity of food to such an extent that we were forced to buy our food in the canteens. This costs our families something like 1,000 shekels a month.
> *Hassam, Jenin, February 2008*

This is a situation that Hassam believes should not be tolerated – and he blames both the Israelis and the PA for allowing it to develop:

> But this is a situation we cannot simply put on the Israelis. Our own organisations are failing to resist and fight on the issues of prisoners. This was always a central part of our resistance for 40 years of occupation: the struggle against the humiliation and suffering of prisoners. We should not have allowed the Israelis to push this burden of prisoner's food onto the Palestinians.
> *Hassam, Jenin, February 2008*

Mahmoud and Omar both spent time in prison in the Negev desert in the south of Israel. Conditions there were even worse:

> I was in prison in Israel – in the desert. We had to live in tents. The tent was 15 square metres and for 20 people. In the winter it was tough as the tents would flood. We had rats, insects, snakes. But at least we didn't have to stay in the tent all day, like you do in the cells.
> *Mahmoud, Tulkarm, September 2006*

After three months in Ofer I was transferred to the Negev. The conditions were terrible. There were no mattresses in the tents, we had no covers. All we were given at first was some plastic sheeting to put on the ground.

In the desert it was like being in a hot shower in the day and a cold shower at night. We were made to sit in a particular uncomfortable position many times during the day when they counted us. All the time we were surrounded by soldiers armed with rubber and live bullets. These guards seemed very rough towards us as if they had been criminals themselves and they had no hesitation in beating us.

Omar, Jenin, June 2008

Omar here alludes to two important features of the prison regime: first, the mundane routine and endless counting of prisoners, and second, the constant threats and intimidation that Palestinians face from the guards. Rouwa also described the daily routine of the prison regime:

Every day we are woken at 7am for counting. Then we have a one and a half hour break. Morning break is used for study. We then go back to the cells which are locked and we have breakfast – and they give us breakfast and lunch together, it's just one meal.

At 1.30pm there is another break. This time we use to play with the youngest prisoners – those who are 13, 14 and 15 years old. We play sports and other games. There were around 25 young children in the prison with us.

One of the women in our prison had a son who was 15 and he was sentenced to 15 years.

At 3pm we go back to the cells and are locked in again.

The dinner is pushed through a small window in the cell door – we eat in the cell.

From 3pm we are locked in till 7am again. We were locked in for 21 hours a day.

Rouwa, Tulkarm, February 2008

But as Ahmed points out, into the prison regime the prisoners have inserted their own educational and cultural activities:

Each day has a routine: cleaning the rooms, making the beds, getting counted, some exercise, then some cultural sessions. After a poor lunch, you have to clean your plates. Then rest, then workshops in groups organised around different topics. These workshops last for one month. If you pass your exam you can go on to the next level. But if you fail you have to do it again. And in the evening maybe cultural events such as a play. Every day we listen to Egyptian singers on the Israeli radio between 6.30pm and 7.30pm.

Ahmed, Balata, June 2008

The fact that the prisoners organise their own cultural and educational activities raises one other important aspect.

Palestinian prisoners locked away inside Israeli prisons are not cut off from the resistance struggle but remain a central part of the fight for Palestinian freedom. And this means, of course, that the prisoners are under constant surveillance and threat from the prison guards and wider regime. Jamal raised an element of this when he spoke of the constant threat, both real and implied, from the prison guards:

> I was sent to a prison near Netayana where I spent seven months. It is a prison mainly for young people and very tough. The guards were always provoking and insulting us and they used lots of punishments like putting you in isolation and stopping visits from your family.
> *Jamal, Nablus Old City, September 2006*

Hamad points out that the privatisation of the Israeli prison system has made things worse. Private prison guards were definitely the worst, he argued:

> In the prison I was in there were two types of administration, one run by the military and the other a private company which provided guards contracted by the Israeli prison commission. The private guards had very hard strike teams who used dogs, electric prods, tear gas and pepper bullets. Whenever we protested about anything, some brutality for example, or the food, they would send in these teams.
> *Hamad, Nablus, February 2008*

For young women another aspect of their imprisonment is the threat of sexual harassment. Rouwa told us of her experiences:

> We faced a lot of problems with one Druze guard. He was harassing our women and he used to beat women in sensitive spots and take off their clothes.
>
> But it wasn't just the men. We also had these problems with women guards. Some of the women guards who have to take prisoners to court or doctor or dentists or administration – they strip search the prisoners and sometimes behave inappropriately. If any prisoner goes anywhere they have to be stripped and searched before going.
> *Rouwa, Tulkarm, February 2008*

The issue of sexual harassment and abuse of Palestinian women in prisons has been explored by Elham Bayour:

As punishment for their participation in resisting the occupation…Palestinian women…[have been] imprisoned, humiliated, sexually assaulted and physically and mentally tortured… Palestinian women political prisoners were targeted by policies designed to…humiliate women through physical, mental and sexual torture. They seek to exercise control over women's spirit as well as their bodies, sexuality and reproduction. These policies are designed to dishonour Palestinian men through the brutalisation of Palestinian women's bodies.[21]

Visits

The Israelis will not allow anyone who has ever been a prisoner or in any way regarded as a "security" threat to visit someone in jail. Given the numbers of Palestinians who have had a period in jail, this has a huge impact on visits, especially for young prisoners whose parents are commonly refused permission to visit. Further, many of the prisons are in Israel, and this puts further restrictions on who can visit. According to the UN Special Rapporteur, "family visits remain a serious problem. As prisons are held in Israel and many Palestinians are denied admission to Israel, a majority of prisoners receive no family visits".[22]

All the ex-prisoners we spoke to repeated the same tale – visits, letters and contacts with their families were difficult at best, impossible at worst.

When I was in prison my family were not allowed to visit, not once. I couldn't phone. And most of the letters from my family never got to me.
Riham, Tulkarm, February 2008

I had little contact with my family. I was imprisoned in June 2003 and it was not until 2005 that I received a visit from my younger brother. Other than that I got some short letters – five or six lines from my family through the Red Cross. This was every six months. That was all.
Jamal, Nablus Old City, September 2006

They wouldn't let my father visit me because he was an ex-prisoner. He tried five times and each time they threw him back. I did have a visit from my sister, it was just one day before my release.
Ahmed, Balata, June 2008

Contact with our families was difficult. There was one time
when the ICRC collected letters from us to send to our families. My letter arrived six months after my release!
Omar, Jenin, June 2008

If contact with families is hard for prisoners, it is equally difficult for family members trying to visit a relative. Manal told
us of her experience:

My father is in prison. When we go to visit him we have to
leave at 1am. We wait in the buses for a very long time – hours
– and then we eventually get a short visit with him. They want
to make the visit a big burden.
Manal, Nablus, September 2006

Even when she got to visit, Manal was separated from her
father by a glass screen and had to speak through a phone
handset which was so poor that they could hardly hear one
another and had to keep repeating themselves. We were constantly reminded of the extent to which the Israelis seek any
means, however small, to assert their power and to add new
layers of humiliation and suffering. This process continues
beyond the imprisonment itself; Mohammed describes his
release:

When I came to be released they dropped me at a checkpoint
15 kilometres from Hebron. It was August and very hot and
I then had to walk to Hebron. I was very scared and thought
they would pick me up again. When we got into Hebron we
went to the municipality and were given 100 shekels to pay for
our fares back to Nablus. The taxi drivers were very kind. I had
24 hours to get home. This was set down on the paper to get
me through the checkpoints.
Mohammed, Nablus, September 2006

Riham's parents were informed that she was going to be
released, but the authorities changed the notified location of
her drop-off.

On the day of my release the authorities told my family I would
be at the checkpoint at Nablus. My family went there. But they
actually let me out between Tulkarm and Nablus. So there was
nobody there to meet me.
Riham, Tulkarm, February 2008

Imprisonment
and arrest

In the face of constant threats the prisoners respond by organising collectively to offer support to each other. Such solidarity networks are vital to help the prisoners through their time in prison. Riham told us of her experience:

> [After I left the hospital] they transferred me to the women's prison. I was the youngest person in the women's prison; I was 15 years and four months old. I was very afraid. I had no experience of prisons or political organisations in the prisons. I didn't know that political prisoners were separate from the criminals… [But] after a few days they [the other prisoners] made me welcome. I built strong friendships, they looked after me. You feel as if you are one of them – we are all together. My psychological and medical condition was very bad. I had a colostomy. But they made me feel I was among "family" and comrades. They gave me support and solidarity. We were able to create a bit of life in the prison, to create our own space. We had religious and political sessions. There was teaching, culture, language learning. I learned Hebrew. I learned about our history. There were sports. Once I left, I missed my friends.
>
> They were very close to me, they looked after me and I was sorry to leave them. And I think, in a sense, they were sorry for me to go.
>
> *Riham, Tulkarm, February 2008*

The family homes of those who are imprisoned are often destroyed. This is in Jenin. The eldest son was imprisoned, the family home blown up

Rouwa made similar comments:

> There is a very strong feeling that we are one, we are a unified group of Palestinian prisoners. We stand together and we fight together and struggle together for our rights as prisoners – no matter which organisation we are affiliated to.
>
> *Rouwa, Tulkarm, February 2008*

Support and solidarity is embedded within the prisoners' culture. All the main Palestinian political organisations are represented within the prisons and prisoners nominate which organisation they want to look after their interests on entry.

Table 3: Political affiliation of
Palestinian prisoners (percent)[23]

Fatah	44
Hamas	26
Islamic Jihad	14
Popular Front	5
Democratic Front	1
Undefined	10

Within the cramped confines of the prison regime the political organisations play a highly significant role in the day-to-day life of the prisoners and are the source of the cultural and educational activities mentioned by Ahmed, Omar and Rouwa. The political parties determine who should perform which jobs on the wing – collecting and distributing food, laundry work, keeping the communal areas clean, etc – and also coordinate the various acts of resistance carried out by prisoners.

Imprisonment and arrest

In the Negev all the groups were present and active. For me it was like being in a family again and my spirits were lifted. All the autonomous groups were represented on a central prisoners' committee and this made decisions for all the prison and were binding on all the groups and prisoners.

Of course we would take account of differences among the prisoners. Those who were sick or children were not expected to take part in hunger strikes. Others were expected to strike for a certain number of meals and no more. Then there were those who worked in the kitchens or laundries who were expected to take action at certain times. For those coming to the end of a period of administrative detention we would keep them low. In this way it was possible for everyone to have a role in the resistance.

Omar, Jenin, June 2008

Hassam makes some very similar points:

Each prisoner nominates a political organisation to look after their interests – Fatah, Hamas, PFLP, etc. Each organisation has a camp committee and links with the outside world and each organisation views the prison as just another site of struggle. As part of that struggle we act collectively to push our demands – for better food, for more access to phones for longer and more frequent visits, against the brutality of the guards. The

Khaled's story

I was first imprisoned in 1982 at the age of 16. In prison I found what I was not
expecting to find: I found inside the prison what I could not find outside of it. In
prison I found Palestine's political, national, revolutionary university. It was in
prison that I realised that knowledge is what paves the road to victory and
freedom...

Through the will and perseverance of the prisoners, prison was transformed
into a school, a veritable university offering education in literature, languages,
politics, philosophy, history and more. The graduates of this university excelled
in various fields. I still remember the words of Bader al-Qawasmah, one of my
compatriots who I met in the old Nablus prison in 1984, who said to me, "Before
prison I was a porter who could neither read nor write. Now, after 14 years in
prison, I write in Arabic, I teach Hebrew, and I translate from English." I
remember the words of Saleh Abu Tayi [Palestinian refugee in Syria who was a
political prisoner in Israeli jails for 17 years before being released in the prisoner
exchange of 1985] who told me vivid stories of prisoners' adventures smuggling
books, pieces of paper, and even the ink-housing tubes of pens.

Prisoners passed on what they knew and had learned in an organised and
systematic fashion. Simply put learning and passing on knowledge and
understanding, both about Palestine and in general, has been considered a
patriotic duty necessary to ensure steadfastness and perseverance in the struggle
to defend our rights against Zionism and colonialism. There is no doubt that the
Palestinian political prisoners' movement has played a leading role in developing
Palestinian national education.
Badil Resource Centre [24]

comradeship, solidarity and steadfastness of the prisoners allow
us to survive these difficult days.
Hassam, Jenin, June 2008

The activism within the prisons places a great emphasis on education, ranging from basic literacy and numeracy
to the learning of languages, Palestinian history and culture.
Mohammad, for example, our erstwhile guide and translator
had learnt his excellent English while in prison; Saeed who we
met in Qalqilya in 2008 had learnt to read and write while in
administrative detention – as well as his considerable skill in
origami! For Kareem, his five years in prison was his university education:

I got to read books on politics and history in prison that I
would have never been able to get hold of in Nablus where the
Israelis stop such books from being sold. I was amazed at the

stuff that got smuggled into the prison. When the book was
popular some of the prisoners would write them out so we had
extra copies and even then we might have to wait for weeks
before we could see them. In the prison we had so many educated people who could teach us things from science to politics
to poetry. I was educated in prison.

Kareem, Nablus, 2008

From arrest to release the Israeli authorities attempt to isolate, humiliate, intimidate and break the spirit of those they
incarcerate. The experience of Palestinian political prisoners
is traumatic, but the solidarity and support inside the prison
regime means that most prisoners survive the experience and
come out more educated, more politicised and more aware
of their collective plight than they were before they entered
prison. The prisons act as a "university in the struggle". Of
those we spoke to, Hossan and Saed used the experience of
prison to learn to read and write, Riham decided to pursue a
career as a lawyer and to fight for prisoner rights, Rouwa joined
the Palestinian security services, Ahmed became an activist
within Fatah, and Mohammed and Omar became community activists within their refugee camps. None of those we
spoke to was ashamed or embarrassed that they had spent time
in prison; indeed they were proud that their period in prison
marked them out as resistance activists. Prisoners, like martyrs,
are highly revered in the West Bank and are never forgotten.

Notes

1 Addameer, "Political Detention: The Infinite Violation of Human Rights", www.addameer.org/detention/background.html (accessed 14 May 2009).
2 *Palestine Monitor 2009 Fact Book*, p32, www.palestinemonitor.org/spip/IMG/pdf/factbook_Final_online-2.pdf (accessed 1 October 2009).
3 PLO Negotiations Affairs Department, "Palestinian Political Prisoners", www.nad-plo.org/facts/others/Political20 percentPrisoners percent20-percent20August percent202008.pdf (accessed 1 October 2009).
4 Information Clearing House "Resistance to Israeli occupation – a right?", 29 December 2008, www.informationclearinghouse.info/article21559.htm (accessed 1 January 2009).
5 Addameer, "Political Detention: The Infinite Violation of Human Rights", as above.
6 *Palestine Monitor 2009 Fact Book*, as above, p33.
7 That the Israeli army was raiding his house so soon after his return from the aborted mission was put down to the work of collaborators who are a ubiquitous presence

across the West Bank. For many of the young people we met the issue of collaboration was sensitive and complex and it was an area that we were never able to explore in any depth.

8   M Frykberg "Israelis continue to abuse Palestinian prisoners", *The Electronic Intifada*, 17 December 2008 electronicintifada.net/v2/article10034.shtml (accessed 13 May 2009).

9   V Trojan, *Child Rights Situation Analysis: Right to Protection in the Occupied Territory – 2008* (Defence for Children International – Palestine Section and Save the Children, 2008), p64, www.dci-pal.org/english/publ/ research/SRSAReport.pdf (accessed 15 May 2009).

10 There are countless sources which provide detailed evidence and testimony to the use of torture by the Israeli state against Palestinians. Useful starting points are Addameer (www.addameer.org) and DCI-Palestine (www.dci-pal.org).

11 E Bayour, "Occupied Territories, Resisting Women: Palestinian Women Political Prisoners", in J Sudbury (ed), *Global Lockdown: Race, Gender and the Prison-Industrial Complex* (Routledge, 2005), p208.

12 M Frykberg, as above.

13 International Commission of Jurists, Swedish Section, *Palestinian Children Behind Bars* (Gothenburg, 2005), www.dci-pal.org/english/doc/reports/2005/apr03.pdf

14 Addameer, addameer.info/ (accessed 1 October 2009).

15 Defence for Children International – Palestine Section, "Palestinian Child Detainees, Administrative Detention",

October 2008, www.welfareassociation.org. uk/forms/DCI_Briefing_Paper.pdf (accessed 8 October 2009).

16 Defence for Children International – Palestine Section, "Palestinian Child Detainees, Administrative Detention", as above.

17 B'Tselem, "Statistics on Administrative Detention", www.btselem.org/english/ Administrative_Detention/Statistics.asp (accessed 14 May 2009).

18 Addameer Case-studies and Testimonies, addameer.info/?p=1321#more-1321 (accessed 1 October 2009).

19 *Palestine Monitor 2009 Fact Book*, p32, www. palestinemonitor.org/spip/IMG/pdf/ factbook_Final_online-2.pdf (accessed 1 October 2009).

20 United Nations, "Report of the Special Committee to Investigate Israeli Practices Affecting the Human Rights of the Palestinian People and Other Arabs of the Occupied Territories", 26 September 2005, para 96.

21 E Bayour, as above, p202.

22 United Nations, "Report of the Special Committee", as above, paras 91-96.

23 *Palestine Monitor*, "Palestinian Prisoners: The Facts" www.palestinemonitor.org/spip/ spip.php?article9 (accessed 19 May 2009).

24 Khaled al-Azraq, "The Prison as University: The Palestinian Prisoners' Movement and National Education" (Badil Resource Centre, 2009), www.badil.org/en/al-majdal/ item/1267-the-prison-as-university-the-palestinian-prisoners percent5C'-movement-and-national-education

Chapter 4

Weapons of occupation

Poverty is now extreme for many. We have no state. We have no social security system. We have virtually no civil infrastructure. We are reliant on the United Nations Relief and Works Agency for food, for NGOs to help us with some projects, but always the Israelis interfere. Many people I know start each day with nothing and not knowing how they are going to eat. The reason we have such deep poverty here in the West Bank and Gaza is the occupation, plain and simple. It has destroyed our economy, our trade, our agriculture and our means of moving around. We have no natural resources like the Gulf. We have just our lands and our skills and the lands they are taking. We had our labour and we had our land. They don't want our labour but they want our land. But the occupation is not just about land. It is about every aspect of our life that they want to affect and destroy. That includes us: socially, economically, individually and politically.

Muhammad, Tulkarm, February 2008

The consequences of the economic war waged by Israel are as brutal and damaging as the military incursions and leave no part of Palestinian society untouched.

The demographics of the West Bank don't help, with over 45 percent of the population aged less than 16 years. As a result the International Labour Organisation estimated that "every employed person in the region supports six persons in the total population, and the majority of them are working poor struggling for survival".[1] There is now a large and rich range of research data available (much of it accessible through the internet) emanating from NGOs, the UN and a variety of solidarity groups which highlight the manifest consequences of deepening poverty and mass unemployment in the West Bank.

While the data is graphic in illustrating the depth of Palestinian poverty it is through the testimonies of the people

UNICEF data on poverty and well-being on the West Bank[2]

1 While infant and child mortality rates have stagnated since 2000, other long-term indicators such as stunting rates, reflecting chronic malnutrition, now affect 10 percent of children, up from 7.6 percent a decade ago.
2 Households have become significantly and rapidly poorer in recent years, and food insecurity is on the rise, affecting more than a quarter of households in the West Bank.
3 More than 50 percent of children under age five across [the Occupied Territories] are anaemic and many suffer from vitamin A deficiencies, seriously undermining their intellectual and educational achievement and physical development.
4 Around 70 percent of all infant deaths are due to prematurity, congenital malformation and pneumonia...
5 A recent World Food Program Survey reported rising food insecurity among Palestinians, finding that between 2006 and 2007, 75 percent reduced the quantity of food purchased and 89 percent reduced the quality. Food insecurity has been further exacerbated by rising prices due to adverse environmental conditions, including prolonged frost, drought and dry winds. The continuing price rises in 2008 have caused average food prices to reach levels 20 percent higher than in 2007 in the West Bank.
6 46 percent of Palestinians do not have enough food to meet their needs. The number of people in deep poverty, defined as those living on less than 50 cents a day, nearly doubled in 2006 to over 1 million, according to the UNRWA.

themselves that the human impact of the data is revealed. Here is what our interviewees told us:

> The poverty is now very bad. A family near to me is so desperate that they are searching the garbage bins for old bread and vegetables. They soak the dry bread in water and then eat. It is so difficult. Many of those with some money will give help to neighbours. It might not be much but it can buy some food. People help each other. This is how we get by.
> *Hebab, Nablus, September 2006*

> Many of my friends' families are paying for their children's university fees not from their income but from selling things. One friend's mother sold her gold jewellery, another sold some land. This is happening more and more.
> *Abla, Nablus, September 2006*

> Families have turned to the home economy to survive. We make our own bread. Some of us keep chickens, a cow or a

goat. We grow things to eat and we have our own olive oil. But we cannot afford to buy any seeds now. When we need to buy our seeds we won't be able to afford them. I don't know what will happen then.
Kareem, Jenin, September 2006

Again and again we were told how community and family solidarity was now more critical than ever to survival. In 2006, for example, the international blockade following Hamas's election victory meant that there was no money to pay the wages of PA employees, whether they were teachers, nurses, police or security personnel. As the largest employer in the West Bank the lack of any significant income for over six months for its workers was devastating. Yet although there is a great deal of extreme poverty we saw no people starving. There were no people begging on the streets such as we had encountered in Tel Aviv or Jewish West Jerusalem. Instead, what we saw were shops and traders giving extended credit at immense cost to themselves and

The remains of the soap factory in the old city of Nablus, bombed by the Israelis in 2003

mutual support systems at all levels from food to cash. This included Hamas and Fatah providing emergency aid and support as well as money sent from those in the Palestinian diaspora who were able to do so. The significance of such remittances is indicated by the Western Union signs that can be seen even in small agricultural villages. All these are significant factors in surviving unrelenting and deepening poverty, but in common with many other impoverished peoples it is the family, both immediate and extended, that is the key survival mechanism for many in the West Bank.

In a society in which the average family size is over six persons, where multiple-family households are common, and where most relatives live in close proximity, it is often possible to find at least one or two people who are able to garner some form of paid work. Family responsibilities are taken seriously and those who have something are expected to help those who have nothing. As the Institute for Middle East Understanding noted:

Family identification and solidarity can be seen as the one traditional structure to have survived the Nakba. Even in refugee

Coping mechanisms

According to the International Committee of the Red Cross "poor" and "very poor" households use a number of "coping mechanisms" to meet their basic material needs. These included:

Diversification of income: Growing vegetables or olives, keeping a few sheep or chickens and engaging in small-scale selling of surplus provisions and goods.

Engagement in "marginal labour": Households often had one or two members looking for work opportunities either in construction or in agriculture (including illegal work within Israel). In addition, women increasingly looked for work as cleaners and domestics and children sold sweets on the streets.

Kinship support: Although difficult to quantify, "poor" households did benefit from kinship support from abroad and support from wealthier relatives nearby. This support was, however, greater in rural areas than in urban areas, as members of households in small villages were more likely to be related through birth or marriage. However, support from abroad and from Arab-Israeli villages (on the other side of the West Bank barrier) was also affected by restrictions on banking between Palestinian and Israeli institutions.

Obtaining loans and credit.

Selling off property, including productive assets such as agricultural land.

Delaying the start of university studies: Students admitted to university were postponing their enrolment in order to contribute to their family's income or to work and save enough money to pay for their studies.

Begging and stealing: Focus group discussions noted that there was a small rise in these activities.

Selling off humanitarian assistance: This was seen mainly in the Beach Camp and included the sale of food and other items of aid.

ICRC, 2006[3]

camps, far from their villages or towns of origins, Palestinians continue to live, work and socialise within the confines of the family. Many men from the Occupied Territories or refugee camps in neighbouring Arab countries often leave behind wives and young children to work in the oil-rich Gulf States. They send money home to support the extended family. And these extended families pool their resources and provide for each other when money is needed for medical reasons or for college expenses.

Palestinian children are raised with a keen sense of responsibility to family members. Older parents and grandparents rely on the financial support and care of their children and grandchildren. Though this responsibility usually lies with the eldest son, it can typically be borne by those who are most financially able or by the family as a whole.[4]

While some men may leave home to work in the Gulf States, the women of the West Bank rarely have such opportunities to travel given the prevailing attitudes and social conservatism. We discuss this in more detail later, but the simple truth is that women are at the core of the Palestinian household and family. They are the ones who have to find ways of meeting the household's basic needs and for large numbers of women this is now done in families where the (traditional) male wage earner is either unemployed, imprisoned, injured, dead, disabled or out of the country. Thousands of women have also had their homes demolished. At the same time opportunities to find employment, mainly in the low-paid agricultural sector, have been decimated by the occupation's destruction and confiscation of land.[5]

The Wall

The economic war against the Palestinians has many layers and fronts and is waged on an entire people. The destruction of the indigenous Palestinian

The "Separation Wall" at Qalqilya

economy through checkpoints, confiscation of property or the encroachment of the settlements is one of the principal forms of collective punishment which characterises the Israeli occupation of the West Bank. During the period of our visits the construction of the illegal "Separation Wall"[6] added a new layer to this economic war. Although not yet completed at the time of writing, the construction of the Wall, especially in the northern areas of the West Bank, and especially in cities such as Qalqilya, which is now "bottled in" by the Wall, devastates already vulnerable and struggling Palestinian villages and communities.

It is now well established that the Wall, as it weaves its way from north to south, is not primarily a security measure to prevent the entry of "suicide bombers" into Israel, but an explicit establishing of facts on the ground of the boundaries of a core Israeli society, which takes in the major Jewish settlements that have been built in the West Bank since 1967. Through this means, and by consistently building the Wall on the West Bank side of the "Green Line", Israel has confiscated a further slice of shrinking Palestinian territory. Israel initially insisted that the Wall was both temporary and only concerned with protecting its security; this pretence is now dropped, as the Israeli deputy

More annexations

The Wall is not being built on, or in most cases even near, the 1967 Green Line. Rather it cuts deep into the West Bank, expanding Israel's theft of Palestinian land and resources.

When completed, the Wall will de facto annex some 47 percent of the West Bank, isolating communities into Bantustans, enclaves and "military zones".

Nearly 16 percent of Palestinians in the West Bank will be "outside" the Wall in the annexed areas and living in unbearable conditions. They will face loss of land, markets, movement and livelihoods – and also "expulsion" from Israel where they are now de facto located.

This includes over 200,000 residents of East Jerusalem, who will be totally isolated from the rest of the West Bank.

In contrast, 98 percent of the settler population will now be included in the annexed areas – within Israel's new "borders".

The Wall's total length will be some 730 kilometres.

The Apartheid Wall will cost in excess of $3.4 billion, approximately $4.7 million per kilometre.

In places the Wall is 8 metres high – twice the height of the Berlin Wall – with armed watchtowers and a "buffer zone" 30 to 100 metres wide for electric fences, trenches, cameras, sensors and military patrols.

Anti-Apartheid Wall Campaign, 2005[8]

prime minister, Dan Meridor, openly acknowledged in November 2010: "I think the new border has to be based on the principle of the security fence route and the settlement blocs. That is what we have to aspire to. In addition, we are insisting that Jerusalem remain the capital of Israel and are opposed to the right of return to Israel [of the Palestinian refugees], and of course [will insist on] security arrangements".[7]

Although there has been much huffing and puffing about the illegality of the Wall, even from traditional core supporters such as the US and British governments, this has had virtually no impact on its construction. Israel, as ever, demands that its security overrides every objection, and repeats claims that the Wall is temporary and only concerned with preventing terrorist infiltration. Yet, as Weizman has persuasively demonstrated, the route of the Wall has been influenced by many factors and not simply security. He wrote, for example:

...that one of the primary reasons for the Wall's routing in the area of Alfei-Menashe was not only to surround and grab the settlements themselves, but also to grab hill tops intended for their expansion, and that this route was dictated at the expense of the very security principles, defined by the military, that formed the whole basis for the Wall's conception. In some cases...reasons for routing the Wall reflected the interests of real estate companies with existing construction contracts... The annexation of colonised lands had the potential to yield enormous profits.[9]

The Wall absorbs some of the richest agricultural lands on the lower slopes of the West Bank where it was possible to grow cereals and to support thousands of horticultural small-holdings growing vegetables and salad crops as well as citrus orchards. For the Israelis every metre of land on their side of the Wall brings rich rewards in terms of land prices and opportunities for settlement building and industrial zones.

The reality of this theft of the land was movingly told to us to by two young farmers from Qalqilya, where the Wall has not only encircled the city but has led to the devastation of its traditional farming economy (see overleaf).

This discussion with the young farmers was difficult as their anguish was so evident. Farmers and gardeners everywhere develop deep and multidimensional relationships with the land they work. This is no less true in Palestine where reverence for the land is deepened by the occupation and the persistent threat of its confiscation. Its theft is like an amputation and its mutilation – whether uprooting olive trees or citrus orchards to make way for roads, settlements, so-called "nature reserves" or the Wall – is experienced personally. This is how the mother of a farmer in a village near Jenin described her feelings in 2009 at losing 600 of the family's olive trees:

> As a girl I planted many of these trees with my own hands. I carried the saplings on my head. When the fence was put up I wept because I felt I had lost all my efforts... Our life, our identity, is in the land – even our destiny. We won't leave it.[10]

Olive trees

During the Second Intifada between 2000 and 2004 Israeli troops uprooted 1,145,154 trees and levelled 6,185 hectares of land, according to the Palestinian Ministry of Agriculture. The destruction continues unabated as Palestinian trees and land are stolen for roads, settlements and military areas.

"I planted my olive trees when I was only 20 years old. Fifty-six years later, I saw them being recklessly cut and uprooted." In remembrance of the many decades he tended to his trees, Kasem placed the remaining roots of the trees in his yard. "I look at the roots every day. I will always keep the roots to remind my grandchildren what the IDF did to me and to them".

Harvard International Review, March 2004 [11]

It is punishing to watch your land, which has been tended by your family for generations, lie wasted and ruined, uncultivated in the shadow of the Wall. The cruelty is compounded as the Israeli state has dredged up an old Ottoman law from 1858 which was applied historically in the region, whereby land left uncultivated for longer than three years passes into the ownership of the state. Through this law Israel has confiscated over 900,000 dunams of Palestinian land in the West Bank and the figure continues to climb.[12] This is what Ibrahim and Ahmed expect to happen to their stolen lands – the Israelis have blocked them from farming the land

Farmers' tales

Ibrahim: We have both lost our land to the wall. I had 25 dunams and Ahmed 15 dunams. At first, when the Israelis issued a lot of permits to all the farmers who had had land on the other side of the Wall, I was able to continue to farm, but when they reduced the number to 5,000 permits I have never since been able to get a permit. So my land is lost.

When we were first told about the Wall we had already planted the land. It's good fertile land and with irrigation. We were promised by the Israelis that we would have permits to continue with our crops, but then they changed their minds and told us that we had to go away that this was not our place anymore. We lost all that crop. My father persuaded me that we should replant the land. So we went back. It was an act of steadfastness and resistance. And we did replant. But then we got shot at by soldiers one day when we working the land and we never went back.

Ahmed: I lost all my land. First they took four dunams to build the road by the Wall and then later the other 11. This I had planted about half with tomatoes and the rest with green vegetables. I had many difficulties getting by the soldiers but I was able to irrigate and grow my crops. But when we came to harvest they stopped me with a tank and took me to the land where a bulldozer was smashing up everything. All the crops, the pipes, everything smashed and pushed into a heap. I went back later to get my pumps and generator. At least to try and save something. I saw that they had destroyed the well and all my machinery was destroyed. This land has been with my family for over 100 years. Now it is standing empty and doing nothing.

It drives us crazy to see this Wall every day but what can we do? Even before the wall the Israelis were against the Palestinian farmers. This was a big farming area and we took our crops to markets in Hebron and Bethlehem. With all the barriers and permits it became impossible and Qalqilya is too small for all the produce. Before I was sending all my crop of aubergines to Hebron but when that stopped I still grew 12 dunams of cabbages but I sold only two containers to a local trader. It was nothing. I was really destroyed and had bad debts.

Ibrahim: My life is now utterly miserable. I see no end to my problems. The land gave me income, my family's prosperity, our life, everything. It has been taken. I am in debt for seeds and fertilisers and other things. We have sold all our properties and even the gold of our women. We have nothing.

There is some agricultural relief but it is very poor. They provide sugar, rice, flour and other basics but it is not reliable. But I and many other farmers have our dignity – as young farmers who were good producers. This gave us social position and I and many others refuse to have any of this assistance. Now I look for work anywhere, on a daily basis with other farmers who can still afford to pay. I am lucky only in that my creditors are all very patient and understand my position. They don't press me as they know I have nothing.

Qalqilya, June 2008

so it will be deemed uncultivated and so in time declared state land. The imposition of this law explains why so many farmers and their families try so hard to get to their land.

It is often in the minutiae of policy that the power, arrogance and impunity of the Israeli state is revealed. In Qalqilya we were told that whether one got a permit to pass through the Wall to tend the land is a lottery – usually with a cruel twist, as in Ahmed's case where he was allowed to continue to cultivate and irrigate his lands only to watch bulldozers tear it apart just as he was about to harvest. We heard of permits being given to grandfathers too old to work the land rather than their farmer sons. There seems to be no limit, as far as the Israeli state is concerned, to the "messing about" of Palestinian lives. No opportunity, it seems, is ever lost to assert domination, and to make life unpredictable and miserable.

Ali works for the PA as one of the district coordinators in Qalqilya. His job involves meeting with the Israelis over any matter which brings West Bank residents into contact with Israel including access to Israeli hospitals, land disputes with settlers and/or the military, and above all, the 11,000 farmers in the area who have been affected by the Wall and who now require permits from Israel if they are to farm their land on the other side of the Wall. It is, as he depicts below, a deeply depressing job.

Qalqilya is not unique. Wherever the Wall passes through the West Bank similar stories abound. In 2006 we went to the Christian village of Aboud, close to Ramallah, where we learned that the village had lost thousands of dunams to the Wall. As well as land that was used for vegetables and fruit, the village had lost hundreds of dunams of olive trees. Much of the land which was stolen by the Wall is now under the control of the Jewish settlements which encircle the village. Kareem, a university student, told us what this meant for the village:

> Our biggest problem is that they are taking our land. We have lost 6,000 dunams to the Wall, which runs right through the middle of the village and its land. Many of the families here now have olive trees on the other side of the Wall. But whenever we try to go to collect our olives the settlers attack us with stones and tell us to go away, that this is not our land any more and no longer belongs to us. We can no longer go there.
>
> The settlers have a big impact on our ability to live from our olives. After we were attacked many times by the settlers, the army intervened and cut the olive trees down in order to protect, they said, the security of the settlers. This has had a

Ali's story

Before the Wall was completed there were 11,000 permits for 11,000 farmers. Everyone who needed a permit got one. Even in the cases where the registered owners were dead!

The Israelis wanted to show the farmers that the Wall would not stop their access to the land. They didn't want a lot of local opposition. The Wall here was attracting a lot of international attention so the Israelis wanted to use the permits to show that the Wall would not affect the Palestinian way of life.

Now the Wall is finished, and now the Israelis issue 6,000 permits.

But it is not just the reduction in numbers of permits that causes problems but all the other obstacles and frustrations placed in the way of the farmers.

So for all the farmers with less than two dunams of land there are no permits. For those with more it is almost impossible to get permits on a regular basis so farmers miss out on months of access to their land as they appeal decisions and wait for renewals.

If your land is filled with olive trees then the permits are only issued at harvest time. There is no care for them other than at that time.

For those who grow vegetables it can be very difficult – like the farmer who had five dunams of plastic tunnels growing cucumbers. They need great care and attention. But when he got his permit renewed they did not allow permission for his pick-up truck so he had no way to get his crop to market.

Many people lose their crops. It is so common now. Then the farmer might work his land with, say, four sons but he can only get permits for two of them, so he has further difficulties.

Now they want farmers to get licences for donkeys and carts and they say that without a licence they will not be allowed to pass. And all this takes much time.

People have to wait and wait for these decisions. For example, we have a file for urgent cases. These are supposed to be dealt with in 48 hours. It is a lucky case if it is seen to in two months. And these are the urgent cases.

We were once well known in Qalqilya for the production of oranges and lemons. Now it is for the Wall.

Ali, Qalqilya, June 2008

tremendous impact on Aboud and the ability of families to survive as we are reliant on olives and the oil. And another very important issue is that we have lost control and access to our water. We used to have enough but no longer. They have fenced off our main spring supply and locked all access. This is a big problem for an agricultural village. Every Friday we make a protest at the Wall. We often get gassed and beaten with batons but we still go every Friday.

How can we have a country when we are cut up into pieces?

Kareem, Aboud, September 2006

The recent closure of the Israeli labour market to West Bank workers has been devastating. Since its inception, Israel has relied on large numbers of Palestinian workers both from within its 1948 borders and from the West Bank. It is probably not an exaggeration to say that most of the roads, homes, factories and shops of Israel were built by Palestinian workers. Construction work in Israel, as Firas told us, is Palestinian work. "The Israelis consider it as 'dirty work' and beneath their dignity. I don't think like that. I like construction even if the wages are poor" (Jenin, September 2009). For Israeli society, the availability of a pool of construction workers at wage rates much lower than would be demanded by Israeli workers has been enormously beneficial.

For the West Bank economy such employment was hugely significant. In 2000 it was estimated that 25 percent of the West Bank labour force was employed in Israel with thousands of workers travelling to and from the West Bank on a daily basis. But following the outbreak of the Second Intifada in 2000 things changed. The Israeli state, anxious that this large flow of labour from the West Bank compromised its security, embarked on a policy of limiting access to the Israeli labour market both as a collective punishment and as a security measure. New systems of work permits were introduced which not only regulated and reduced the flow of labour but also added new layers of irritation for West Bank workers, who were forced to go through lengthy bureaucratic processes to secure permits which only lasted for three months at a time.

Protests at the Wall provoke a vicious response. This picture is from Bi'iln where the weekly protests are met with sound grenades and CS gas – these are the spent canisters that litter the ground around the protest site).

No sooner had we got a permit for three months when we had to start applying again for another three months, and just because we had got permits earlier we were never sure if we would get another. And if you or any of your family had been in trouble or arrested then you could be sure that would be the end for you. Even with a permit, the Israelis were closing the West Bank so many times during the Intifada that we went for weeks at a time with no work as all the gates were closed.

Firas, Jenin, September 2009

The official Israeli position hardened even further and in 2008 it declared that it would no longer issue work permits for work in Israel, although it has not yet been able to impose this ban totally due to its ongoing need for Palestinian labour. But for the West Bank economy, the reduction to around 10,000 permits in 2009 had a dire impact in exacerbating poverty and unemployment.

I worked in Israel, in Ramat Gan near Tel Aviv, for 20 years in a meat and chicken factory. Now the Israelis have replaced us with Russians and Chinese. Every man in this camp used to work in Israel. Now they get sick because they worry too much – how to get money, how to support their children... Before, you could help yourself, but now we are down to zero. If children ask for fruit we can't give it to them. We can't afford medicine for our child.[14]

The collapse of the West Bank economy combined with the loss of legal employment in Israel had led to the creation of an extraordinarily vulnerable pool of Palestinian labour. Through desperation to feed themselves and their families they are driven to work on jobs and in conditions that no human should ever be expected to withstand. This is exemplified in the key areas of waged work still available to West Bank workers, which includes illegal working within Israel, working in factories in the industrial zones and working in the Jewish settlements.

One of the cruellest consequences of deepening poverty in the West Bank is that many Palestinians took jobs helping to build the Wall itself. Bassam, a 20 year old studying at the university in Nablus, told us about the Wall and his isolated village:

When the Wall came to our lands the Intifada was one year old. The poverty in the village was very hard and people had no idea how they were going to get money. There were two main sources of income. One was the land, but this was never enough on its own. Then there was the work in our occupied 1948 lands [Israel]. Since the Intifada we have lost both

"We built Israel," says Abbas. He has been travelling illegally to Tel Aviv to work on a building site since 2001. In the 1950s, Palestinians crossed borders into Israel to work on their former fields. After 1967 those borders were erased. Now, with the Separation Wall, those borders exist again – if you have the wrong ID papers... In 2009, there [were] between 35,000 and 40,000 illegal workers – ghost workers – according to the Palestinian Workers' Union. "They [Israelis] can't get by without us and we can't get by without them," says Hassan, who works in an upscale Tel Aviv restaurant on a forged Israeli ID.
Russia Today, 2009[13]

sources. This was the issue for many in the village and led to them working on the construction of the Wall.

Bassam, Nablus, September 2006

We asked whether there had been any resistance to the Wall that had devastated the village:

The village is isolated. There have been no internationals visiting the village and no press or TV journalists. So we are very concerned about holding demonstrations against the Wall because the army will deal with us very hard, maybe shooting and certainly making arrests. We need to have the media and international witnesses because then the army won't be so tough with us. My village and those around us feel very isolated.

Bassam, Nablus, September 2006

Extreme and acute poverty drives Palestinians to work on and in their own jails, whether it is building settlements, working in factories and industrial parks in the settlements, or constructing the Wall. Much of this work is not only characterised by low pay, toxic environments and no protection, but is also humiliating and demoralising. In report after report the workers make clear that it is poverty which compels them into this soul-destroying work:

Mustafa, who is working in an Israeli settlement in the West Bank, has been helping to build the Wall for three years. With eight children to feed and no work in the Palestinian areas, he says he has no choice. "I betrayed my country, my religion, my ideas, my law, but I have to feed my people, I have to feed my children," said Mustafa.[15]

It is the sheer desperation to survive and to provide for their families that now

A worker's tale

"I feel like a slave," says 21 year old Palestinian Musanna Khalil Mohammed Rabbaye.

"But I have no alternative," he says, as he waits among a group of sun-beaten men in dusty work boots outside the Jewish settlement of Maale Adumim.

The phrase comes up again and again as the labourers try to explain why they spend their days hammering and shovelling to help build the Jewish settlements eating into the land they want for a future state of Palestine.

Mr Rabbaye wants to be a journalist and is trying to fund his studies.

Jaffar Khalil Kawazba, 24, says he is supporting his ten brothers and sisters as his father is too ill to work.

Fahd Sayara, 40, is trying to fund treatment for his disabled child.

"It's a very bad feeling – you can see how we're losing our land, bit by bit," says Hossam Hussein, a Palestinian labourer.

"I'm not the only one. My whole village works in the settlements," says Mr Rabbaye. "Everything, all the settlements – even most of the Wall – was built by Palestinians," he says.

BBC News, 2009[16]

drives many Palestinian workers to take on work that is quite simply lethal:

> Nizzane Ha Shalom, which is situated between Tulkarm on one side, and the separation wall and the Israeli Highway 6 on the other, was established in 1995 as one of nine planned industrial estates in the West Bank. There are seven factories, which provide jobs for some 700 Palestinians in various industries such as the production of cartons, plastic spare parts, pesticides and poisonous liquids.
>
> "It's better than no work at all," comments M (35) on his job at the carton factory Tal El Iesoef Ve Mihzoer Ltd. M urges us not to publish his name. This father of five comes here every day – six times a week, nine hours a day – for an hourly wage of 11 shekels; that is more than 7 shekels under the Israeli minimum wage. And for this salary M literally works himself to death.
>
> Why? Because he is a privileged man, he says. "Of course I know the situation is bad, but at least I have a job. I can feed my family and send my children to school".[17]

According to Dania Yousef:

> The labourers that [we] interviewed had reached a point of desperation that negated their national identity. They no longer viewed themselves as Palestinians fighting for autonomy, but rather as fathers fighting to feed their families. As research was conducted on the political and economic circumstances surrounding their situations, it became painfully clear that they were victims of an intricate political game between the PA and the Israeli government. The coupling of PA corruption[18] with Israeli occupation created an atmosphere that made it nearly impossible to survive economically.[19]

We, however, did not meet any workers in the West Bank who had abandoned their Palestinian identity. All those we met who had been compelled to work for their jailers expressed anguish at their plight. There was no pride or dignity in the work; all acknowledged that it was demoralising and many were ashamed that they had been forced into it. The PA itself, while unhappy about the situation, felt unable to condemn the workers – although crucially they failed to provide any tangible help.

> "We do not condone it, we would like them to stop," says Bassam Khoury, the Palestinian Authority's Economy Minister.

"But as a human being I cannot tell them 'Go hungry' at a time when I am not able to provide them with jobs," he says.[20]

We were with a group of university students in Nablus when Bassam recounted his story about how some of the men in his village went to work on building the Wall which has so damaged the village. It was a hard story to tell, but while there was a sense of shock among some, the overwhelming response was sympathetic. If anything, they were more critical of the PA for not providing them with financial help so as to avoid this dilemma.

We learned much from Jamil, now 20 years old, about working in Israel illegally, that is, without a permit. His family home is in the Tulkarm refugee camp and he has been travelling to work in Israel for the past three years. "Jamil's story", overleaf, contains an extract from our interview.

Jamil, as he noted, was luckier than many as his skills as a plasterer were in demand. Unlike many unskilled workers he was not forced to seek work through one of the number of Palestinian labour contractors that also profit from their exploitation. But as Jamil notes, everyone working illegally in Israel faces high financial costs as they can't ever afford to argue about the exorbitant costs of travel and accommodation on account of the fear that they will be "turned in". It also involves a complete distortion of one's daily life, living in fear of being caught and imprisoned, and spending countless hours out of sight.[21]

But for Jamil the risks and costs of illegal working were much better than trying to find work in the Israeli industrial zone established in Tulkarm in the mid-1990s.

Industrial zones: bringing the factories to the workers

Everything about the Tulkarm industrial zone is disturbing, from its chillingly inappropriate name – "Nizzane Ha Shalom" (literally, buds of peace) – to its location by the Wall and its close proximity to the centre of Tulkarm. This zone, which now includes 12 Israeli-owned factories, is one of the older zones in the West Bank, although many more are now being planned or built in and around Israeli settlements and along the Wall. Their advocates claim that they will be able to employ up to 100,000 Palestinians when completed. [22]

In Tulkarm four of the 12 factories were involved with plastics and chemicals considered by local people as especially

Jamil's story: illegal worker

CJ: Where are you working now and what is your job?

Jamil: I am working as a plasterer over in Taibe. [At this point Jamil walks to the window and points out the lights of Taibe. They are very close to Tulkarm where we meet.] I have relatives there who are able to find me work.

ML: How do you get to your work? Can you get through the Wall?

Jamil: Although Taibe is only 5 kilometres from my home, the journey takes all day and is expensive and often dangerous. I leave here at 6am and we drive on the back roads to Al Quds [Jerusalem]. I pay the driver and he gets me into Jerusalem. From there we take another taxi, again travelling on back roads over the mountains, to Taibe. The whole journey takes around 12 to 13 hours.

The car I travel in is meant to take four people – but there are usually nine or ten of us crammed into the car. Two weeks ago there was a group of workers trying to get into Israel and their car crashed. They were all killed. This is because they have to use back roads that are not very good – and they have to drive very fast, so they don't get caught.

I don't know how many people travel this way – but I think it's a lot. Every time I travel I see maybe 200 to 300 people trying to get into Israel for work. Because of the difficulties of getting there I don't come back every weekend, I usually stay for three months and then come back for a few days.

CJ: What are the wages for this kind of work?

Jamil: About 8,000 shekels a month – this is a very good wage compared to people on the West Bank. I am a skilled worker and I am never short of work and I do better than many of the labourers who work with me. I work for five days, ten hours a day.

ML: It is illegal work – so there is no tax and no insurance?

Jamil: I pay tax, but there is no insurance. I am on three-month contracts. I have to pay tax, but I'm not allowed to claim any benefits or use any facilities in Israel – so I pay tax for nothing. When I'm in Israel I'm a non-person. And also I use a different name – I call myself Ahmed in Israel. And because I have no papers I have to pay more for everything. If I get a taxi – they might charge five or ten shekels to someone else – but because they know we shouldn't be there they charge us 50. It is the same with accommodation. I rent a flat, but I don't have permission to be there. So I have to pay a lot. I pay 3,000 shekels for a room, and a shared bathroom and kitchen which I share with four others.

CJ: What is it like working and living there?

Jamil: It is very dangerous. I'm usually just in the flat or working. If you decide to go to the shops or the cafe it is dangerous and a big risk although it is easier when I am in the [Palestinian] village where my relatives live, but I still have to be careful so when I am not at work I am mainly in the flat watching TV.

If I'm working – and all my work is in the houses of Jewish Israelis, they are the ones with the money! – then I have to be very careful. I cannot go out of the house or flat where I'm working. The security officers who work there know that we are there and, okay, they turn a blind eye as we do the work. But if they see you outside the workplace they will stop you and send you to prison.

ML: Have you been caught?

Jamil: I have been caught on three occasions – working illegally. They have told me that if I get caught again I will go to prison for a long time.

The previous times I was caught the soldiers took me to the jail and I had to stay for three months, the second time it was nine months and the third time it was for three months. They beat me badly when I was in the prison – but they also made me sign a sheet of paper saying that I had been treated well and not beaten.

The last time the authorities caught me inside Israel I was in my working clothes on my way back to the flat. I told them that I was just doing my work. The interrogator and the police had an argument – the policeman wanted me to go to court and the interrogator said it was obvious I was not a terrorist and should be allowed to finish my work.

But I was sent to court and then to jail. The prison was inside Israel and was mixed. There were Jews – Israelis and Russians, Palestinians, Druze inside. They put criminals and illegal workers all together.

CJ: So is it worth the risks?

Jamil: If you don't work, life will be miserable – but where can you work in the West Bank? There are no jobs. I have 12 friends who have just graduated from university. Only one of them has a job. How can we live? My family needs my support. I have five brothers and two sisters, my father is also a construction worker but he is too old now to come with me and he has no work in Tulkarm.

ML: How long will you continue going into Israel?

Jamil: No one can guarantee how long you can do this back and forward into Israel. Many times I have tried to get to work and couldn't get across and so had to come back home. My plan is that if it is possible to go back to Israel I will. My salary is good and I can save money. I will do this for two more years and then I will come back, get married and set up a business here. But you know it is very difficult to think and talk about the future – there are so many things that can change and happen: planning is very difficult. It is difficult to plan ahead for four days, not four years!

Jamil, Tulkarm, September 2009

---

hazardous. The factories work 24 hours a day, seven days a week. The men work between nine and 11 hours a day for 9.7 shekels an hour (the Israeli rate is 19.7). We met with a group of trade unionists in Tulkarm who told us about the dangers and hazards:

> Much of the work in the factories is dangerous. Many of the men are working inside pipes cleaning and preparing them. They often use sand in this process but they have no safety

equipment at all even though they are working with chemicals, fertilisers and hazardous gases. They have no masks provided for example.

We believe we have in this area one of the highest rates of cancer in the world. The environmental risks to this area are very bad indeed. At night especially you can smell the gases and chemicals coming from the zone throughout Tulkarm.

Ahmad, Tulkarm, June 2008

For these trade unionists, there was no question that:

Above, the Wall snakes around the Tulkarm Industrial Zone

Right, the Tulkarm Zone

All of these factories benefit from the occupation and the miserable situation and poverty of Palestinian workers. Their position is so hard now they are prepared to work in these dangerous places. And the workers themselves know the dangers. But if there is ever a vacancy there are tens of unemployed workers waiting to start.

Muhammed, Tulkarm, June 2008

The threat to the workers and to the people of Tulkarm from the industrial zone is measured by the climbing rates of various cancers and skin and respiratory problems. Public health officials in Tulkarm identified the industrial zone and the dump where the factories dispose of their waste as the principal agents responsible. They told us:

We have no rights of inspection in the zone. When we analysed the water near the zone we found very high levels of sulphuric acid and ammonia. It has been like this since 1991. We know that Israeli businesses from the zone and from within Israel are dumping their solid toxic waste on our dumps. The Israelis won't allow a 24-hour guard or a gate to the dump.

When the wind blows over us they open their chimneys and filters. When it blows over Israel they close them down. We now have big numbers of cancers in the southern area of Tulkarm. Many people have respiratory problems. We don't have the resources to keep full statistics but some are being collected by the PA and the Ministry of Health in Jordan.

Mr Abu H, Tulkarm Local Health Officer, June 2008

The combined hazards of both the festering waste dump and the industrial zone in the Tulkarm area pose a significant threat and are already taking their toll on people's health. It is an aspect of the occupation little commented upon but its consequences are as deadly as the weapons of the Israeli army. Not only are the people of this area penned in, impoverished and subject to daily Israeli incursions, they are also being poisoned.

The industrial zone in Tulkarm foreshadows a more generalised future for many West Bank workers, with industrial zones being built and planned alongside the Wall as it threads through the West Bank. In addition, there is ongoing industrial and horticultural development taking place within the West Bank settlements with an estimated 12,000 West Bank workers now employed in them, producing goods and foodstuffs, many of which end up in large British supermarkets and similar outlets across Europe.[24] Irrespective of their location, all these industrial zones share the same characteristic – the super-exploitation of Palestinian workers under Israeli state protection. The Palestinian workers are funnelled in one entrance directly from the West Bank and the goods flow out

Working in an Israeli/Palestinian zone

"In my place the boss can find ten others immediately," M explains.

And therefore he leaves his home by five in the morning, does not ask for the minimum salary, works when he is ill or during the holiday of Id Al Adha and has never had a vacation.

His older colleague J knows what happens if you protest.

"I have worked already ten years in the Israeli wood factory here. The company doesn't have a name and I doubt that it is even registered. I get 100 shekels per day for nine hours of work. We work here with 30 employees. There's hardly any protection against the sun or rain and the factory hall has no flooring. In the winter we stand all day in the mud. There is no toilet and we are not allowed to go out, because this iron door only opens at four. Can you imagine how dirty it gets, with 30 men? Two years ago I finally found the courage to complain. You know what happened? I was sacked on the spot and sent home without pay. Two weeks later the phone rang. It was my boss. He said he would give me a last chance, but I had to shut up."

And that's what J does. He doesn't complain about the lack of protective clothes and he was silent when the boy Namer accidentally shot himself in the abdomen with the electric stapler and was sent home without pay.

But he admits he's furious. "The worst thing is that the manager doesn't really care. It's not that he treats us as animals. He just doesn't see us at all."
Jerusalemites[23]

from another, either through the Wall or along the reserved Israeli-only roads that link the West Bank settlements directly into Israel. These factories and companies have none of the hassle of checkpoints and barriers which has done so much to destroy the indigenous economy. Moreover, as they are working in the West Bank, they do not have to comply with Israeli environmental or health and safety legislation and the companies are exempted from a range of business taxes applicable within Israel.[25]

Both the PA and the Israeli state share a mutual anxiety that

The smouldering dump (above). The waste ash and smoke engulf the surrounding villages, the chemicals drain from the dump into the water basin

Right, the smoke and poisonous gases blow down onto the village's crops

persistent mass unemployment and a labour pool that is being continually swelled by young people reaching working age feeds into "radicalisation". Wertheimer, who is behind a programme for the construction of up to 100 industrial zones in the West Bank, reflected, "It is better to occupy people with work rather than let them turn to terrorism".[27]

In similar vein Qadoura, a Fatah member, claimed that the planned zone for Jenin will help bolster moderates among Palestinians and weaken support for Hamas: "We have our radicals and it is of concern, but when we have over 50 percent unemployment and 6,000 graduates without work, then they become targets for radicals".[28]

However, as Rapaport observed in his article on the zones, philanthropy plays no part in their development or operation. As one Israeli involved in the zones asked him, "Why do you think the Erez industrial estate is still attractive for 200 factories that have stayed put despite all the terrorist attacks?... The most important motive is the low wages paid to the workers: around 1,500 shekels ($332) as against 4,500 shekels ($995), which is the minimum wage in Israel. What is more, the employers don't have to abide by Israeli labour laws".[29]

"Bringing the factories to the workers" is attracting major international support with consortia of governments (including France, Germany, Turkey and Japan) leading on the fastest-developing zones in Bethlehem, Jenin and Jericho. Some have estimated that the zones will eventually employ 500,000 Palestinian workers and that the significance of the zones will mean that over three-quarters of all economic activity in the West Bank will be oriented to the needs of the zones.[30] As in the case of other similar zones in Mexico, Jordan and Egypt, these Palestinian zones, which are actively encouraged by the PA, are characterised by low paid, hazardous and menial employment. They will further disrupt and damage the traditional agricultural economic base of the West Bank economy as has happened with the Jenin zone, which is being built over some of the richest farming land in the country. But above all, they will entirely subordinate the West Bank economy to the needs and interests of Israeli capital which will exercise ultimate control.

Pressures

The fallout from this massive onslaught on the condition of the Palestinian working class within the West Bank is ubiquitous. There is now, for example, a growing phenomenon of children dropping out of school. According to Rashad, a social work student at the Al Quds Open University, "We can see more and more children not going to school. The average family may have five children in school. They all need pencils, copy books, colours and one shekel as pocket money every day. That's five shekels a day immediately, but they don't even have one shekel! So school stops" (Tulkarm, June 2008).[31]

Israel's Free Trade Zones

The zones are being actively supported by the World Bank and Israel's core international supporters in Europe and the US.

Central to World Bank proposals are the construction of massive industrial zones to be financed by the World Bank and other donors and controlled by the Israeli occupation.

Built on Palestinian land around the Wall, these industrial zones are envisaged as forming the basis of export-orientated economic development. Palestinians imprisoned by the Wall and dispossessed of land can be put to work for low wages.

The post-Wall MEFTA [Middle East Free Trade Area] vision includes complete control over Palestinian movement. The report proposes high-tech military gates and checkpoints along the Wall, through which Palestinians and exports can be conveniently transported and controlled. A supplemental "transfer system" of walled roads and tunnels will allow Palestinian workers to be funnelled to their jobs, while being simultaneously denied access to their land.

Sweatshops will be one of very few possibilities of earning a living for Palestinians confined to disparate ghettos throughout the West Bank.
Project Censored, 2007 [26]

The familiar sight of children selling chewing gum, tissues and lighters on the streets of the West Bank towns, at the bus and taxi stations as well as around the fixed checkpoints, was for many of the young people we met a stark indicator of their society's desperation. Commonly referred to as "one-shekel kids", because that is the price they charge for their cheap goods, their increased presence on the streets is a direct impact of poverty.

Even for those who had made it through school and to university, the prospect of no work on graduation casts a deep shadow. This is what Ali, an IT student at the private American University near Jenin, told us:

> One of the problems is that there are no jobs or careers here. The occupation now means no work. So we stay on at university and we get really good qualifications, but then we have no choice, we have to travel out of the country to get a job. I'd say about 99 percent of students I know want to leave Palestine. They have had enough.
> *Ali, American University, Jenin, February 2008*

His friend Usman, a business studies student, was supported by all the group when he noted that lack of jobs and the daily experience of the occupation was a lethal combination:

> Of course the job situation makes me want to go and the job situation is bad because of the occupation – but so does the occupation itself make me want to go. They are both factors making me want to go. The future is not great. It is so bad and has been for ten years. We want to leave because elsewhere we can do things.
> *Usman, American University, Jenin, February 2008*

The issue of whether to stay in the West Bank or to leave is both a complex and controversial issue especially for many middle class Palestinians. It is, however, not a choice available to most Palestinian young people. Even those who have the resources and contacts outside Palestine may lack an ID, which allows them to leave or, more importantly, to return, as Ibrahim explained:

> Many of the students hope that with their degrees that they will get work. Most of us now will go out because it is so difficult to get any work here. But not all of us are able to do this as

we don't have any ID. This is my situation. I have a Jordanian passport from before but now it has expired and until I get a Palestinian ID I cannot travel out of Nablus. If I do leave now, I won't be able to get back.

Ibrahim, An-Najah University, Nablus, September 2006

And this is what Rasha, a 20 year old student from Nablus, told us about her friend:

We have so many difficulties when we want to travel. My friend who is a journalism student got a scholarship to study in Germany for a year. When he came to leave for Germany he was stopped at the checkpoint and he was held for eight hours while the soldiers looked into his situation and then told him that he couldn't go and had to return to Nablus. When he returned he got a lawyer to help him. After long negotiations the lawyer reported that my friend would be given permission to go to Germany. The condition was that my friend would have to sign a paper which said that he could only return to Palestine with the permission of Israel. He didn't sign as he knew that the Israelis would never give him this right to return. He was terribly upset and stressed by all this and became ill. He died in a month.

Rasha, An-Najah University, Nablus, September 2006

One-shekel kids

Ala is a 14 year old boy originally from Gaza. His family moved to Ramallah eight years ago. He has eight brothers and sisters and his father is unemployed.

Ala works after school and during his summer holidays, he sells gum and sweets around the restaurants in Ramallah for two shekels each; he says some people are nice to him and give him extra money when buying but some others yell at him and ask him to stay away from them.

Ala says sometimes he makes 25 shekels and some other days he makes 100 shekels. He saves up the money to give to his family, as his father has lost his job due to the current political situation and his mother doesn't work. It is up to him and his brother to make sure that there is enough money to pay the school fees.

Those children not only suffer from the people who humiliate them in the street but also from the Palestinian police who beat and humiliate them. The restaurant managers and store owners where the children are selling their stuff are always shouting at them and kicking them from one place to another.

ITUC, 2008[32]

The students we met at the American University near Jenin were drawn from predominantly professional family backgrounds (engineers, doctors, dentists, business owners) who could afford the costs of private university education and in the main were "returnees" who had foreign passports which allowed them and their families to move around. In this group there were students whose Palestinian parents had worked and lived in the US, a number of Gulf States, Turkey and North Africa. They were very different from the students we met on the same visit who were studying through the Open University in Tulkarm and at An-Najah in Nablus. Few of these students were from professional middle class families and none of those we met at the Open University had families or relatives outside of Palestine with whom they could stay. In addition, they were concerned that the Israelis, who control all international travel in and out of the West Bank, would prevent their return. The American University students did not have such fears and most of them spoke of leaving the country to find work which would be sufficiently lucrative to enable them to return home and live in comfort, as Norisa, a 20 year old dental student, explained:

> One of the problems for the young here, is we sometimes feel we have to leave to get a job, to make money and get a life. But we are also dreaming of coming back and building a nice house, starting a family and settling back here in Palestine. I am increasingly thinking that I will have to leave the West Bank to develop my career but I intend to make it temporary. I intend to come back, but then who knows what will happen when I live outside.
>
> *Norisa, American University, Jenin, February 2008*

But some sense of the tensions over leaving or staying is evident in Amal's response to her friends at the American University:

> I will not migrate! This is my country. Most young Palestinians say they will leave. But for political reasons, from my point of view, I agree and disagree with emigration. I agree that it is not fair to expect young men to stay here without a job, but at the same time I feel we need those young people to stay. The situation is so bad, families struggle to send their children to get their degrees and then if they leave they take all that money, all that training, all that education – they take it all out of Palestine and use it to help develop other countries. This means our resources – which we need to develop – are being exported.
>
> And, if we do leave our place will be taken by Israelis! They want to replace us. The Israelis want us to go, to leave – we have to stay so they know that they cannot just take all our land.
>
> *Amal, American University, Jenin, February 2008*

Many in the West Bank recognise that their dire economic realities and poor prospects are an inextricable aspect of the Israeli occupation and are weapons as powerful and destructive as the Israeli apache helicopters and F16s. As Rashad told us:

Poverty, lack of jobs – these are weapons of the occupation. They want to show us that without them, without their help, without their investments – without all this…we will be nothing. This is war in another way.

Rashad, Tulkarm, February 2008

Notes

1 International Labour Conference, 93rd Session, Report of the Director-General, 'The Situation of Workers of the Occupied Arab Territories' (Geneva, 2005).

2 UNICEF Annual Report 2009.

3 International Committee of the Red Cross, 'Household Economy Assessment: West Bank and Gaza' (2006), p11.

4 Institute for Middle East Understanding, 'Social Customs and Traditions' (2006), imeu.net/news/article00249.shtml (accessed 15 April 2007).

5 For further detail see Amnesty International, *Israel and the Occupied Territories: Conflict, occupation and patriarchy. Women Carry the Burden* (London, 2005), www.reliefweb.int/library/documents/2005/ai-opt-31mar.pdf

6 On 9 July 2004 the World Court in The Hague ruled that Israel's construction of its proposed 720km barrier/wall on occupied Palestinian land was illegal.

7 S Bannoura, 'Israeli Deputy PM: Wall should become Official Border for Israel', 15 November 2010, www.uruknet.info/?p=71878 (accessed 26 January 2010).

8 Anti-Apartheid Wall Campaign factsheet, 2005: 'The Apartheid Wall', www.miftah.org/Doc/Factsheets/Other/NewWallFactSheet.pdf

9 E Weizman, *Hollow Land* (Verso, 2007), p168.

10 J Blythman, 'Palestinians Find a Harvest of Hope', *Guardian Weekly*, 16 October 2009, pp28-29.

11 R Sarafa, 'Roots of Conflict: Felling Palestine's Olive Trees', *Harvard International Review*, 22 March 2004.

12 H Ofran, 'Despite Promises – Land Confiscation Continues Throughout 2008 – January 2009', Peace Now Reports, www.peacenow.org.il/site/en/peace.asp?pi=61&fld=495&docid=3497 (accessed 3 March 2011).

13 'Under Cover of the Night: Palestinian Ghost Workers in Israel', Russia Today, 9 November 2009, rt.com/Top_News/2009-11-09/cover-night-palestinian-ghost.html (accessed 15 Jan 2010).

14 Cited in M Howell, *What did we do to Deserve This?* (Garnett Publishing, 2007), p170.

15 'The Ultimate Betrayal? Palestinians Work on Israeli Wall Construction', Russia Today, 24 August 2009, rt.com/Top_News/2009-08-24/israel-wall-construction-palestinians.html?fullstory (accessed 15 January 2010).

16 H Sharp, 'Dilemma of Palestinian Settlement Builders', BBC News, news.bbc.co.uk/go/pr/fr/-/2/hi/middle_east/8220680.stm (accessed 17 March 2010).

17 S Korkus, 'Back to the Wall: a Study of Palestinian Working Conditions in Israeli Settlements', Jerusalemites, www. jerusalemites.org/reports/84.htm (accessed 15 January 2010).

18 We discuss PA corruption in more detail in chapter 5, but a flavour of what is involved is given by Makdisi: " The Oslo arrangement did, however, benefit the small Palestinian elite centred on Yasser Arafat and his associates in the Fatah party. Members of this elite gained financially from the monopolies granted by the PA to various loyalists and from general corruption, cronyism and mismanagement that was endemic in the Authority. Nearly half of the PA's 1997 budget, for example, was lost to corruption and financial mismanagement, according to an internal auditor's report." S Makdisi, *Palestine Inside Out* (W W Norton, 2008), p85.

19 D Yousef, 'Palestinian Laborers on the Israeli Separation Wall', *The Electronic Intifada*, 10 May 2006.

20 H Sharp, as above.

21 It is difficult to estimate the numbers of Palestinian workers without permits in Israel but according to Israeli Internal Security minister Avi Dichter, between 1 January 2006 and 14 June 2006 some 51,000 Palestinians were caught in Israel without permits. See G Alon, "Dichter: Since Beginning of Year 51,000 Persons Staying Illegally Caught in Israel", *Haaretz*, 15 June 2006 (Hebrew), www.haaretz.co.il/hasite/ pages/ShArtPE.jhtml?itemNo=727227&co ntrassID=2&subContrassID=

22 M Rapoport, 'Israel: Industrial Estates Along the Wall', *Le Monde diplomatique* (English edition), June 2004, mondediplo. com/2004/06/05thewall. (accessed 15 June 2010).

23 S Korkus, as above.

24 Corporate Watch, 'Profiting from Occupation: UK and International Companies complicit in Israeli War Crimes Against Palestinians' (2009), www. corporatewatch.org.

25 Corporate Watch, 'Occupation Industries: The Industrial Zones', News, 2 December 2009, www.corporatewatch.org. uk/?lid=3477 (accessed 15May 2010).

26 Project Censored, 'The World Bank funds Israeli-Palestinian Wall' (2007), www. projectcensored.org/top-stories/ articles/9-the-world-bank-funds-israel- palestine-wall/

27 Cited by M Rapoport, as above.

28 'Jenin Leads Effort in Israeli-Palestinian joint Industrial Zone', *Jewish News*, 3 September 2009, www.ijn.com/ business/1197-jenin-leads-effort-in-israeli- palestinian-joint-industrial-zone

29 M Rapoport, as above.

30 S Bahour, 'Economic Prison Zones' (Middle East Research and Information Project, 2010), www.wearewideawake.org/index. php?option=com_content&task=view&id= 1896&Itemid=239 (Accessed 19 November 2010).

31 "Rising poverty and unemployment is affecting school attendance across Palestine. In the 2005/6 school year the number of students whose families could not afford the NIS 50 ($11) school fee doubled from 29,000 to 56,000." *Palestine Monitor Children Factsheet*, updated 18 December 2008.

32 N Shabana, 'Child Labour in Palestine' (International Trade Union Confederation, 2008), www.ituc-csi.org/child-labour-in- palestine.html?lang=en (accessed 15 June 2010).

Chapter 5

Palestinian divides

The Israeli occupation of the West Bank envelops everybody and distorts every aspect of Palestinian life. It has also engendered a refusal to buckle under or surrender to the Israelis and levels of solidarity that form the core of a remarkable resistance. Nevertheless, from the very beginning of our visits, we were aware of divisions and differences in the West Bank. The first thing that struck us was the range of housing, suggesting that some Palestinians lived in homes that those in the refugee camps could only dream about. Likewise, the strangled economic base is built on a large agricultural sector with almost feudal overtones of land control in the hands of a few large families. Palestine has only a tiny manufacturing sector, but it has enriched a small number of exceptionally wealthy Palestinian businessmen.

Our first experience of the West Bank was Ramallah, where we were astonished to see the stark contrast between the conditions in the refugee camps and a number of large and opulent houses spread throughout the city. In the former, thousands of people were corralled in cramped and overcrowded housing. Many of these houses had been made into beautiful homes inside, with modern kitchens and welcoming lounges decorated with great care, but outside the front door there are narrow and dark alleys with drain water running down the centre, and houses so packed that there is barely a metre separating one building from another. Many of the refugees had, over generations, transformed their homes into oases of comfort in what can only be described as a ghetto.

The contrast with large lavish mansions, some in very close proximity to the camps, is extreme. During the course of our visits the number of such properties in Ramallah multiplied and the hills of the city are now dotted with grand houses standing in their own sculptured grounds.

Ramallah provided us with the clearest example of such

disparities in living conditions, but examples exist across the West Bank in both rural and urban areas. At this very basic empirical level it is clear that there are some significant differences in West Bank society.

When we explored what these differences meant to young people we were surprised by their defensiveness and insistence that such divisions did not reflect a problem for West Bank society. The box overleaf reports an interchange with some of the volunteer workers in the Balata refugee camp.

This toleration of disparities in wealth was also evident from

Al-Amari refugee camp, June 2008 (right) and September 2004 (left)

the absence of the usual security systems that bristle around the houses of the rich in the west. There were no signs of alarms or CCTV, even where the houses were only separated by a road from a refugee camp. The acceptance of this contrast was explained to us on the basis that the wealthy who could afford such homes had shown their commitment to Palestine: "They have returned to the West Bank and often left very good lives in the Gulf or America and shown their confidence in our struggle," as were told by university student Najwa (Nablus, 2006). For whatever reason, these Palestinians had choices and had chosen to return to the West Bank. Furthermore, we were reminded that many who had left Palestine to work and live outside were living their dream when they returned to build a home big enough for their large or extended families.

Fatima did recognise that the endless poverty of the camps is hard to endure, but in the final analysis sees the Palestinian diaspora as positive:

Poverty makes the people in the camps feel down. They struggle to live each day – and then you have people who have left and return here to build big homes. But sometimes they come

back and build businesses in the West Bank which brings benefits to those who live here. And many people send money
home, or they sponsor students to come to university. The
diaspora does send money back and this helps those that stay.
Fatima, American University, Jenin, February 2008

Given the Israeli restrictions on the rights of Palestinians
to return to the West Bank it is no surprise that those able to
return tend to be the wealthy rather than those in the refugee
camps of Jordan, Syria or Lebanon. Many were professionals

– doctors, lawyers, academics – who thought that Oslo would
bring new opportunities. Although significant numbers have
since left as Oslo failed to deliver, those that remain consti-
tute a significant proportion of the wealthy in the West Bank,
as Nadia told us:

Examples of the
lavish new mansions
in Ramallah

> There are wealthy people here but nearly always they are from
> outside, like the US or the Gulf States. Many of them help peo-
> ple with money, but not all. It just depends on their outlook
> and their feelings.

She continued:

> The issue of poverty here does not attract the same attention
> as other aspects of the occupation like the so-called peace proc-
> ess. Many families are shy about talking about their poverty and
> problems or about their wealth and their advantages.
> *Nadia, Nablus, 2006*

There is a wealthy elite in the West Bank, an elite which
would like to secure its position and extend its power in any

On poverty and inequality

Sami: We are not the only side – as refugees – who take all the responsibility for the resistance. Others resist as well. Of course in the camps we have our particular problems. But they have problems in the cities and villages as well – but they are different problems.

Hamed A: The refugee camps in the 1950s had tents; now the refugees have achieved a house. We have managed to build these.

Hamed R: In our actual life, as refugees, we are different to other people. There are poor people in the cities and the big houses only belong to a few people who maybe have goods jobs in the government, or those who have sold their land, or perhaps they are migrants from the US.

Sami: We have to look at ourselves. We can't get angry because he has a big house or something. In fact you could say we have a better situation as refugees compared to Palestinian refugees in Lebanon or Syria. In Lebanon Palestinian refugees are banned from all different types of work, for example.

Hamed A: You know in Britain and America you can find people who are homeless or who are poor. The richest countries have this problem of poverty – we are not different.

Balata, February 2008

future settlement. However, the abject poverty of the West Bank is not of their making. The relationship between this elite and the majority of the population is not simply rooted in economics. It is also shaped by the occupation, in which traditional customs of charitable giving take on added significance as the formal economy collapses and poverty deepens. Although not easily quantified, the inflow of support from the diaspora has been crucial to the survival of the West Bank. The result is that most Palestinians take the same view as Nadia, who told us:

So many of the poverty problems are directly due to the occupation. This is why we must fight to end it for when we are free we will overcome these difficulties.
Nadia, Nablus, 2006

While most young people we spoke to saw class and wealth inequalities within Palestinian society as part of the normal order of things, or at best something to be dealt with after the occupation is ended, some recognised a greater significance, both in the experiences of occupation and in the prospects for a future free Palestine. These attitudes were most clearly evident in the distress caused by the corruption within sections of their own economic and political elite

At a meeting at the Friends School we were told that many of the large homes that we had seen were the fruits of corruption within the PA and many of the large and numerous NGOs operating out of Ramallah. Houses are not the only fruits of corruption. One of the students whose father was a senior hospital consultant told us of her father's dismay over the cronyism involved in the purchase of expensive medical equipment whereby valuable contracts were given to "friends" rather than subject to open

tender. Raja Shehadeh provides a clear example of such cronyism and its consequences:

> My school friend Victor was among the first from my genera-
> tion to decide that he would not be able to survive under the
> new regime [post-Oslo]. He had spent the best years of his
> life establishing a computer company under the most gruel-
> ling of circumstances, under the restrictions and obstructions
> of the Israeli occupation and the first Intifada. With the expec-
> tation of peace he had ambitious plans to expand his business
> regionally and had enough talented people around him to
> manage this. One day he was called to a meeting, along with
> other owners of computer companies, to one of the Palestinian
> ministries that needed new software. They were asked to sub-
> mit bids. He along with his staff worked day and night and
> produced the best offer, but they did not win the tender. A rel-
> ative of the minister got it. This was a blow to Victor, who had
> pinned much of his hopes on this big job. This incident was
> followed by other depressing experiences of corruption and
> foul play.[1]

Palestinian divides

Victor and his family closed their business and migrated
to Australia. Shehadeh's disappointment and bewilderment
with many of the developments in the PA following Oslo
echo throughout his book, especially with respect to the way
in which the monies that flowed into the Occupied Territories
following Oslo were used to sustain and support what another
critic described as a "a thin tier of Palestinian capitalists, allied
to the Israeli upper classes…creating ripe grounds for political
and economic corruption and nepotism".[2]

Many spoke of the corruption and nepotism rife in the PA
and Fatah and argued that it was widespread dismay with this
state of affairs which had been one of the significant factors
in the election victory of Hamas in 2006. After the election
the attorney general discovered that over US$700 million had
been siphoned out of public accounts in 50 different cases
under review.[3] It was this kind of money which was finding itself transmuted into some of the lavish properties we
saw in Ramallah and supporting the development of a small
but significant capitalist class in the West Bank closely allied
to the PA and Fatah. As we noted earlier with respect to the
newly forming industrial zones being constructed alongside
the Wall, there is now an emerging layer of Palestinian businesses more than prepared to collaborate economically with

the Israelis to exploit the miserable condition of the people. The corruption of the elites in a context of suffocating occupation is one of the clearest signs that the resistance is not experienced equally.

For such a small society there are some stark divisions; these are illustrated by Ben, the son of a returning US businessman, and Jamal, the same age as Ben but living in the Tulkarm refugee camp. When we asked Ben what he hoped to be doing in five years time he replied:

> In five years time I want to be back here in business and making money. I want to build the economy. This is the best way I know how I can help make Palestinian life better. As for resistance this is not for me. For some fine, but with the chances and connections that I have in my life it means that I can try in business and make my contribution this way.
> *Ben, Ramallah, June 2008*

Jamal was not optimistic that he would be able to find work on completion of his degree at the Open University:

> The job situation is critical for all graduates. The occupation is the major factor here, but the social system and how it works in Palestine is also responsible. If you know someone, if you have relations – you might be able to get a job. But for most people like me living in the refugee camp this is not possible.
> *Jamal, Tulkarm, February 2008*

The importance of these networks and connections should not be underestimated, even though in the present context of distorted economic activity even the best connections may not guarantee a job and career – even Ben may be thwarted. But in 2008 when we met him, his life and his opportunities far surpassed Jamal and his friends in the Tulkarm camp. Both had experienced curfew, one in a spacious home the other in a room; for Ben to have soldiers in his neighbourhood was rare, and in his home unheard of, whereas for Jamal both were common. Reem, Ben's friend at school, gave us this illustration of the divisions within Palestinian society:

> My mother is well educated and known all over Ramallah for her work at the University. The Israeli soldiers always treat her better than less well educated women. They are frightened of being exposed. When IDF soldiers wanted to come into our

house one night my mother refused and said that there was a
child in the house. They went away. They never tried to force
the issue. But for others it is very different. Like for the woman
in the camp who had gone for a robe before answering the door
and was blown up and killed as the soldiers blasted the door
down. There is a big class difference here.

Reem, Ramallah, 2006

Ashraf, from the Al-Amari refugee camp in Ramallah and
a volunteer worker in the youth centre, was more prepared
than many to speak out about his experiences and the necessity
for any future intifada to tackle both the occupation and the
behaviour of their own elites:

I work as a volunteer in the camp – at the disability project.
I've worked here since I got out of prison 18 months ago. There
are no jobs in the camps and it is difficult for me to work anywhere. You look outside. Look at the buildings – there are very
rich people here. And yet we have nothing in the camps – we
struggle to feed ourselves and yet they make more and more
wealth. Is that right?

There is money in the PA but Fatah and government officials use this corruptly. The government has their big projects
– they're very prestigious and they get money from the international community and the Americans. Yet the people have
nothing. Why the big buildings when we are starving and have
no jobs? And as with the buildings individuals misuse their
position to get rich, they use their money to buy influence and
support. We have a big and growing problem of corruption.
This happens at all levels.

Let me give you two examples. First, I volunteer in the
camps, I work hard for my community. Yet if there is an invi-
tation to go abroad I never get invited. Why? It is because I am
Hamas and these trips only go to Fatah – as a reward, as something to keep them in Fatah and because Fatah members will
be politically safe. Second, my brother. He is in jail. He got a
25-year sentence during the First Intifada and has been in there
for 20 years. Yet when they talk of prisoner exchanges or prisoner benefits he is never included. Why? Because he is Islamic
Jihad and both the Israelis and Fatah see him as dangerous.
There is much talk about a third intifada. I believe it is coming but this intifada will be different. It will be against both the
Israelis and the PA and its corruption.

Ashraf, Ramallah, April 2010

Ashraf drew attention to a further fissure in the West Bank that was discussed on many occasions, namely the plight and treatment of the refugees, especially those living in the refugee camps.[4] This, as we were to discover, has a number of dimensions. The refugees of the camps are among the poorest people of the West Bank. The majority depend on the food aid provided by UNRWA. Although a significant number have jobs with the PA, as part of its policy of support for refugees, for the majority casual and menial day work tends to be the only waged work available, and that is diminishing. The populations of the camps for over 60 years have experienced the full force of the occupation – socially, economically and militarily.

Their resistance and steadfastness is the source of enormous pride and solidarity within the camps. They are rightly proud of their steadfastness in the face of sustained Israeli oppression, especially since the First Intifada when the camps were such an important source of resistance and subsequently a target for the IDF. The heroism of the camps, their casualties and martyrs, is lauded throughout West Bank society. In so many ways the camps provide the vanguard of the Palestinian resistance, but in many ways their position is not secure, even within the struggle for national liberation. While their right to return has been emblematic throughout the struggle against Israel, enshrined in United Nations Resolution 194, it is clear from the Oslo Accords and all the subsequent efforts in the so-called "peace process" that Israel is never going to honour this obligation. More significant and disturbing for the refugees is the preparedness of the PLO and then the PA to negotiate over their right to return. For the refugees the right to return can never be a matter of negotiation. The large banners and painted murals stating that there can be no peace that does not enshrine the rights of the refugees, which can be seen close to many West Bank camps, are not only for Israeli consumption!

The issue of the right to return is invariably presented in the Western media as complex, given that the lands and homes people fled in 1948 and 1967 have been under Israeli occupation for decades. It suits the Israeli case for such an understanding to take root. It is such a fundamental right – the abrogation of which for over 60 years has condemned millions of Palestinian refugees to misery – that it can not be diluted or compromised. Interestingly, we heard from many

Palestinians in the West Bank and within Israel that a surprising number of the villages destroyed in 1948-49 have never been developed by the Israelis. Within the camps all the families we met were aware of what had happened to their homes and lands and it became evident that the return of the refugees to their lands – if not to their homes – is nothing like as difficult as Israel contends.

Within the camps we met many third and some fourth generation refugees, young people, for whom the right to return to their former family homes burned as strongly as it did for their parents, grandparents and great-grandparents.

The drawings and paintings by young refugees commonly included the keys which were symbolic of their lost homes and land. In camps such as Balata regular attempts (some successful) are made to organise trips to their lost lands. For these young people the right to return is inviolable.

Seventeen year old Ahmed from the Jenin camp spoke for many when he insisted:

حق العودة خط أحمر لا يمكن تجاوزه
The Right of Return is a Political Red Line that Can Not be Crossed

One of the many banners proclaiming the importance of the right to return

> The refugees must be part of any solution. The right of return must be part of any solution. Abu Mazen must not suggest there is a peace if it does not include refugee rights. If refugee rights are not part of the solution, there will be another intifada.
> *Ahmed, Jenin, 2008*

Ahmed and his friends in the camp recognised the massive popular support for their rights but there was not the same confidence when it came to their representatives in the PA and among the small political and economic elite. Their preparedness to negotiate on the principle was alarming enough, but we came across other examples which suggested that refugees, especially from the camps, experienced discrimination.[5] Abla's story, below, is one such case.

In a depressing conversation we had with four young men who had just transferred from the UNRWA school in the Balata camp to a governmental school in Nablus to complete their high school education, it was all too clear that the schooling provided in the camps was in every sense inferior to that experienced by the rest of the population.

Ameen: I had the highest average in my class at the UNRWA school. But when I went to the governmental school I found I was last in the class. The dreams I had of being a doctor suddenly disappeared.

Hussan: I would like to be an engineer but because of the situation I think I will struggle to get an average that will get me into the university.

Hamed: I was first or second in my class at UNRWA, my average was 98 percent, but when I went to the governmental school I found that the level was much higher. It is not that we are

These two photographs show the village of Saffuriyya on a hill just 6 kilometres north of Nazareth, as it was in 1947 (left) and as it is today. The village was occupied and "cleansed" in July 1948

lazy, we worked hard at school but when we arrived at the governmental school we found we were way behind. This is very frustrating. The level of the curriculum is limited in the UNRWA schools and they get fewer resources. There are 50 to 55 students in the class. There are also incursions, killings and so on in the camp and this also affects our schooling.

ML: So there are two problems: first, the incursions, etc and second, the system of education which discriminates against kids from the camp?

Ameen: The huge number of students in the class is a problem.

Hussan: The number of students is also a cause of disorder in the class. The teacher can't keep control. And all the time people are looking outside waiting to see if there will be any trouble, so the students' attention is sometimes elsewhere.

CJ: If you had gone to a governmental school for the first nine grades, would the class size have been smaller?

Hamed: Yes. Perhaps 25 students in each class, the maximum is 35. In the city there are many governmental and private schools. In the camps there are a limited number of schools with large numbers.

Balata, February 2008

As Ahmed summarised:

Regarding the education process. After 9th grade we have to leave the UNRWA school for the 10th, 11th and 12th grade. And you find that students who transfer to the governmental school always struggle. Life in the camps is much more difficult than in the towns and villages and the effect is much greater on the students.

Ahmed, Balata, February 2008

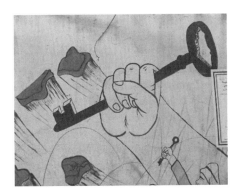 

These examples point up some of the faultlines that exist within the West Bank. One cannot read off a seamless and undifferentiated solidarity, especially with respect to the position and prospects of the refugees, and particularly those living within the camps. For many, these were not easy conversations as they perceived such divisions as constituting a weakness which undermined their unity, which in turn had bedevilled their struggle historically, as 12 year old Mohammed told us in Tulkarm:

The mural, left, is from the edge of the Palestinian refugee camp Bourj al-Bourajni in Lebanon

The group of young people, above, had just returned from a trip to Yaffa where they had seen their ancestral homes and land for the first time. They were ecstatic!

We are all Palestinian. I don't say I am first from Tulkarm or Qalqilya, but that I am Palestinian. Just as all of us here are refugees. But there are no differences between refugees and others. We are all Palestinian. All of us equal. Too often we Arabs are weak because we are not united.

Mohammed, Tulkarm, June 2008

Mohammed is in many ways correct. West Bank society exudes a sense of solidarity. There are evident linkages between those in the camps and those outside and countless examples of inter-class solidarities. Our identification of faultlines is not

Abla's story

CJ: There are some gaps we are trying to fill in our research. Can you help? Are young refugees treated the same as non-refugees?

Abla: There is a big difference between how refugee young people and non-refugee children are treated. In school we have different equipment, we are treated differently by teachers, and we have different and older books, for example.

CJ: Can you give me an example that directly relates to you?

Abla: One day, when I was in 8th grade, I was sitting next to a colleague at our desk. She was not a refugee. The sun was coming through the window – it was very strong – so my fellow student and I agreed that we would change places daily. We both agreed and thought this was fair. But the teacher refused to accept our solution and told me to stay in the sun. She came over to the desk and then she noticed our books. My book was quite new and clean. My father had covered it to keep it good. But the girl next to me, her book was old. The teacher took my book and gave it to my friend and gave me the old book in its place.

ML: What did the teacher say when she did this?

Abla: The teacher claimed that I wasn't using the book in a good way. She said I was underlining things in the book – but this wasn't the case. The underlining was there before I got the book.

I went to the head teacher and she told me that this school was originally a very distinguished one. It was a school for the daughters of engineers, lawyers and other high-class people. It was not a school for people like me.

I then told my mum and she told dad. He was so angry and he went in to the school to fight against this discrimination. He demanded that I got the book back and that me and my fellow could continue to change our seats as we'd agreed. He also demanded that the teacher apologise to me in front of the class. Which she did, but not very well.

CJ: Abla, how did you understand this behaviour? The refugees suffer a very big burden – the biggest – from the occupation. So why would a Palestinian teacher treat a refugee like this?

Abla: I was astonished at what happened. They thought we were very poor and that we wouldn't say anything. They are not refugees and they are not suffering like us. They don't relate to us.

CJ: Is this something that students talk about? You mentioned your colleague who sat next to you. She had no problems. So this wasn't a problem among the students.

Abla: These attitudes are not a problem with the students, but they are held by the teachers. When it first happened my colleague said, "Abla just give me the book for the class, when we leave the class I'll give you it back." So she tried to compromise the situation.

ML: How many refugees were in the school?

Abla: It was 50:50

ML: How do you know this? How can you tell who is, and who is not, a refugee?

Abla: The names of people make it very clear. People's family names make it clear. And also in the register of the school it tells that, before arriving at the high school we went to a UNWRA school [for refugees only]. I left the UNWRA school after 7th grade at age 13, but most come at the end of the 9th grade.

CJ: In Balata we talked to people who had been to the UNWRA school in the camp and been top of the class. But when they went to the governmental school they found themselves at the bottom of the new class and struggled to catch up. Is this the same here in Tulkarm?

Abla: Yes, it was the same. When we transferred from UNWRA to the governmental school we feel we get treated differently. The teachers put more effort in because of the other children: some are the children of doctors or lawyers – we are just refugees so why bother?

You know the UNWRA schools are very over-crowded. At least 50 people in a class. There are not enough computers to go around – we had one computer for every nine students. The material you cover is the same – but the administration is different; the style of teaching is different – they are quite different places.

CJ: How did it make you feel?

Abla: Sad. Going to school should be a happy thing. But it isn't always.

Tulkarm, September 2009

---

intended to exaggerate difference but rather to point to issues which we believe need to be addressed and not left to some future date. If not, the goal of national liberation will not lead to a land where all people can live with justice and humanity.

Gender

From the very beginning of our work in the West Bank we were repeatedly told that it is a society which favours boys over girls. We were given many examples. Twelve year old Selma in Qalqilya told us in 2006 that her hobby was swimming, but when we asked her where she swam she told us that she didn't as the swimming pools in Qalqilya were only for boys and men. When she dreamed of a free Palestine, she said, it included not only freedom from the Israeli occupation but also a place where girls like her could go swimming. Likewise, many young women spoke of their envy of the young men who could go out with their male friends, drink coffee and stay out during the evenings enjoying their company. This was not an option for the young women, especially in conservative places like Tulkarm and Qalqilya, where such behaviour is regarded as bringing shame on them and their families, and in turn impacting on their future prospects of marriage. Public life for many young women in the West Bank is chaperoned. Teenage girls in particular are closely watched and are expected to behave at all times in ways which honour their families.

Geography plays a part, even in such a small place as the West Bank. Villages and small towns tend to be socially conservative with traditional values continuing to exert considerable influence over girls' and women's behaviour. Rema from the Friends School told us:

*Voices from
the West Bank*

We can go out [with boys] but Ramallah is well known as a liberal city not like the rest of the West Bank. There are many Palestinians here from abroad, like America, and that has an effect. They have more money than elsewhere in the West Bank and they tend not to be so religious and so not as conservative. It is so different from Qalqilya. There girls are definitely not allowed to date. You can go to the same restaurant but not sit at the same table as boys. To be at the same table would be seen as shameful. Wrong. My girlfriend from Qalqilya has been dating a boy for two years now and they have never yet been alone together. They relate mainly online or through texting on their phones.

Rema, Ramallah, June 2008

Norisa in Jenin made a similar point, noting that being a young woman in Qalqilya was more difficult than being a young woman in Jenin:

How you are treated depends on your family and their location. In Qalqilya, when I lived there, it was harder. There were stricter controls. I'm a Muslim, I have my beliefs but I don't agree with the rules as they are applied in Qalqilya. Here in Jenin, it is not so conservative.

Norisa, Jenin, September 2008

This was our experience too, not just with respect to Ramallah and Jenin but in Nablus and on many of the university campuses we visited, where it is not unusual to see young men and women sharing conversations, walking together and drinking coffee. Moreover, even in the more conservative places, we never once had a meeting with mixed gendered groups where the women or girls were deferential to boys or afraid to express their opinions and views, whether it was about personal relationships or broader political issues. This was typified by Mira's comments to us when she said:

The women of Palestine don't need anyone to tell them about their role and importance in the resistance. We know. What we do need to do though is to put ourselves forward to become leaders. I believe that we need more women in the legislative council and in politics in general. We don't need NGOs telling us about the importance of voting!
Mira, Jenin, September 2006

But, as Said Madhieh noted with respect to Hebron – which applies to other similar towns and villages in the West Bank – socially conservative attitudes to women still prevail and impinge adversely on their life chances and participation in society:

Palestinian divides

Social solidarity and nepotism are still apparent within the Arab community in Hebron and the surrounding villages. Individuals, especially women, feel that they are constantly being watched. They are expected to know the traditions and abide by them, otherwise they risk being ostracised. There is an elite group of male elders in Hebron who are experts in clan or tribal laws and regulations in the areas of social conflict and murder. The rulings of this group have the authority of the law and are obeyed and revered by all people – young and old alike. They are even more effective than the decisions taken by civil courts.[6]

In a discussion with a mixed group of students from the university in Nablus, Jumana, a final year medical student, was insistent that as a young woman she felt continually "watched" when she was not at the university.

It's only here [university] where I feel free and can breathe. At home in Tulkarm, I am a different person.
Jumana, Nablus, June 2008

Jumana, as a doctor, is almost certain of a decent job on graduation. But the near destruction of the West Bank economy means that many women graduates have no option but to return to their families and wait for marriage. This came home to us when we met for the third time a group of three young women who had just graduated from the Open University in Tulkarm in the summer of 2009. As with many other young women, they were confident and assertive with strong views on a wide range of issues. They spoke with candour about their lives on graduation and how, having left university, they were once more expected to see their main activity as within their family and its domestic economy. The friendships they had developed in university were likely to fade as they waited in their homes for marriage. Their opportunities to socialise were once more highly restricted. They still met one another, but less frequently. Most of their time – given that there were no jobs available to them in Tulkarm – was spent in the home. Their evenings and leisure time were often solitary with the internet or mobile phones being the main channels for talking with old friends. When their former friends married, their friendships came to an end, as they would be expected to devote themselves to their new husbands and families. There was some sadness at this prospect, but there was an underlying confidence that things would change; after all, they said, look at the differences between them and their mothers, none of whom had gone to university. Fareeda told us:

> I am not saying that we are asking for equal rights with men. This is not possible as they are stronger than us. But I want us women to have more rights, to be given a place in society, to express our thoughts and opinions, and the right to work. We are becoming more powerful and you will see women taking a leading role in cultural centres.
> *Fareeda, Tulkarm, September 2009*

Life in the West Bank is highly gender differentiated, from schooling, to social activities, to employment opportunities, and within domestic arrangements including housework, cooking, eating and leisure time. The occupation reinforces such gender divisions and inequalities. In a society distorted by the occupation, the pervasiveness of traditional cultural practices works to the disadvantage of women. The much-lauded honour of a family is determined by the behaviour of women, who alone bring either honour or shame. The consequences for Palestinian women are many, as Hadi and Engler noted:

> Social traditions also make women more vulnerable to isolation due to lack of freedom of movement. Families worry about the honour of the women in their household and are reluctant to allow them to run the risk of harassment at checkpoints, or of being unable to return home due to the unstable

political situation. In addition, transportation and travel time has become more costly. This means that women have less access to their personal support network of friends and family who live in other areas. Nor do they have access to activities, services, and household decision-making that take place outside the home.[7]

There are countless ways in which women and girls are disadvantaged when compared to men and boys. Some of these are familiar throughout all societies, but in the West Bank the occupation and the resistance have added a distinctive dimension to gender relationships. Whereas the resilience of women in male-dominated societies often goes unnoticed and is kept private and largely hidden, in the West Bank women's capacity to hold households together in every sense (often in the absence of key male figures due to imprisonment or injury) is widely understood as being crucial to the resistance and its steadfastness.[8] In a society that has no formal welfare system of any significance it is the capacity of the family and the household, and especially of the women who manage this, which ensures the fundamental survival of the people, placing "women's work" at the core of community and family resistance.[9] Caring and healing the wounds of occupation, especially long-term disability, falls disproportionately on women. Women and girls are as much a part of the resistance as men and boys. In the mass civil uprisings of the First Intifada women were fully engaged and during the more militarised Second Intifada, where male fighters predominated, women continued their protests against the IDF incursions, especially in the refugee camps. Above all, the Israeli occupation is not gender specific and while women are less likely to be killed and imprisoned than men they are no less in the front line of resistance.

Against this background, it was no surprise that we came across much resentment to the prevailing Western media that simplistically portrayed Palestinian women – as with women in all Islamic societies – as downtrodden, passive and weak. In the West Bank we found much of this anger directed at those NGOs that insisted on targeting women and girls as though they needed salvation. According to 20 year old university student Nisreen:

> Many NGOs want to come and run projects that will "save our women". They have an idea that we treat our women so badly;

that they are just breeding factories; that they are weak and have no voice; that they have no place to meet and to raise their own issues. Of course there are issues here – like there is in your country or in America, but they exaggerate. You wouldn't guess, for example, that in An-Najah University in Nablus 60 percent of the students are female. It is not as simple as they make out.

Nisreen, Nablus, September 2008

Dana, another 20 year old student from Jenin, similarly told us about how distorted views of women in the West Bank were leading to inappropriate NGO projects being imposed on Palestinian women:

We have many projects which are funded by NGOs and aid organisations such as USAID. Many of these are aimed at women. But they choose these projects and they decide which are suitable rather than because they have been asked for. We simply implement their project whether we want it or not. There are many local projects like this, especially in the villages where they fund initiatives to do with women's participation in village councils or getting involved in things like embroidery which they can then sell to raise income. At the election, there was a lot of NGO activity again encouraging women to get involved and vote. But we know about voting. So many of the projects reflect their own thinking – their Western perspective – and I don't think they are useful for Palestinian society. USAID is especially like this. They hold the view that women in the Arab world are oppressed. I am not saying that there are no problems facing women. Of course there are, here as everywhere in the world. But they are nothing like what USAID implies.

Dana, Jenin, February 2006

The "oppression of Arab women" occupies a particularly potent place in the West's lexicon of justification for its policies in Palestine and elsewhere, in Iraq or Afghanistan, just as it constitutes a central role in Israel's claim to be an advanced, modern Western society in contrast to Palestine's backwardness.[11]

The burqa and the hijab worn by many Palestinian women are often seen in the West as a feature of women's oppression, but in our interviews and conversations with young women dress emerged as an issue which once again highlighted the paradoxical nature of gender relations in the West Bank. One of the families we stayed with had two teenage daughters, aged 15 and 17. Their mother wore traditional dress but the girls wore Western clothes, jeans and the like. While we were staying the girls were deciding whether or not to follow their mother's example or to stick with Western fashion. Their father insisted that the choice was theirs to make with only one stipulation, namely that whatever they decided they must stick with, especially with respect to traditional clothes. There was to be no chopping and changing. When we saw them six months later, the older girl was wearing traditional dress. We discussed this with a group of students at the university in Nablus, and Manal's comments reflected the views of many of those students wearing traditional dress:

I started wearing the hijab just five months ago and I have felt a big difference. Before, when I didn't wear it I felt that many men would be looking at me on the street. The same with the soldiers at the checkpoints. Now with the hijab I feel much less exposed. Okay, some men still look but it is not like it was before. But there were many reasons why I decided I wanted to wear the hijab. First I wanted to be a good Muslim. And I wanted to stop all the teasing from men. It was annoying me and I didn't like it. Wearing the hijab makes me feel more self-confident and gives me self-esteem.
Manal, Nablus, September 2008

13 March 2005: In the West Bank village of Bil'in, Palestinian girls and women chant slogans in protest at the construction of the Wall[10]

This particular discussion among women university students was concluded by Jumana, who clearly lost patience with the discussion over the dress she could choose.

Yes! As young women we can make choices about what we wear in many families today. But so many of our choices are within a framework determined by men. This is the problem. We are defined by our relationship to men.
Jumana, Nablus, September 2008

No one in the group disagreed. These comments were reinforced by Rasha's experiences, which highlight the reality of women's oppression. Rasha, 28 years old, has three children and lives in a camp:

I've worked since I got married. I love working and I love my job. If I stay at home it's as if I've dropped out of life. Getting out of the house gives me opportunities for different ways of seeing the world. Working is very important for women. It builds character and gives a woman self-esteem... If my husband told me to stop working I would accept his decision passively and stay at home. I might try to talk with him gently but I wouldn't carry it further than that because I wouldn't want it to reach the stage of divorce. The problem, you see, isn't just between my husband and me; the problem is the whole society. If I were to go to my parents and complain in such a situation, everyone – my father, my brothers, my uncles – would tell me that the issue [of my working] is my husband's responsibility. He is the man of the house. It's his right to make all decisions concerning me, I shouldn't even try to discuss his decision with him, and I should be contented at home. This is not the way I think it should be, but it doesn't matter what I think, it's much bigger than me. Here the norm of male dominance is extremely strong – no matter what class, educational level, social or geographic location, it's the same, and it's overwhelming.[12]

Rasha undoubtedly speaks for many women in the West Bank. But unlike our discussions around class and wealth inequalities there was a greater recognition among all the young people we spoke with that this was an issue which needed attention now.

All the younger girls we met expected to go to university, an aspiration which would have been meaningless for many a generation before. University for many was a unique experience where young men and women worked and learned together and often resisted together. These experiences can be expected to play out further in shifting entrenched gendered values and expectations. But it was also clear that this was for them to do and not have some version favoured by the West imposed upon them. As Sami (male) from the Yaffa Centre argued:

If we want to rebuild our Palestinian character this means more than working just with the children. We want to involve the fathers, but we know that they are constantly on the run trying to provide money for the family. So we concentrate on the mothers. And this is important for another reason. Palestinians are not a backward people; we have always been open to new ideas. And that involves promoting gender equality. We want

women workers, we want adult women in our classes, involved
in all our activities – so that all the children see this and just
think it's normal. This is a very important issue for us. We
want to change and challenge the assumed position of women
in society. We think this is an important part in building their
character as Palestinians.

Sami, Balata, June 2008

Enduring change which meets and speaks to the needs of
Palestinian women must come from below and can never be
imposed from above, and certainly not via Western NGOs.
For as Eileen Kuttab, a veteran left feminist and director of
the Women's Studies Centre at Birzeit University in Ramallah,
observed:

> After the first Intifada, the women's movement lost its connec-
> tions to the grassroots. In the early 1990s, and especially after
> Oslo, women's issues became institutionalised, professional-
> ised and NGO-ised [with the consequence] that the women's
> organisations have separated women's issues from the political
> and national issues, which in turn deepens their marginalisa-
> tion from the grassroots struggle...when these NGO women
> want to go to a village and talk about women's mobilisation,
> they have great difficulty. The people are depressed and frus-
> trated; they see corruption all over and identify these NGO
> women as an elite. They therefore challenged their capacity to
> speak with them about their problems and advise them what to
> do to solve them.[13]

Our concern with divisions and faultlines is because without attention in the here and now there is a grave danger that
a free Palestine might not be a place where children such as
Selma in Qalqilya will be able to swim and where women will
determine their own lives. This is also the concern of Eileen
Kuttab:

> We always used to say that we wanted a state. But we don't want
> any state. We want a democratic state because we have strug-
> gled for a long time now and people deserve to be rewarded
> with good governance. We also used to say that we would not
> follow the path of the Algerian women, who, after liberation,
> went "back to the kitchen" and are now suffering the conse-
> quences of an oppressive fundamentalism that has demolished
> their achievements.[14]

Kuttab's comment about fundamentalism takes us naturally to the issue of the faultlines and divisions that took place following the victory of Hamas (and the defeat of Fatah) in the legislative council election of January 2006. This was at the beginning of our research and since then relations between Fatah and Hamas have deteriorated. We anticipated that these divisions and acrimonies would dominate many of our discussions with young people in the West Bank but this was not our experience, even when we sought to explore them in our conversations. There are a number of possible explanations, including the enduring dominance of Fatah in the West Bank (unlike Gaza) and that we rarely met active cadres of either political grouping. It is also possible that it was a topic of such sensitivity that those we met were reluctant to express their position and sentiments.

However, our conversations did reveal once again that the prevailing Western presumptions about the rise and nature of Hamas in particular were both exaggerated and simplistic, especially with respect to Hamas's Islamist agenda. The response during 2006 to our questions about the implications of the Hamas victory ran along four main channels. The first was that their victory was not a result of a turn to Islamic fundamentalism but rather support for Hamas's rejection of Oslo and its so-called peace processes which had seen not progress but rather more oppression, more settlements and significant loss of land.

The second was that Hamas was a "clean" party and that Fatah needed to be "punished" for its corruption and nepotism. Thirdly, there was anger at the hypocrisy of the international community, which lauded democracy but then proceeded to punish the Palestinians by a blockade and starvation of funds, when they voted for Hamas in what all – including international observers – determined was a fair and free election. And finally, deep sadness, especially when fighting broke out between Fatah and Hamas activists in Gaza, resulting in deaths and injuries. This is what Rasha, a 17 year old school student told us in 2006:

> The vote for Hamas was a vote against corruption which was so obvious in Fatah. Hamas felt more like the voice of the people, not that we all want an Islamist state, but we wanted an end to corruption and we wanted resistance. What we need

most is decent government. We need fresh new leaders who are
not corrupt.

Rasha, Ramallah, September 2006

Her friend Nadia added:

I was really proud about the legislative elections. It shows the
depth of the democracy here, if we had a chance. Unlike many
other Arab societies we are much more open and here can freely
curse the government in the street.

Nadia, Ramallah, September 2006

And another friend, Suha, continued:

Palestinian divides

I don't believe that Hamas won the election because of people turning to religion. They wanted a change after what Fatah
had been doing for ten years. For me it was the wrong choice
but people wanted change. Enough is enough. We don't want
them stealing from us, or seeing people killed. This is why
Hamas won.

Suha, Ramallah, September 2006

By 2008, relations between the two groups had descended
into violence, and in the West Bank, where Fatah is generally
stronger, we heard accounts of Hamas activists being harassed
and imprisoned by the PA. For the students at the American
University near Jenin this was a cause of deep sadness:

Ibrahim: All young people are very sad about this. Myself, I
cried about the conflict. We are used to being killed by the
occupation, but not by ourselves, not by other Palestinians.
    In the refugee camp I have friends from Hamas and from
Fatah. We used to have discussions, we agreed that we had
all made mistakes and our organisations had made mistakes.
But now the discussions are limited. Here we try not to talk
about it too much because we feel we have to be together
and not get into conflict with each other.

Fatima: We are doing what the Israelis and the Americans want
us to do – fighting among each other. We have to work
together. We dream about ending the occupation – we have
to be together.

Ali: Now I have my cousins and they ask me are you Fatah, why
aren't you Hamas. Other people ask the reverse. This should
not be like this.

Usman: We are fighting each other, it is terrible. It hurts me personally when I see Palestinians fighting Palestinians. At the leadership level they are both as bad as one another. But among the members hopefully we can still work together. The most important thing is to think as a Palestinian, act as a Palestinian and not get down to fighting each other because he is Hamas or he is Fatah.

Jenin, February 2008

By 2010, it was clear that this internal conflict was impacting upon the deep-rooted solidarity of the West Bank society. The students in Jenin reported that there were now occasional clashes between Fatah and Hamas supporters on the campus, which were roundly condemned by those we met. The sense they gave that this is precisely what the Israelis and their international supporters desired seemed to fuel their determination not to take sides, just as it informed the approach of the youth centres in the camps we visited where participants were asked to "leave their politics at the door". The impact of this conflict, while significant, did not appear to dominate the lives of those we met in the West Bank, although it provoked deep sadness that the unity of the Palestinian people was threatened.

One noticeable side effect of this political divide was the posthumous rehabilitation of Yasser Arafat, witnessed by the ever growing number of his pictures on the walls of West Bank towns and villages. The earlier critical comments we heard at the start of our research concerning the failure of Oslo and the "peace processes" and Arafat's despotic control of the PA had given way to lauding his ability to control factionalism and be a symbol of Palestinian unity. Mohammed, a student studying in the Tulkarm technical college, exemplified this view:

While we are fragmented as a people it is difficult to fight back. If Yasser Arafat were alive we would not be in this situation and he would have united us and developed a strategy.

Mohammed, Tulkarm, June 2008

Certainly in terms of charisma there is no contest between Arafat and the grey Mahmoud Abbas, his successor as president, who, to many, has always been a "suit" and a technocrat, closely identified with the Oslo Accords and the ongoing failure of the peace process to halt the erosion of Palestinian rights, land and property. But Arafat's rehabilitation has much more to do with the fundamental sense on the street that divisions between the Palestinians and the resulting internecine killings and injuries are a source of deep dismay.

The rise of Hamas did not appear to signify an upsurge of militant Islam in the West Bank nor herald any division between the majority Muslim and the minority Christian populations.[15] But it is the case that Islamic belief in its broadest sense is a crucial aspect of West Bank society and underpins social relationships and daily life. It is particularly significant in terms of shaping gender relations, attitudes to wealth – a gift from God – and not least solidarity. This is how Rashad explained its importance:

> In terms of how we survive this situation our religion is very important. Islam places great importance on cooperation and solidarity throughout the Muslim community. You can't leave your brother or neighbour without food and basic things. So we show solidarity and support. In addition we know that Israel uses poverty as a major weapon against us so we respond politically. Survival in poverty is a sign of our steadfastness. We reduce our needs. We continue.
> *Rashad, Tulkarm, June 2008*

Religion, from what we perceived, is not one of the faultlines in West Bank social relations. On the contrary, attitudes to religion seem to be based on a mutual respect and tolerance typified by Joseph, from the largely Christian village of Aboud near to Ramallah, when he said, "We live in the same situation as the Muslims. There is no difference. We are one people, Palestinian, and it makes no difference if you are Christian or Muslim" (2008). Equally, we also met with a general insistence that the conflict with Israel was not a religious one of Muslims against Jews, however much the Israelis and the Western media wish to portray it as such. Here is Nadia, again from the Friends School, who spoke for many when she told us:

> This has never been a war about religion between Jews and Muslims. This is a war between Israelis and Palestinians. Our problem is with Zionism and their belief that this is their land and we have no right to be here. This is the problem. But it is complicated further because Israel declares itself as a state for the Jews. And they use religion to stir other Jewish communities across the world to raise funds because they say they are being threatened by Muslims.
> *Nadia, Ramallah, September 2006*

Jamil, her classmate, similarly recognised:

> There are anti-Zionist Jews. My grandfather was part of the
> resistance and now lives in the US. Last year he went on a dem-
> onstration against the Israeli occupation of Palestine and he
> walked hand in hand with a rabbi. So we know there are Jews
> who support our cause and condemn Israel.
>
> *Jamil, Ramallah, September 2006*

Comments such as these typified the high levels of political awareness that infused so many of the testimonies we were
privileged to record. They also reflected the extraordinary
humanity which we encountered and is so well expressed by
Cairo, a child psychologist based near Ramallah:

> Here there is a humanity and sense of community that no
> longer exists in the West [Cairo was born to Palestinian par-
> ents in the US and returned when she was 15]. Our people
> are incredible survivors. They have lived under occupation for
> more than 35 years and have had to learn to survive under the
> worst of conditions. The Israelis want to dehumanise us and
> make us despair so that we give up. But we know that if we
> keep our hope alive, they can never win. Unless they kill us all,
> that is!... Another vital thing is that we don't have the feeling
> of inferiority that colonised people often have. We have never
> wanted to be like the Israelis. They are who they are, we are
> who we are, with our own values. They are perhaps in a better
> situation, but that does not mean that they are better people.
> We like who we are. That is very important... There is pride in
> being Palestinian, and as long as that exists, the Israelis will not
> be able to finish us off. We see families who find it very hard to
> survive but we don't see people collapsing. They are not ready
> to give up.[16]

We share this view. Like many other outsiders who have
had the opportunity to spend time with the people of the West
Bank we fell in love with their sense of humanity and resilience
which contrast sharply with the individualism and isolation
that have been so deeply attenuated by rampant neoliberalism
and greed in much of the West. The qualities we applaud in the
West Bank have been forged under the most severe occupation
and repression. They are no less noteworthy for that, but it has
meant that differences and inequalities have been elided and at
times submerged.

For nearly every Palestinian we talked to, and for obvious reasons, the ending of the Israeli occupation is by far the over-riding priority. But how the resistance is organised, who is included in the struggle and on what terms, are likely to deter-mine not only its success but also the type of society that is to take its place. The danger is that those who are accorded a priv-ileged position in the struggle, whether because of their class or gender, are likely to remain in that position when the struggle ends. This was one of the harsh lessons of the early years fol-lowing Oslo when significant elements of the returning PLO leadership enriched themselves and reactivated old patterns of power and privilege to the benefit of the few.

What kind of society a future liberated Palestine might become does not depend solely on defeating the Israeli occu-pation. Discrimination, poverty and inequality also have their roots and structures within Palestinian society, and throw-ing off one oppressor does not necessarily mean freedom for all. A foretaste of this is evident in the PA's decision to build, with Qatari finance, Rawabi, a new city primarily for the mid-dle and professional class. Ali Abunimah cites the Rawabi Newsletter of the development company:

Unlike any other [city] in Palestine, Rawabi will be charac-terised as a modern, high-tech city with gleaming high-rise buildings, green parks and shopping areas. Located 6km from Ramallah, Rawabi is sure to become a future social hub for young professionals and families, offering a higher quality shopping experience, entertainment facilities and serving as an overall social and business networking destination in the West Bank... The city will also promote and support the transfor-mation of Palestine into a more investor-friendly region by building on the assets of the first Palestinian planned city.[17]

Quite rightly Abunimah concludes his article by arguing:

Rawabi represents an entirely top-down, profit-driven approach to the development of Palestine where the "vision" created by financiers, marketers, international investors and "peace proc-ess" officials is substituted for the aspirations of the broader community. Palestinian nationalism is transformed into a zeal for real-estate deals and the establishment of gated communi-ties rather than a focus on liberating human beings and giving them the chance to decide for themselves how they want to live and what they want their communities to look like.[18]

The route symbolised by Rawabi will be a disaster for the Palestinian people. The foundations of the resistance, its blood, its energy, its steadfastness reside in the "people of the street" – not with the tiny financial and political Palestinian elites. Its heart is in the refugee camps and the yearnings of a Palestinian diaspora to return home, and not in the boardrooms of multinational banks. The struggle is universal and that means its outcomes must be equally universal, otherwise the suffering of the Palestinians will have been for naught and young girls will still not be able to swim.

Notes

1 R Shehadeh, *Palestinian Walks* (Profile Books, 2007), p134.
2 T Honig-Parnass and T Haddad (eds), *Between the Lines* (Haymarket Books, 2007), p39.
3 T Honig-Parnass and T Haddad (eds), as above, p320.
4 The West Bank has 19 UNRWA-maintained refugee camps with a total population of just over 194,500 people in May 2010. The largest camps include Balata in Nablus with over 40,000 and the camp in Jenin with 35,000 people. The Tulkarm camp has about 11,000.
5 For an informative summary of the right to return and the position of the refugees, see S Cypel, *Walled: Israeli Society at an Impasse* (Other Press, 2005), pp253-256.
6 S Madhieh, 'Social Life in Hebron', in *This Week In Palestine*, 4 April 2008.
7 I Abdul Hadi and Nadya Engler, 'Women and poverty: the high price of occupation' in *Social Watch: Poverty Eradication and Gender Justice* (2005) www.socialwatch.org/node/10964 (accessed 6 June 2006).
8 As Joharah Baker noted in 2006, "The fact that throughout the Intifada, approximately 8,000 Palestinians have been imprisoned in Israeli jails means the burden of family responsibilities have fallen on the woman of the house. With their husbands in jail, Palestinian women find themselves having to play the role of mother and father and provide food and clothing for their children, often having to seek work outside the home for the first time in their lives. According to a UNFPA situation analysis report, approximately 11 percent of all Palestinian households in the West Bank and Gaza are run by women." 'Palestinian Women and the Intifada', in MIFTAH, 5 July 2006, www.miftah.org/Display.cfm?DocId=10709&CategoryId=21 (accessed 19 March 2011).
9 J Baker, as above.
10 L Nessan, 'Women in Palestine', in *Monthly Review* (March 2006), mrzine.monthlyreview.org/2006/nessan080306.html (accessed 19 March 2011).
11 See, for example, S Faludi, *The Terror Dream* (Metropolitan Books, 2007), where she observes that one of the key justifications for the US invasion of Afganistan and Iraq was to liberate women.
12 C Rubenberg, *Palestinian Women: Patriarchy and Resistance in the West Bank* (Lynne Reiner, 2001), p31.
13 E Kuttab, 'Gender, Class and Representation in the Al Aqsa Intifada', in T Honig-Parnass and T Haddad (eds), as

above, p74.

14 E Kuttab, as above, p77.

15 As Cypel also argued, "Its strong nationalist identity is the reason why the Palestinian Islamist party won the votes not just of the religious but also of a great many Palestinians who wanted to punish Fatah for its negligence in meeting the basic needs of the population, and, even more, for its negligence in the face of Israeli policy. Why vote for a party that calls for making peace through negotiating with a state that takes no account whatsoever of the wish for peace, and ignores the leaders making such an appeal if it does not hold them in utter contempt? Worse, a state that, as the Palestinians see it, never acts except in relation to force, never evacuates a territory or settlement except under constraint". S Cypel, as above, p467.

16 From K Mourad, *Our Sacred Land* (Oneworld Publication, 2004), p110.

17 Quoted in A Abunimah, 'Role of Israeli firms raises boycott concerns about Rawabi', in *The Electronic Intifada*, 30 December 2010, electronicintifada.net/v2/ article11706.shtml

18 A Abunimah, as above (accessed 3 January 2011).

Chapter 6

Resistance

Recently I read an article by a really good Israeli journalist. She asked, "Is it true that the Israelis are winning?" It made me think. With all their power and military might, we are still here: 60 years after the Nakba and we're still resisting. Could it really be said that the Israelis are winning? I think we underestimate our strength and at the same time overestimate the strength of the Israelis. We are a really strong people and we should take great pride in our resistance.

Samia, Ramallah, June 2008

We have spent a long time under occupation – 60 years. But this is a small period in our total history – and we have nowhere to go. When we realise this we know that when we are patient, and keep our memories and traditions alive we become strong and resilient.

Sami, Balata, February 2008

Palestinian resistance arises out of...[an] oppressive situation. The degree of violent response varies from case to case, indeed in many instances resistance is mainly non-violent. Despite all the odds against them, people resiliently continue to live, study, pray and plant crops in occupied land. In a few cases, they actively resist and resort to violence. This violent resistance may be defensive (and, thus, to my mind, morally accepta-ble), such as the resistance of the Jenin refugee camp fighters as Israeli death machines approached; or it may take the form of...offensive acts, such as the bombing of Israeli civilians... As we have seen, both peaceful and violent resistance are met with sanctioned, deliberate state violence by the...Israeli gov-ernment and its forces.[1]

This chapter deals with our interviewees' attitudes towards, and involvement in, resistance to the Israeli occupation.

Since the Nakba the Palestinians have found themselves dispossessed, marginalised and unwanted in their own land. Throughout this period they have shown remarkable resilience in continuing their struggle for nationhood. Palestinian oppression and Palestinian resistance form two sides of a common whole, perfectly captured by the graffiti on the Wall in Qalqilya which adapts Camus' famous dictum that "I rebel therefore I exist" and turns it into "To exist is to resist".

Yet an obvious question is, how do we conceptualise resistance? This is not a straightforward issue. As we have already noted in earlier chapters the young people we met described a wide range of activities as "resistance" from "surviving the occupation" to engaging in military acts against the occupier. But if we define everything as resistance, are we not in danger of losing any specificity the term may hold? On the other hand, the testimony of the young people is compelling, especially in a West Bank context where the Israeli occupation is so all-embracing and affects almost every aspect of daily life.

Graffiti on the Wall in Qalqilya

The extent of this definitional problem was revealed on our second trip when we asked the young people the question, "what is resistance?" Here are some of the less obvious replies we received:

Resistance is the signal that we refuse to accept the bad situation we have under Israeli occupation.
Khaled, Nablus, September 2006

We believe that so many things are done under the occupation to make us miserable, so this is our challenge – to keep smiling.
Nida, Jenin, September 2006

Our smiles reflect our steadfastness. We will never be on our knees.
Ja'far, Jenin, September 2006

We have two things: tears and smiles. I am sure the Israelis would like to stop us from smiling. Maybe a curfew on smiling? I think our smiles are part of our resistance, especially among the children.
Soona, Nablus, September 2006

Teaching your own children about their plight is resistance.
Mayada, Qalqilya, September 2006

Patience is resistance.
Aysar, Qalqilya, September 2006

Jokes. We laugh because we can't spend all day crying. This is part of our resistance against their attempts to grind us down.
Haya, Qalqilya, September 2006

Smiling and telling jokes are unlikely to appear in many political or sociological accounts of "resistance strategies" or part of the "repertoire of contention" of marginalised and dispossessed groups discussed by sociologists of social movements.[2] Recently there has been some debate between sociologists of social movements over how we should understand resistant acts. The problem is summed up by Rose Weitz who argues that "the term resistance remains loosely defined, allowing some scholars to see it almost everywhere and others almost nowhere".[3] According to Michael F Brown, "the indiscriminate use of resistance and related concepts undermines their analytical utility".[4]

For writers like Brown the term resistance should only be applied to a relatively narrow range of overt, intentional and oppositional activities carried out against a powerful opponent. The list of "legitimate resistance activities" would include a range of consciously political acts of collective contention, such as strikes, marches, demonstrations and protest actions, as well as a range of individual acts against the authority of the powerful, including both passive and violent acts of rebellion. The key determining factor of "resistance" for authors like Brown is that they should be purposive acts, clearly recognised as resistant acts by other protesters, by those on the sidelines and by opponents.

It is our belief that it is appropriate to describe a wide range of activities that the Palestinian young people are involved in as "resistance acts". These activities and actions are located within the totality of the social relations of exploitation and oppression that dominate in society and reflect a refusal to accept the Israelis' right to rule and dominate society as they wish. They thus reflect the complex, contradictory, shifting reality of class-divided, unequal societies located within the hierarchy of the global state system.

The responses of the young people we met reflect a deep-seated recognition that Israel's ultimate aim is the destruction of Palestinian society and the expulsion of Palestinians from the "Jewish state". Israeli academic Baruch Kimmerling called this "politicide": "a process that has, as its ultimate goal, the dissolution of the Palestinian people's existence as a legitimate social, political and economic entity".[5] Thus surviving, staying on the West Bank, taking part in everyday life and holding on to Arab traditions in the face of the occupation – and doing so in a way that "denies and mitigates" the claims made by Israel and rejects their attempts to grind down Palestinian community – are consciously defiant acts. Hence Samia's rejection of Israeli claims to be winning because "after 60 years…we are still here" and Sami's assertion that 60 years is a small period in the history of the Arab peoples. What these quotes reflect is a spirit of refusal and defiance, encapsulated within oppositional acts, which include a rejection of authority (here, of course, Israeli authority) and would be recognised as acts of resistance by most sociologists of social movements.[6]

The resistance of everyday life

The literature on "covert forms of resistance" includes a vast range of actions and deeds that become embodied with a spirit of defiance. Examples include activities such as African-Americans singing spirituals in church during the heyday of American slavery,[7] the actions and cultural practices of indigenous peoples in the face of annexing and colonising powers,[8] the history of the blues and jazz,[9] the dress codes and practices of various youth subcultures,[10] and the art and literature of the "Cultural Front" in 1930s America.[11]

Our quotations from earlier in the chapter indicate that Palestinian young people explicitly and consciously interpreted an equally broad range of activities as part of their "resistance". Surviving the occupation is part of resisting the occupation. Moreover, as we noted in chapter 1, when young people talked about surviving the occupation this was much more than simple endurance – getting by day to day – it also involved what John Berger has called "undefeated despair".

In this context survival takes on many dimensions including holding on to your identity, your dignity, your humanity and your inalienable right to live in your own land, and without resistance this form of survival is simply impossible. This steadfastness and resilience – "*sammoud*" – in the face of Israeli provocation and harassment is absolutely central for

Palestinians. Here is Saud from Tulkarm describing what *sammoud* means to her:

> Our belief is that we have to put up with a lot, a lot of trials and pressures. Life here for us is very testing. But despite these pressures we have to stay, we have to wait to get our land back, we have to continue our life, we have to move forward with our life and our families. We have to be steadfast – that is *sammoud*.

In part this means facing each day, one at a time:

Seven levels of despair

To search each morning
To find the scraps
With which to survive another day.

The knowledge on waking
that in this legal wilderness
no rights exist.

The experience over the years
Of nothing getting better
Only worse

The humiliation of being able
To change almost nothing,
and of seizing upon the almost
Which then leads to another impasse.

The listening to a thousand promises
Which pass inexorably
Besides you and yours.

The example of those who resist
being bombarded to dust.

The weight of your own killed
a weight which closes
innocence for ever
because they are so many.
    John Berger[12]

I live for the moment – I don't think too far into the future. I think this is a necessary philosophy, "live life for today".
Manal, Tulkarm, February 2008

Palestinians have a strong will and we have lived this way for 60 years or more. So we work where we can, we study and we live for the moment. In other parts of the world people "plan for the future" but in Palestine this is not how we think.
Ibrahim, Al-Amari, February 2008

This should not be interpreted as fatalistic passivity. As earlier chapters have shown, there is something essentially realistic about young Palestinians' recognition that their life could be dramatically altered by the Israelis' actions at a checkpoint, by arrest, injury or the death of themselves or a loved one. Not planning too far into the future but instead concentrating on the present is a perfectly rational response to a life of such uncertainty. But it also reflects a degree of *sammoud*: for despite all this we carry on!

It also means that overcoming such obstacles becomes a victory.

We achieve impossible dreams by becoming students and overcoming the checkpoints and the hassles associated with the occupation. Students in

other parts of the world think about studying and parties. But
we have to think about checkpoints, eating…everything. And
overcoming these obstacles is part of our resistance.
Usman, American University, Jenin, February 2008

The resistance of everyday life is encapsulated in the vast
range of activities that we also discussed in chapter 1 – taking part in sporting activities, involvement in writing clubs,
playing drums and music in celebration of Arab culture and
keeping alive traditional Palestinian handicrafts – these are all
activities that young Palestinians on the West Bank are engaged
in, which fill their time with social and leisure activities, and
which do so in ways that are imbued with a sense of defiance
against the occupier. Here is 12 year old Rashad:

We are living to challenge all the difficulties of the occupation.
This is our life… Despite all the difficulties we are working, we
are challenging how they want us to live and we are succeeding.
Rashad, Jenin, September 2006

This also means that helping and supporting others during difficult times becomes an important source of solidarity.
Hassan expressed it this way:

The important thing is not to be isolated. We try to make sure our
friends are not isolated or feeling down. It strengthens our spirit.
Hassan, Tulkarm, June 2008

Fatima told us:

There is a lot of solidarity. You should see the shopkeepers gath-
ering the children into their shops when an attack comes, to get
them off the streets. Neighbours give food to each other and
help one another out. I remember my aunt during the siege of
Nablus in 2002 where she worked with all the people in the
block to survive and live. She was a teacher so in the mornings
she would work with the children.
Fatima, Friends School, Ramallah, June 2008

Jamal made a similar point:

There is much cooperation in this area. In the camp it is important we help each other. That way we keep our lives.
Jamal, Jenin refugee camp, September 2006

Supporting others – materially and emotionally – to enable them to survive the occupation shows *sammoud* and solidarity.

Jamal's point is also important – his stress on the "necessity of solidarity" in the camps – because it raises (once more) the differing impact of the occupation on different sections of Palestinian society. It is a theme taken up by others:

> The greatest solidarity and steadfastness is in the camps.
> *Rashad, Tulkarm, June 2008*

> Their situation [in the refugee camps] is much more difficult than ours. They have to be much stronger.
> *Jumana, Friends School, Ramallah, June 2008*

> All the camps are targeted; they are the centre of the resistance. Life in the camp is more extreme. We were deported, we are refugees, all our land and property is in Israel and we have to live in this confined space.
> *Crusoe, Jenin, February 2008*

> We are not the only side – as refugees – who take all the responsibility for the resistance. Others resist as well. But in the camps we have our particular problems.
> *Sami, Balata, February 2008*

Our interviewees, from right across the West Bank, also discussed their individual activities and actions within a framework of conceptualised resistance. In other words, living, working, going to school and university are activities that are located within the general struggle against the Israeli presence.

For many of the young people we spoke to, getting an education was viewed as part of the resistance struggle.

> Education is about more than getting a job. It is to show the world that we continue to struggle through our education. In the past our parents weren't educated and the Israelis and collaborators were able to rob their lands or whatever by getting them to sign forms when they didn't know what they meant. So we need to be educated so that we know and can have some control over what is happening and know when and why things are wrong.
> *Fatima, Al Quds Open University, Tulkarm, February 2008*

So for Fatima an educated Palestinian population will be clearer about their rights – and this will serve the struggle

for nationhood. Mohammed had a slightly different take on
this issue:

> I believe that many of us want to go to university because it is
> a type of resistance. We believe in overcoming all the obstacles
> put in our face by the Israelis. Getting an education feels like
> having a weapon that we can use against the occupation. It will
> also help us in finding work in the future even if we have to
> leave Palestine for a few years to support our families.
> *Mohammed, Nablus, September 2006*

For Khadija education was particularly important for
women. The constant threat of imprisonment facing Palestinian
men means, she argued, that women must educate themselves
to ensure they can cope and survive if their husbands are taken
from them.

> We try to fight and struggle through our education. As females
> we know that we must also be educated for the benefit of our
> families. Men and women believe that education and certif-
> icates benefit us in the "fight for life" – the fight for a better
> life, to improve ourselves and our families and our society. But
> then women also have to think – my husband may be killed
> or imprisoned or whatever... Under these circumstances the
> educational certificate helps women find work and look after
> themselves and families.
> *Khadija, Al Quds University, Tulkarm, February 2008*

And for all three, their decisions meant, as we saw in chapter
3, almost daily hassles at the checkpoints and closures during
examination periods. For students who have to travel to university they can be assured that their courses will be longer and
more difficult to complete. It is just one more example of the
everyday resistance which characterises the West Bank.

"Irrational" resistance?

> We are raised with a lot of anger inside us. Even kids as young
> as five hate Israelis. They may not know why but they hate
> them. We see people shot and killed as we grow up. It's nor-
> mal. It changes us. It makes us different from other teenagers...
> People react in different ways. Some want revenge, many
> want and do fight back, others want nothing to do with it,

others want to leave and others join political groups. But what is common to us all is our bitterness. It may not always be good but what can we do?

Firas, Friends School, Ramallah, June 2008

Everyday life on the West Bank is part of a struggle to survive and to reject Israeli control, authority and legitimacy. But it also creates a situation where Palestinian actions are often incomprehensible to Israelis – a feature that Albert Memmi described as part of the mindset of all colonising peoples:

Voices from the West Bank

[Through the colonisation process] all the qualities which make a man of the colonised crumble away. The humanity of the colonised, rejected by the coloniser, becomes opaque. It is useless, he asserts, to try to forecast the colonised's actions ("They are unpredictable!" "With them, you never know!") It seems to him that strange and disturbing impulsiveness controls the colonised.[13]

To the coloniser, the acts of resistance, therefore, appear irrational or reinforce racist stereotypes of the lazy, idle, stupid, obstinate Arab. Lorenzo Veracini[14] discusses this aspect of Israeli response to Palestinian resistance. Quoting an article by Israeli journalist Yoel Marcus, entitled "Get Down from the Roof, you Crazies", Veracini explores Marcus's inability to grasp why Palestinians might want to resist the continued colonisation of their lands. Marcus wrote:

What is the matter with these people? Why, every time the door opens a crack for some Israeli compromise or concession, do they suddenly have this urge to maim and kill?[15]

It was a theme Marcus returned to in a further article discussing the plans for Israeli withdrawal from Gaza:

As we watch the Palestinians acting crazy a month before Israel's withdrawal from the Gaza Strip… How many more times do these poor people intend to screw themselves? How much more killing and bloodshed must there be before they take the advice… Get down from the rooftops, you loonies.[16]

As Veracini argues, there is a complete failure to detect any "rational agency informing Palestinian actions".[17] In the case Marcus was discussing – the removal of settlements from

Gaza – the Israelis' actions were matched by a rapid expansion
of settlements on the West Bank and led to greater isolation
and military control over Gaza; they were not moves towards
establishing two viable states, as Marcus suggests, but a change
of tactic whose purpose was the further "bantustanisation" of
the Palestinians – and thus resistance was perfectly compre-
hensible in these terms.[18]
Some aspects of this "irrational" resistance was captured by
Manaal when she told us:

> Many people have sacrificed much in the Palestinian struggle.
> Some have fought and been hurt, even killed. Others have sac-
> rificed other things. My parents could have a much better life
> abroad; they could have taken us to live in peace and protected
> our family from the Israelis. But they have chosen to work and
> stay here. Some people might not understand that – but it is
> our land and our home.
> *Manaal, Friends School, Ramallah, June 2008*

In the abstract it might seem much more "rational" to
remove oneself and one's family from the front line – but
this is a "rationality" that always bows down to the power of
the rich and powerful and denies legitimacy to any form of
resistance.

In this sense, as Frantz Fanon noted in the 1950s, "the
natives' challenge to the colonial world is not a rational confrontation of points of view".[19] Indeed Israel and its supporters
often highlight the "backwardness" of Palestinian culture (and,
more generally, of Arab societies) in terms that are often rem-
iniscent of an older discourse about "the white man's burden"
during the era of European colonialism. Israel defines itself as
an environmentally conscious, liberal, gay-friendly, democratic,
"rationalist" island in a sea of "irrational" Arab traditionalism.
Yet defence of Arab culture, cultural practices and traditions
needs to be located and understood within the clash between
coloniser and colonised.

The historian Edward Thompson, in an important study
of the customs and cultural practices of increasingly prole-
tarianised communities in 17th and 18th century Britain,
described "customary consciousness and customary usages"
as "claims to…'rights'." Thompson saw these practices as part
of a Europe-wide "stubborn resistance" of "plebs to patrician
culture". And, Thompson claimed, such "resistance" often
embodied "a paradox: a rebellious traditional culture":

Resistance

The conservative culture of the plebs as often as not resists, in the name of custom, those economic rationalisations and innovations (such as enclosures, work-discipline, unregulated "free" markets in grain) which rulers, dealers or employers seek to impose. Innovation is more evident at the top of society than below, but since this innovation is not some normless and neutral technological/sociological process...but is the innovation of capitalist process, it is most often experienced by the plebs in the form of exploitation, or the expropriation of customary use-rights, or the violent disruption of valued patterns of work and leisure... Hence the plebeian culture is rebellious but rebellious in defence of custom.[20]

*Voices from
the West Bank*

And so it is the case in Palestine. Defence of traditions and cultural practices may seem "irrational" to the Israelis and their supporters – defence of a "pre-modern past" at the expense of the rationalities of a new world – but the defence of culture is framed in terms that reject Israel's right to determine what happens on Palestinian land and to determine and interpret Palestinian history.

So, for example, some people might think it crazy that Palestinians even reject such "neutral" artefacts as Israeli maps or school history books, but from the standpoint of the Palestinians these artefacts are far from being neutral but are the documents of the oppressor. Hence Sami, who is a youth worker in Balata, outlines why teaching history and geography in independent youth centres is important.

> The geography curriculum at the UNRWA school defines Palestine as Gaza and the West Bank only... It doesn't include the rest of Palestine, the place where the majority of families in our camp come from. So we have to teach the full geography of our land and country. And this means knowing about our history and the fact that Palestine exists from the river [Jordan] to the sea [the Mediterranean] and that is what we must strive to get back: all of ancient Palestine.
>
> *Sami, Balata, February 2008*

He goes on to argue why resistance also means a fight over history and culture:

> Any people who have had their history ignored or wiped out have this need. We cannot deal with the problem of Palestine and the occupation and the refugees without fully

understanding our history. There are millions of refugees as
part of the diaspora. There is always talk of just making them
part of Jordan or Lebanon or whatever…but with historical
and political education and awareness we can show how these
solutions are not solutions that can work.

Sami, Balata, February 2008

Hamed, another youth worker, proceeds to explain why they
put such an emphasis on cultural practices and traditions:

We have…courses teaching handicrafts, traditional dance, oral
history, music. The historical or cultural…are just part of what
we do. We do this because our children must know about our
history and connection to the Palestinian land. The Israelis are
in the process of inventing their own history. They try to give
the impression that there is a link between everything they do
today and events from Ottoman or whatever. They try to sug-
gest there is a continuous Israeli history here, but there isn't.

Hamed, Balata, February 2008

One area where resistance is often viewed as being particularly "irrational" is in its recent fusion with religion.
Historically the resistance movement in Palestine has been
dominated by secular and leftist organisations, but like the
Middle East region as a whole, the last 30 years (at least since
the Iranian Revolution of 1979) has witnessed the growth both
of groups attached to political Islam as well as of a more general and open religious affiliation towards Islam.[21] Nada made
a comment to this effect in 2008. Her comments drew general
agreement from the other young people (eight of them) who
were also involved in this group session:

People have become much more religious recently and I am
sure that this turn to religion is the result of more people thinking that this is the only way which is left for them. We have
tried everything else, let's try this.

Nada, Ramallah, June 2008

On an earlier trip Ghaada made a similar point, but she also
included her take on the US:

Everybody seems to becoming more religious, but not just here
in Palestine or Israel, all over the world. Look what's been happening in the US with the fundamentalist Christians. It seems

Resistance

to me that people have given up hope and are turning to religion as the last resort.

Ghaada, Ramallah, September 2006

For many liberals in the West the rise of political Islam has been treated as the growth of an irrationalist (for some, even fascistic) politics. For writers such as Christopher Hitchens, Sam Harris, Will Hutton and Martin Amis[22] the rise of political Islam (and for some, the spread of Islam in general) is viewed as a throwback to a pre-modern restrictive age that is obscurantist, oppressive and violent. So Harris writes:

"Muslim extremism" is not extreme among Muslims. Mainstream Islam…represents an extremist rejection of intellectual honesty, gender equality, secular politics and genuine pluralism.[23]

Hutton argues:

Muslims want to build mosques, schools and adhere to Islamic dress codes with ever more energy. But that energy…derives from the same culture…that produce[s]…suicide bombers. The space in which to argue that Islam is an essentially benign religion seems to narrow with every passing day.[24]

The anxieties of the Western liberal intelligentsia reflect, ironically, their belief in the power of religion and religious ideas. Religion, therefore, becomes a major barrier to modernisation and, in the form of "political Islam" (or "Islamic fundamentalism"), involves an attempt to move society "backwards".

There are a number of problems with such a conceptualisation. First, it's not the case that political Islam simply wants to move back to a pre-modern era. Political Islam sits perfectly easily with nuclear power stations in Iran, with stock exchanges, oil production, global television stations and media outlets and a range of other economic, political and cultural artefacts of the modern world. Political Islam is perfectly malleable to the needs and demands of modern capitalism.[25]

A further problem with the critique of political Islam developed by the likes of Hutton and Harris is its perception of those who hold religious ideas and beliefs. It portrays religious people as empty vessels who are filled with irrationalist ideas after listening to the sermons of charismatic leaders and preachers who urge them to adopt their extreme values and perspectives on life. By depicting the religious in this way, the

Western liberal critics deny the religious any agency, or reject any possibility that religious ideas may offer a critical interpretation of the world or an interpretation of the source of the problems people face.

It also ignores the flexibility of religion and its ability to appeal to different sections of society by stressing different aspect of its message. Traditionalist Islam can appeal to the conservative instincts of the powerful and their hostility to any form of social change but, at the same time, by appealing for a return to traditional practices and removing outward signs of religious corruption and cultural invasion it can offer a vague promise of improving people's lives by removing those "alien" institutions, leaders and practices that have brought pain, poverty and inequality to the Umma.[26] Thus it is important to locate the growth of Islamist political currents in the Middle East in their appropriate social context. Rather than simply seeing religion (all religions) as a set of false or irrational ideas – "the opium of the people" – it is important to recognise that the ambiguities of religious ideas, and the way those ideas change historically, mean that they offer an expression of the suffering of the oppressed and the exploited in society – the sigh of the oppressed in a heartless world.[27] In other words, religion can offer an interpretation of the world that articulates, albeit in a disjointed way, the social and political problems confronting the poor and dispossessed.

One of our interviewees, Hajar, explained that she had recently decided to wear the hijab. She saw this as an expression of her cultural resistance to the occupation:

I wear the hijab because Islam is important to me and it is part of our identity in this land. The Israelis try to use all kind of differences to try and divide us. For example it is not unusual for them to separate the Christians from the Muslims at checkpoints. They will let the Christians through and hassle the young Muslims for an hour or so. Christians and Muslims – we are all Palestinians, but I'm happy to wear the hijab and I don't care if it brings more difficulties for me.
Hajar, Nablus, September 2006

There is no doubt that part of the appeal of political Islam in the Middle East is its articulation of anti-imperialist sentiments and hostility to the existence of Israel and the support it receives from the US and other Western powers. And it is more than just words: the Iranian regime, Hezbollah, Hamas,

Muqtada Al-Sadr's militia and the other elements within the Iraqi resistance have all posed a challenge – a physical challenge – to Western imperial interests in the region.

Hezbollah's open letter to the "Downtrodden in Lebanon and in the World" published in February 1985, for example, argues that the world is divided between the oppressed and the oppressors; dismisses the countries of the "arrogant world" (especially the US and, at the time, the USSR) as offering any solution to the problems of the Umma; calls for struggle against the local imperial proxy the "Zionist entity" which is usurping "the holy land of Palestine"; and, in the letter's final section, calls for unity between Muslims and Christians – making it clear that it doesn't support an enforced Muslim caliphate – against the corrupt and sectarian regime dominant in Lebanon. It is therefore, in large part, a political document outlining social and political grievances and arguing for a political reform to Lebanese society to improve the lives of the poor and the dispossessed.[28] This ideological engagement is combined with a political practice which provides a range of welfare services for the poorest sections of Lebanese society.[29]

Hamas is similar. In the West discussion of Hamas rarely moves beyond the accusation that they are an extremist organisation which expends most of its energies recruiting suicide bombers. However, Hamas grew out of the first Intifada and its early declarations placed it firmly within the boundaries of the Palestinian liberation movement (early statements about establishing an Islamic state were quickly sidelined).[30] But when Fatah signed up to the Oslo Accords Hamas made clear their opposition to any dilution of the demand for a single Palestinian state – and raised their profile and popularity among the refugee population whose position had become much more fragile as a result of Oslo. Like Hezbollah, Hamas also have a social programme. Their manifesto for the 2006 elections, for example, demanded an end to corruption (a huge problem among leading layers of Fatah), an emphasis on "social solidarity and [expansion of] the Social Protection Network", the creation of a "unified pension system so as to achieve equality and fairness among pensioners", investment in schools and hospitals and the provision of social and public services "to all citizens without discrimination, favouritism or partisanship", combating poverty by wealth redistribution, support for the families of prisoners and martyrs, and support for institutions which provide care for those with special needs.[31] Badi'a told us why she thought Hamas won the January 2006 elections:

The vote for Hamas was a vote against corruption which was so obvious in Fatah. Hamas felt more like the voice of the people, not that we all want an Islamist state, but we wanted an end to corruption and wanted resistance.
Badi'a, Friends School, Ramallah, June 2008

Fatima added:

Many of the people who got corrupted under Fatah were resisters. Some had been in prison. When they went into the government they were people we looked up to. But they became corrupted inside government and not before. We no longer have so many people we can look up to. The good ones are in prison.
Fatima, Friends School, Ramallah, June 2008

Our interviewees clearly plot the growth of Hamas as a reflection of both a growing "religiousness" in Palestine and elsewhere and the linked political programme of addressing imperialism, poverty, inequality and corruption within the West Bank and Gaza. All in all, this is a more complex understanding of the world and of Hamas's position within it than you get in much of the Western media.

Collective resistance

So far we have looked at the extent to which everyday life can be permeated with a spirit of resistance. But we also have to recognise that there are different levels of engaged resistance. In his history of resistance in the Nazi concentration camps, Hermann Langbein notes:

No definition of "resistance in the concentration camps" is universally valid. Narrowly defined, it means only active resistance to guards. Interpreted in the widest sense it encompasses everything that was done or planned to subvert the aims of the camp administration.[32]

The problem with the "widest definition", he suggests, is that it includes every instance of someone sharing their bread or whispering words of support to a fellow inmate and, while we should never disparage the "personal heroism" of those who "carried out such feats", we have to recognise these activities as

being of a different nature to examples of "active resistance…
[as] an organised activity with far-reaching goals".[33]

Langbein draws a distinction between different types of
resistance activity. It seems only right and proper to do so.
Hence, as well as the resistance of everyday life we have to
acknowledge the importance of various forms of overt resistance to Israeli rule. These are much more recognisable forms
of contentious political action.[34] During most periods of history "overt" collective resistance to authority is less common
than the "covert" resistance of everyday life, but, nevertheless,
history points to regular periods when such overt resistance
– in different guises and forms – has burst onto the political
stage. Thus strikes, demonstrations, individual and collective
acts of defiance, community organisation, and involvement
in the armed struggle all represent different forms of such
overt resistance. In the context of Israel/Palestine, however,
those who engage in overt resistance find themselves labelled
as "terrorists".

> The [Western]…media call our search for freedom "terror-
> ism", thus casting the Palestinian in the role of the international
> prototype for the terrorist. This has shaped Western pub-
> lic consciousness… But "terrorism" is a political term used by
> the coloniser to discredit those who resist, as the Afrikaaners
> and Nazis named the Black and French freedom fighters,
> respectively.[35]

The labelling of all forms of Palestinian overt resistance as
"terrorist" also glosses over the widely different perspectives
on Palestinian resistance politics. A useful distinction can be
drawn between "popular resistance" and "armed resistance'.

Popular resistance

Popular resistance is an alternative to either armed resistance
or passive acceptance of the status quo. As Nadia Hijab has
argued:

> The armed struggle is the least effective source of power avail-
> able to the Palestinians. Yes, it is legitimate under international
> law for people living under military occupation to take up
> armed resistance, so long as the tactics chosen do not violate
> those laws. But the Palestinian situation is very different to

that of other guerrilla struggles that succeeded against supe-
rior forces. This does not mean that Palestinians should give up
their arms. They do provide a deterrent, however modest, and
an irritant to the established order. Yet the question of whether
the struggle is armed or not is a distraction from the real issues.
There is more than one "s" in resistance, and any party that
wants to lead the Palestinian national movement needs to recognise that resistance must be strategic, solidly based, and
sustained towards a clear set of goals.[36]

"Popular resistance" is a phrase that is often used, but
little defined. In the Second Intifada "Popular Resistance
Committees" were established as a coalition of various factions
opposed to the conciliatory approach adopted by the PA and
Fatah towards Israel. Their conceptualisation of resistance was
primarily framed in terms of military engagement with Israel
and IDF troops.

However, in more common usage the term applies to the
aspects of general political resistance and opposition that developed in Palestine during the First Intifada.

The First Intifada started in Gaza on 8 December 1987
after the driver of an Israeli tank transporter aimed his vehicle at a line of cars carrying Arab workers who were returning
home after a day's work within the borders of 1948 Palestine.
Four workers were killed and seven seriously injured. The
funeral later that night turned into a mass demonstration.
In the days that followed there were clashes between Israeli
troops and Palestinian marchers – and the rebellion spread
from Gaza to Nablus and then, by 21 December, to Arabs
within 1948 Palestine.

At the time, like many governments facing mass protest,
the Israeli authorities looked to blame a small minority of
troublemakers. Yitzhak Rabin suggested the movement was
inspired by Iran, Iraq, Syria and the PLO.[37] But as Marshall
points out:

In fact the Uprising made no use of Palestinian guerrilla forces;
its activists were unarmed youth… The movement brought a
sense of hope to the people of the Occupied Territories and
there was a rapid increase in morale which recalled other periods of mass struggle.[38]

In the context of mass participation and mass protest there
was a revival in a range of Palestinian organisations: trade

Omar's story

I was at high school in November 2002 and I was about to sit the final school examinations. I was 17 years old.

This is a very serious time for all of us as these exams are tough and the results decide whether we can go on to university. At that time there were many incursions so I decided to stay at my aunt's home as it was safer. Where we lived was next to the main entry route used by the Israelis into the town. I was afraid there and my mind was so full of anxiety that it was hard to concentrate on my studies. So I decided to move to my aunt's to be safer and to prepare for my final exams.

Omar (centre), with Chris (left) and Mohammed

One day the headmaster announced that we had to leave the school and go home because of an Israeli incursion. I took my school bag and started to make my way to my aunt's house. It was on the way that I came face to face with a heavy tank and Israeli soldiers. The tank just opened fire without warning and began to shoot randomly at the students who were going home. I was one of the wounded. I believe that they targeted us. They fired because we were students. It was deliberate.

I was hit in the neck and through the spinal cord and I am now paralysed from my upper chest downwards. I have a little movement in my hands but it is very limited.

I was taken by the Red Crescent to the hospital in Tulkarm but only for a few minutes before being moved to a hospital in Israel through an organisation of doctors in Palestine and Israel. I was in a coma for ten days. When it became clear that I would live I was transferred back to Tulkarm. From here I was sent to three different hospitals in Jordan all paid for by the PA. Then I was sent to Germany for three months' physiotherapy. It helped, as before I was totally paralysed from the neck but I do now have some movement in my hands.

My house has been simply adapted so I can get in and use the toilet. This has been paid partly by UNRWA and mainly by my family. My mother is my main carer and the rest of my family help when they can.

After I was shot and had recovered enough I went back to school and took the leaving exam. I got the grades to go to university. So I am now studying social work but I would prefer to be studying English literature or law but I have to choose subjects that are available in Tulkarm, at the Open University, as it is not possible for me to travel to Nablus where these courses are available.

I feel it is a policy of the Israelis to injure and cripple as many Palestinians as they can. They target all sections of the people. That many are children is because in part we have many children here and they are out on the streets.

My injuries led me to get involved in humanitarian and political issues. I was not involved before the shooting.

I have been elected as a student leader in the university, and I'm a member of the Fatah youth movement. We are well organised and we take part in all forms of campaigns against the occupation.

I have also taken out a legal claim against the Israeli army – but we are still waiting for a final response. When I first made the claim the Israeli military refused to cooperate at all but instead made a counter-charge, claiming that I was throwing stones. They never admit to their mistakes or random shootings.

But I will continue this claim. I will not give up and I will not be defeated.

---

unions, women's groups and a network of committees that sprang up in villages, towns and cities. This network organised first aid, education, youth work and cultural activities; they promoted collective "self-help" welfare; they distributed leaflets that called for regular strikes, demonstrations and boycotts of Israeli goods.

> [Such] a...strategy allows for a broader and therefore larger participation among the citizenry than armed conflict does. This was true in the First Intifada – largely credited with empowering civil society, women, as well as the young and old.[39]

At its high point in 1988 the First Intifada was a mass movement for change that aimed to engage and unite broad sections of Palestinian society into the struggle for national liberation. It harked back to earlier episodes of mass struggle against imperialism – like the great revolt of 1936-39 that was the longest sustained challenge to British imperialism in the interwar period.[40]

Although eventually defeated, the First Intifada left behind a significant tradition of grassroots activism that remains in place across Palestinian society today, and is best seen in the activities of a range of youth and cultural centres across the West Bank.

On our various visits we spent many hours in such centres talking both to the volunteer workers and the young people who use the centres. We asked them how they thought the centres themselves fitted in to the Palestinian resistance. Sami in Balata told us:

> Everything we are doing we consider part of our resistance. We fight to teach our children about their rights and their needs.
> *Sami, Balata, February, 2008*

Another of the young volunteers argued that the centres were important because they helped the young people understand who they were and the significance of their Palestinian identity. He argued:

> This is the most important part of our mission. To know your origin, your history – this is the right of all the young people here. We have other activities and courses about education, rights, drama, sport, IT – but historical and cultural awareness and identity are the most fundamental of our activities and we try to include them in all our work.
> *Hamed A, Balata, February 2008*

While his colleague identified the importance of passing the tradition of resistance on from generation to generation:

> Of course we don't know when Palestine will be reunited, but it will happen. We came here as children and we learned these things, now it is our job to teach the children in the camp today about our history, our culture, our geography… You know there is a simple saying we grow up through the circle of life – we are born and eventually we die. In history we see the same with all the great empires – they start, they seem powerful, but they all end. One day Israel will go and we will have our Palestine again.
> *Hamed R, Balata, February 2008*

We heard a similar story in Al-Amari camp. Ibrahim had started as a "service user" of the centre and its activities, but now he was a volunteer helper.

> I grew up here. I was seven when I first came to the club. I joined everything and I had a good time. And now I'm here to give back to the club and the kids, so they can have a good time like I had. In the hope that we can build a new generation, better than the past, with all their abilities and capabilities, their hobbies and talents, their ideas and thoughts – so that they can feel secure and safe.
> *Ibrahim, Al-Amari, February 2008*

Nadir was a regular attendee of the youth centre and described what he did:

> We do drawing and reading… We have music lessons, learn handicrafts, go on summer camps. We have sports days and

challenges. And we prepare plays and dramas for open days
when our parents come to the centre.

Nadir, Al-Amari, February 2008

Mohammed was one of the volunteer workers at the centre
in Al-Amari. He grew up in the camp during the First Intifada
and pointed out the importance of the "mass participation"
politics of the First Intifada for the establishment of the centres.

Before the First Intifada, when I was growing up, there was
nothing for us. We had no centre, no sports, no sword-fencing, no summer camps – nothing… These things developed
during the First Intifada and now we are fighting to give the
new generation of kids the best we can get. We need to give
them a perspective for the future. We need to show them it
can be different.

Mohammed, Al-Amari, February 2008

The politics of "popular resistance" are based in mass
engagement, involvement and participation. It recognises that
the resistance affects all aspects of life – and thus the struggle must embrace life in its totality and that means engaging
with young people through a variety of means to encompass
the extent of their struggle for nationhood. The following two
extracts cover segments of interviews we conducted at Al-Amari
and Balata and give a glimpse into the activities and the politics of the centres.

Popular resistance stresses collective involvement and collective action – and that includes involvement in marches and
demonstrations against Israeli policies. These, of course, are
often dangerous activities:

We often join demonstrations in Ramallah. Last week for
example we joined the demonstration of the striking teachers.
Sometimes the school supports us and sometimes not. We can
understand the school's position because you never know when
demonstrations can get messy with the Israelis charging in firing tear gas or rubber bullets. The school can't handle this. But
we decide through the student council what action to take. We
meet once a week and it is in cooperation with other schools
in Ramallah. So what often happens is that we get a phone call
asking for our participation in something and then we decide
our action.

Firas, Friends School, Ramallah, September 2006

CJ: When we were here before (in Al-Amari) we saw a wonderful film, *The Cage*.
Ibrahim: I was in that film. We still make films and videos and DVDs. But it was not a story. It was based on living here, on our life in the camp. The film expressed real life and the real need to express our life in a cage. In the film we are looking at the solutions.
CJ: You still make films?
Ibrahim: It depends on financial support and donations. But we like to do this. We have cameramen, producers, directors, actors – but no money.
ML: The film covered incursions and so on, but it also told the story of the Palestinians – their history, culture, struggles – is this important to everything that happens here? Even the sword-fencing – all these activities – do you feel they are part of you asserting who you are?
Ibrahim: Sure, everything – the film, the activities – it all is a part of our identity.
ML: So the centre provides a social space for the children and for a range of activities – but it also has a philosophy that sees the centre connected to the occupation and the struggle for liberation – is that right?
Ibrahim: Yes, it's our response to the occupation. The occupation is ruling over us and this is our response. Whatever they do – repression, destruction, arrest – we still have a buzz and we will still go on. All we do is political. The sport is political because they try to stop us and harass us.

But even if it is just meeting internationals and showing them that we are not what the Israelis portray us as. To show we are cultural, sporting and so on, and we take part peacefully and compete in the way everyone else does. We are just the same; they are trying to make us out to be something else.

The idea is to send a message to everyone: we are celebrating our history, culture and presence. We are still here, they try to stop us, to disrupt us, to chase us off, but we are still here.

The Israelis especially don't like demonstrations about their actions such as the closure of Gaza or the invasion of Jenin. The soldiers are very often violent then. They shoot for no reason even at demonstrators who are non-violent. They don't have a chance.

Manal, Friends School, Ramallah, September 2006

Manal and Firas talk about the centrality of protest within the "popular resistance" tradition, it is a theme taken up by Jaber.

Those involved in such acts of popular resistance are clearly brave, committed activists. Yet the uneasy outcome of the First Intifada meant that when the Second Intifada erupted the dominant political tradition within the resistance forces was that of armed struggle.

International law grants a people fighting an illegal occupation the right to use "all necessary means at their disposal" to end their occupation, and the occupied "are entitled to seek and receive support" (I quote here from several United Nations resolutions). Armed resistance was used in the American Revolution, the Afghan resistance against Russia (which the US supported), the French resistance against the Nazis, and even in the Nazi concentration camps, or, more famously, in the Warsaw Ghetto.[42]

Resistance

In the first few days of the Second Intifada Israeli troops fired off over 1.3 million bullets – which may partially explain the more militarised response of the Palestinians.[43]

Violent resistance arises from an inhuman military occupation, one that levies punishment arbitrarily and without trial, denies the possibility of livelihood and systematically destroys the prospects of a future. The Palestinian people have not gone to another people's homeland to kill or dispossess. Our ambition is not to blow ourselves up in order to terrify others. We are asking for what all other people rightfully have – a decent life in the land of our birth. What is most troubling about the criticism of our resistance is that it cares little for our suffering, our dispossession, and the violation of our most basic right. When we are murdered, these critics are unmoved. Our peaceful, everyday struggle to live a decent life makes no impression on them. When some of us succumb to retaliation and revenge, the outrage and condemnation is directed at us all. Israeli security is deemed more important than our right to a basic livelihood; Israeli children are seen as more human than ours; Israeli pain more unacceptable than ours. When we rebel against the inhuman conditions imposed upon us, our critics dismiss us as terrorists, enemies of human life and civilisation.[44]

The issue of armed struggle was a difficult topic to raise meaningfully with our interviewees. In part this was because our interviewees were "self-selecting" in this regard – to the best of our knowledge we only ever talked to two people who had knowingly joined an armed unit and been prepared to go on an armed mission.

Nevertheless, we lived beside (and sometimes in the homes

CJ: How do you keep your spirits up? How important is the centre?

Hamed: We come here to follow courses to help prepare ourselves for the future. The courses help us with our studies. They tell us about our rights as refugees and our right to return. They prepare us for future work helping our community and fighting for our political rights.

Hussan: the courses here help us to understand our national cause and we learn about the most recent events.

Ameen: One of the courses is called "What kind of solutions are available to the Palestinians – our rights and solutions". I attended this course, but I was convinced that we had no hope, that we would never be successful. But now I feel differently, I feel that one day I will return to Palestine and my land. The course helped me understand our cause much better.

Hamed: Through this centre I have learned how to fight and campaign for my rights.

ML: Can you give us an example of how the classes have led to campaigning work?

Ameen: We were involved in classes working with digital film and photos, the centre got some money from overseas to do this. Those of us that went to the class decided we could make a DVD to give to stall holders and local shops explaining why they should not stock Israeli goods. This was a campaign devised and led by the young people. It gave us skills in planning a campaign, working with shops in our community, filming and working with PCs – so it combined skills and campaigning.

At first we planned everything on paper, then we made our film.

We explained that we were Palestinian young people, and that we were trying to help our cause. Then we explained that they could help by not stocking Israeli goods. We explained that these were grown on our stolen land. That their products were destroying our manufacturing and agricultural companies and efforts. We explained that they could find the same goods made in Palestine, by Palestinians – some were even made locally in Nablus and we could use them instead of the Israeli goods. If the goods were not available locally, we pointed out that they could use goods from other Arab countries. If they were still not available we recommended using goods from friendly European countries.

We then produced another film about our campaign and its impact.

of) those who had decided to take up arms, and among all of those we spoke to there was an acceptance that joining the armed struggle was a legitimate response to the occupation – even if it was a response that most of our interviewees rejected personally. Ibrahim, for example, told us:

> We are not the same in our thoughts. I believe in peace and negotiation and many Palestinians are like me. I believe we

can solve most of the problems this way and that we can have real peace. But others think we should fight and have armed resistance.
Ibrahim, Al-Amari, February 2008

And, of course, this should not in any way be interpreted as "cowardice". As many of the young people made clear in their responses they were prepared to engage in political struggle, even if it meant placing themselves in danger; this is a question of strategy and there is a clear recognition among most Palestinians that their resistance will take a variety of forms.

We are not afraid of the soldiers or their guns. We know they shoot children. This is normal… We are the future defenders of this country. The [Israeli] army kill and wound us before we have a chance to really help this country as men.
Jamal, Tulkarm, June 2008

But as Crusoe, a regional commander in the Al Aqsa Brigades, told us:

People aren't born fighters or "terrorists". If you bring people up without violence, with justice and decency and in a calm way with hope for their future – why will they turn to arms?
Crusoe, Jenin, February 2008

Crusoe the fighter makes it clear – without justice, there will be no peace; at the same time, there is hope for a peaceful Palestinian future if the social conditions of oppression and inequality are fully confronted and addressed.

Crusoe's comments are significant. They emphasise that the struggle has social and political roots, that it is not the result of Palestinian "irrationality" or innately violent disposition.

The social and political roots of the struggle also explain why it is the case that those who join the armed struggle are overwhelmingly drawn from the poorest sections of Palestinian society and particularly from the camps. Here we find those who suffer the brunt of the Israeli occupation and oppression; here are those who live in the deepest poverty; here are those who are systematically ignored by the various and ongoing negotiations about a "road map to peace"; and here are those whose demand for the "right to return" presents such a challenge to the state of Israel, and also to the new Palestinian politicians of the OPT.

Resistance

Jaber's story of civil resistance

Jaber Abu Rahmeh is from Bil'in and is a regular protester at the Separation Wall that divides his village.

How do the Israelis and the wall affect daily life in Bil'in?
Sometimes they put checkpoints in the village—no one can enter or leave. Because of the Wall we started demonstrating every day when it was first being built. We meet at the mosque then go to throw stones at the Wall. One time the soldiers threw tear gas into the mosque while we were gathered there. One man picked up the tear gas canister with his bare hands and threw it back at the soldiers.

Have you been injured before?
Yes. I was shot twice. One time with a tear gas canister in the leg—afterwards I fell on a cactus, which was even more painful, ha ha! The other time was with a rubber-coated steel bullet in the shoulder. I had to hold my arm out to the side for a long time after that. My mum was mad when I came home after that because she told me not to go that day.

How do you think your mum feels when you go to the demonstrations?
She's scared all the time—she asked me not to go any more one time, but then she started going to the demonstrations. But she had a bad reaction to the tear gas and had to go in an ambulance. Since then she cannot go.

Who comes to the demonstrations?
It's mostly men and boys from the village, sometimes a few women, and then the internationals and press—but there used to be more journalists—40 or so, but now there are only about ten.

Does the international presence cause the soldiers to act differently?
The Israeli leader says whether or not to shoot—sometimes it doesn't matter whether there is press or not. The demonstrations usually end with lots of kinds of bullets—rubber-coated steel, rubber, and live ammunition.

What happens in the night raids?
They mostly use rubber bullets—they do these raids just to make problems with the village, to make the villagers react, and when they do they get arrested. They do it to scare people. I once heard an Israeli [captain] say to some other soldiers, "You work on the Bil'in people during the day on Friday and I will work on them at night."

Umm Samara is a mother and grandmother living in Bil'in. She has been attending the demonstrations every week from the beginning. Although there used to be more women who participated in the demonstrations, now she is usually the only woman from the village who goes—and she always tries to be at the front of the demonstration.

How has life changed in Bil'in since the construction of the Wall began?
We have been hurt a lot, and we have lost land. The soldiers hurt us to scare us out of protesting. My house has been raided, they raid daily sometimes. They use

sound bombs in the middle of the night.

Are you ever afraid of getting hurt in the demonstrations?
No. I have a good and strong personality—I love going. I don't like to be at the
end of the demonstration. I like to fight and kick and hit the soldiers at the front.

Why do you think it's important to go to the demonstrations?
To stand in solidarity with the village for our land.

What's the scariest experience you've had at a demonstration?
I have fought with the soldiers. I have been on the ground being hit by the
soldiers. They were beating and kicking my cousin while he was on the ground.
I went in to stop them and got into the fight.

Palestine Monitor, March 2009[41]

As Leila told us:

Very few martyrs come from families who have money and
wealth. Most of them fight because of their poverty and
frustration.

Leila, Friends School, Ramallah, June 2008

The armed struggle is recognised as a legitimate part of the
struggle for nationhood. The streets and camps are full of pictures of those who have sacrificed their lives and martyrs are
treated with the utmost respect: they have sacrificed themselves
for the struggle. But there is a distinction to be made between
support for the right to armed resistance, support for the martyrs and their families and critical engagement over appropriate
liberation strategies – if we were to sum this up, it is perhaps
best understood as "unconditional but critical support" for the
armed struggle.

Conclusion

Resistance is engrained within daily life in Palestine. As
Edward Said noted in a piece about the letters of the activist
Rachel Corrie:

What shines through all the letters she wrote home…is the
amazing resistance put up by the Palestinian people themselves, average human beings stuck in the most terrible
position of suffering and despair but continuing to survive
just the same. We have heard so much recently about the road
map and the prospects for peace that we have overlooked the
most basic fact of all, which is that Palestinians have refused to

capitulate or surrender even under the collective punishment meted out to them by the combined might of the US and Israel. It is that extraordinary fact which is the reason for the existence of a road map and all the numerous so-called peace plans before them, not at all because the US and Israel and the international community have been convinced for humanitarian reasons that the killing and the violence must stop. If we miss that truth about the power of Palestinian resistance (by which I do not at all mean suicide bombing, which does more harm than good) despite all its failings and mistakes, we miss everything.[45]

This is a Palestinian resistance that is constantly looking for new tactics and questioning the dominant strategies being pursued by the main Palestinian organisations. But the search for new strategies has not, as yet, produced any definite alternatives.

Some of the young people we spent the afternoon with in Ramallah in June 2008 spoke passionately about their hopes and fears for the future shape of the Palestinian struggle. They were clear that their aspirations for a "free" Palestine involved: a Palestinian state covering the whole area of 1948 Palestine "from the river to the sea", but more than that it should address a series of social demands such as welfare, health insurance and free schooling and education. Their vision of a better free Palestine involved addressing social issues. But this then came back to a familiar theme:

> What we need most is decent government. We need fresh new leaders.
> *Manal, Ramallah, June 2008*

This raised a further concern; here is Firas:

> We feel linked in our hearts with Arab peoples all over the world. But their governments are another thing. They are worse than ours. So many are hypocritical, speaking out against America but then often using American money to keep them in power. We need a wider Arab solution to our problems.
> *Firas, Ramallah, June 2008*

Though many of the young students weren't quite sure what any alternative would look like, Simira got a murmur of general agreement when she told us:

When we see demonstrations in support of Palestine in other countries it makes me so happy. It really gives me hope as people begin to understand the situation here more clearly. It makes us feel part of something bigger than just us here in Palestine.

Simira, Ramallah, June 2008

For many of the young Palestinians resistance was central, but the question of agency – of identifying the possible social force capable of dealing with the settler state – and, at the same time, addressing the broader social inequalities within Palestine and across the Middle East region is one that they are still grappling with.

Notes

1 S Jabr, 'The Palestinian Resistance: Its Legitimate Right and the Moral Duty', www.ifamericansknew.org/cur_sit/pal-resist.html (accessed 22 Oct 2009).

2 See, for example, S Tarrow, *Power in Movement* (Cambridge University Press, 1992).

3 R Weitz, 'Women and their Hair: Seeking Power through Resistance and Accommodation', *Gender & Society* 15 (2001), p669.

4 M F Brown, 'On Resisting Resistance', *American Anthropologist* 98 (1996), p730.

5 B Kimmerling, *Politicide: Ariel Sharon's War against the Palestinians* (Verso, 2003), pp4-5.

6 See J A Hollander and R L Einwohner, 'Conceptualizing Resistance', *Sociological Forum* 19 (4) (2004), pp533-554.

7 K L Sanger, 'Slave Resistance and Rhetorical Self-definition', *Western Journal of Communication* 59 (1995), pp177-192; A Baraka, *Blues People* (Perennial, 1999).

8 N K Silva, 'Ku'! Hawaiian Women's Resistance to the Annexation', *Social Process in Hawaii* 38 (1997), pp2-15; H Moghissi, 'Away from home: Iranian Women, Displacement, Cultural Resistance and Change', *Journal of Comparative Family Studies* 30 (1999), pp207-217.

9 M Smith, *John Coltrane: Jazz, Racism and Resistance* (Redwords, 2003); A Y Davis, *Blues Legacies and Black Feminism* (Vintage, 1999).

10 S Humphries, *Hooligans or Rebels? An oral history of working class childhood and youth 1889-1939* (Blackwell, 1981); G Pearson, *Hooligan: A History of Respectable Fears* (Macmillan, 1983); D Gluckstein, *The Nazis, Capitalism and the Working Class* (Bookmarks, 1999), chapter 9.

11 M Denning, *The Cultural Front* (Verso, 1996).

12 J Berger, *Holding Everything Dear: Dispatches on Resistance and Survival* (Verso, 2007), pp4-5.

13 A Memmi, *The Colonizer and the Colonized* (expanded edition) (Beacon Press, 1991), pp84-85.

14 L Veracini, *Israel and Settler Society* (Pluto, 2006).

15 Y Marcus, 'Get down from the roof, you crazies', *Haaretz*, 5 October 2004.

16 Y Marcus, 'Get down from the rooftops', *Haaretz*, 19 July 2005, www.haaretz.com/hasen/pages/ShArtDisengagement.jhtml?itemNo=602632&contrassID=23&subContra

ssID=3&sbSubContrassID=0 (accessed 23 Oct 2009).

17 L Veracini, as above, p2.

18 M Lavalette, *Palestine Journey: When Preston went to Nablus* (Respect, 2006).

19 Frantz Fanon quoted in L Veracini, as above, p6.

20 E P Thompson, *Customs in Common* (Penguin, 1991), pp1,9.

21 C Harman, 'The Prophet and the Proletariat', *International Socialism* 64 (Autumn 1994).

22 See, for example, M Amis, 'The Age of Horrorism', *The Observer*, 10 September 2006; C Hitchens, 'Of Sin, the Left and Islamic Fascism', *Nation*, 24 September 2001; S Harris, *The End of Faith: Religion, Terror and the Future of Reason* (Norton, 2004); W Hutton, 'Why the West must stay true to itself', *The Observer*, 17 June 2007; and for a devastating expose of liberal-left irrationalism see R Seymour, *The Liberal Defence of Murder* (Verso, 2008).

23 S Harris, *The End of Faith: Religion, Terror and the Future of Reason* (Norton, 2004), p65.

24 W Hutton, 'Why the Euston group offers a new direction for the left', *The Observer*, 23 April 2006.

25 C Harman, as above.

26 Umma: Arabic word for community, especially the Islamic community or the worldwide community of the faithful.

27 Marx's perspective on religion is often reduced to a quotation (taken out of context) that he viewed it as the "opium of the people"; the full quote is much richer and gives us a flavour of a different approach to religious questions: "Religious suffering is at the same time an expression of real suffering. Religion is the sigh of the oppressed creature, the sentiment of a heartless world, and the soul of soulless conditions. It is the opium of the people." K

28 See J Palmer Harik, *Hezbollah: The Changing Face of Terrorism* (IB Tauris, 2005), esp chapter 5; and A R Norton, *Hezbollah: A Short History* (Princeton University Press, 2007), esp chapter 2.

29 A R Norton, as above.

30 K Hroub, *Hamas: a Beginner's Guide* (Pluto, 2006), chapter 2.

31 *Hamas Election Manifesto for the Legislative Elections*, 25 January 2006, in A Tamimi, *Hamas: Unwritten Chapters* (Hurst & co, 2007), Appendix VI.

32 H Langbein, *Against All Hope: Resistance in the Nazi Concentration Camps 1938-1945* (Continuum, 1996), p51.

33 H Langbein, as above, p52.

34 D McAdam, S Tarrow and C Tilly, *Dynamics of Contention* (Cambridge University Press, 2001).

35 S Jabr, as above.

36 N Hijab, 'More than One S in Resistance', *Agency Global*, 10 August 2009, www.agenceglobal.com/Article.asp?Id=2095 (accessed 24 Oct 2009).

37 Yitzhak Rabin quoted in P Marshall, *Intifada: Zionism, Imperialism and Palestinian Resistance* (Bookmarks, 1989), p13.

38 P Marshall, as above, pp150-151.

39 *Palestine Monitor*, 'Non-Violent Resistance In Palestine', www.palestinemonitor.org/spip/spip.php?article1081 (accessed 23 Oct 2009).

40 T Swedenburg, *Memories of Revolt: The 1936-1939 Rebellion and the Palestinian National Past* (Arkansas Universty Press, 2003).

41 *Palestine Monitor*, 'Meet Bilín: A Village Dedicated to Stopping the Wall', 14 March 2009, palestinemonitor.org/spip/spip.php?article866 (accessed 24 Oct 2009).

Marx, *Contribution to the Critique of Hegel's Philosophy of Right* (1843) in R C Tucker (ed), *The Marx-Engels Reader* (second edition) (Norton, 1978), p54.

42 S Jabr, as above.

43 R Pedatzur, 'More than a Million Bullets', *Haaretz*, 29 June 2004, www.haaretz.com/ hasen/pages/ShArt.jhtml?itemNo=444992 (accessed 17 November 2009).

44 S Jabr, as above.

45 E Said, 'Foreword: The Meaning of Rachel Corrie', in R Sandercock et al (eds), *Peace Under Fire* (Verso, 2004), pviv.

Chapter 7

And so it goes on...

As we noted at the beginning of the book a number of our themes reflected the topics and issues raised by the young people we spoke to. They often led and we would probe. It was no accident that they wanted us to know about the experiences of their everyday life, for this was where they perceived there was the most ignorance about their situation, especially in the West; for them this was an area distorted by anti-Arab racism. The fact that they felt the need to assert their humanity, to show how their dreams were no different from those of young people the world over and how their childhoods are robbed by occupation was in no small measure a result of their refusal to be seen solely through a racist lens, which portrays Palestinians as having little respect for their own lives and an intrinsic hatred for the Israelis.

We noted earlier that despite the ongoing horrors of the occupation many young people insisted that they were not anti-Jewish but anti-Zionist, and in fact most Palestinians see the only viable future as one where they and Israeli Jews can live and work together – albeit in a radically different state formation, one that is secular and democratic, rather than exclusivist and "Jewish".

Given that young people's main contact with Israelis in the West Bank is either with soldiers or with settlers this stance is quite remarkable. For some, such as Manal and her younger brother, it was a matter of incomprehension that human beings could behave so cruelly and violently towards other humans. It was their inhumanity which she emphasised when she told us of their experiences of settlers. Just to be a Palestinian seems enough to provoke their violence.

So many times we were asked in our discussions, is it possible to make peace with a people who don't see you as fellow humans deserving the same respect and consideration? "We are the ones without a partner for peace, not the Israelis," we were told in Nablus in 2008. For these university students, their day-to-day experiences of Israelis, whether soldiers or settlers, were of a people who treated and perceived them as worse than animals. Thus they were clear: there needed to be a fundamental shift in attitude towards them as an Arab people if there was to be any prospect for peace. For all the young people we met – exemplified by many of the testimonies on the checkpoints – this deeply rooted racism towards them is one of the principal barriers to any form of reconciliation. But there are also other obstacles and shadows that lie across a future path to peace.

For the entire period covered by this book, the situation in the West Bank deteriorated.[1] Unemployment and poverty deepened, affecting disproportionately those who lost land and livelihoods to the ever greater development of the Wall, the expansion of settlements and the network of Israeli-only roads which simultaneously links the settlers to Israel and fragments and cantonises the land of the Palestinians in the West Bank.[2] These physical facts on the ground, involving massive state investments which are heavily subsidised by the US, are evidence enough that the Israelis have no intention of seeing a viable Palestinian state.

What was emerging before our eyes as we revisited these occupied territories was a landscape increasingly dominated by settlements, large and small, usually on the high ground, and the squeezing of the Palestinian population into ever smaller areas in and around the larger cities and towns with tight restrictions on their ability to develop, build or expand. Even in Area A towns and cities where the PA has most control, the suffocating nature of Israeli restrictions on land use and development leaves the Palestinians in the administration virtually powerless. The example from Tulkarm where Palestine health workers were unable to do anything in the face of daily poisoning from Israeli waste and factories is common across the West Bank.

Settlers – or, as one of the young students from Hebron rightly insisted, "the colonists" – figured more and more in the lives of West Bank people over the period of our visits. Settlers rarely came into Palestinian towns and cities, with the crucial exceptions of Hebron and East Jerusalem. But all over the West Bank, settlers and settlements were casting an ever longer and darker shadow. Any journey between towns and villages takes one past settlements whose security barriers, lights, observation posts and cameras make powerful statements both about the alienation of these communities from their immediate environment and their intent, at least in the larger settlements, to remain.

One thing that makes settlers so threatening to Palestinians is their tendency to unprovoked violence. We heard many testimonies to this effect: accounts of completely random drive-by shootings of innocent bystanders, and Palestinians attacked with stones and batons as they go to their olive trees close to settlements.[5] There are enough of these incidents for most Palestinians to be fearful of all settlers, especially young male adults many of whom seem to relish the Uzi sub machine gun round their neck and a machine pistol in their belt. What made them especially ominous was their almost total freedom to harass, attack, injure and even kill Palestinians with impunity.

Action by the Israeli authorities to counter the violence of the settlers towards the local people has been and remains derisory.[6] It is clear that one of the principal roles of the IDF in the West Bank is to protect the settlers and the settlements. This intimate relationship is evident in many ways. Army bases are invariably located in the larger settlements, as are detention and interrogation centres as well as military courts. It was commonplace for us to see women from the settlements at the permanent checkpoints supplying the soldiers with drinks and homemade food. From their very origins, the IDF had conceived the settlements in the West Bank as constituting a first line defence/aggression system for Israel which in turn led to the formation of paramilitary units of settlers organically linked into the army and supplied with weapons, communication systems and military intelligence. As former prime minister Ariel Sharon conceived it, settlers and settlements were to be the eyes and ears of the occupier's surveillance of the West Bank with no Palestinian to ever be further than 500 metres away from such a gaze.

The relationship between the IDF and the settlers has however not always been easy, and as Zertal and Eldar have argued there were times before the outbreak of the Second Intifada in 2000 when some leaders of the IDF in the West Bank resented the time, resources and hassle involved in protecting settlements and their various outposts and saw them as inhibiting rather than extending their security capabilities.[8] From the settlers' point of view the IDF is a paradox. On the one hand it is their handmaiden in securing, developing and expanding and then protecting their settlements across the West Bank. But on the other, it is the instrument used by the state when (as

Settlements: the facts

▶ There are currently 121 Israeli colonies, often referred to as "settlements", and approximately 102 Israeli outposts built illegally on Palestinian land occupied militarily by Israel since 1967 (West Bank, East Jerusalem and the Golan Heights). All of these settlements and outposts are illegal under international law and have been condemned by numerous United Nations Security Council resolutions. Israeli outposts are considered illegal under Israeli law.

▶ These settlements and outposts are inhabited by a population of some 462,000 Israeli settlers. 191,000 Israelis are living in settlements around Jerusalem and a further 271,400 are further spread throughout the West Bank.[3] The settler population has grown consistently by between 4 and 6 percent per year over the last two decades, a much higher rate of growth than Israeli society as a whole (1.5 percent).

▶ Approximately 385,000 settlers in 80 settlements will be located between the Separation Wall and the Green Line if Israel holds to projected plans.

▶ In 2008, amidst the "settlement freeze" agreed upon in the Annapolis framework, tenders for new settlement building increased by 550 percent from 2007. Actual settlement construction has increased by 30 percent since the launching of the new round of peace talks. Settlement building around Jerusalem has increased by a factor of 38.

▶ A total of 9,000 further housing units have been approved in East Jerusalem, and approximately 2,600 new housing units are being built east of the Separation Wall, comprising 55 percent of all settlement construction activity.

▶ Settlements are built on less than 3 percent of the area of the West Bank. However, due to the extensive network of settler roads and restrictions on Palestinians accessing their own land, Israeli settlements dominate more than 40 percent of the West Bank.
Palestine Monitor, March 2010[4]

happens occasionally) it wishes to remove or prevent the establishment of a settlement.

However fractured and at times divided, the settlers have proven to be highly effective in securing considerable power and influence far in excess of their numbers. Nowhere is this better illustrated in the route taken by the Wall where we noted earlier that the settlers have succeeded in getting the Wall to incorporate all the principal West Bank settlements into the Israeli "side" and ensuring that many of the more outlying settlements are separately "walled" and tied by way of Israeli-only highways to the hinterland.

They have also succeeded in projecting themselves within Israel as the true descendants of the first Zionist pioneers

– heroically settling and reclaiming their historically given land in the face of considerable hardship and danger. Some groups of younger and even more militant settlers known as the "hilltop youth" have taken this even further by styling themselves on the cowboys of the US West, riding their horses with their rifles across their backs or in their saddle bags searching out new sites for settlements deep within the West Bank.

More menacing in the long term has been the settlers' clear policy of developing a presence within the IDF. In September 2010, *Ha'aretz* noted that 13 percent of all combat company commanders on active service in the IDF came from settlements, a fivefold overrepresentation based on their proportion in the general population of Israel. Commanders from the settlements are heavily represented in the elite Golani brigades, where 20 percent of company commanders live over the Green Line.[11] The growing power of the settlers within the IDF brings self-evident advantages but from the standpoint of the West Bank it makes the settlers more confident, better armed and less fettered.

Why do they shoot us?

In our school we have had attacks from the settlers who have shot at the school buildings. When this happens we are all very scared and the teachers keep us inside the buildings. Why do they shoot us? I can only say that it seems to me that the Israelis, whether soldiers or settlers, see all us Palestinians as the enemy and so they shoot. We don't need to do anything to make them shoot.
Jamal, Jenin, September 2006

This aspect perhaps helps explain our experience when we travelled from Tulkarm to Ramallah on a Saturday in September 2006. The trip took hours and involved negotiating six sets of checkpoints. At one of the random checkpoints in the middle of nowhere the soldier asked us, "Have you enjoyed your trip to Judea and Samaria?" This was an obvious provocation, for these are the Hebrew names for the West Bank. It also revealed the commitment of many IDF soldiers to Eretz Yisrael (a Greater Israel), and the view the West Bank is theirs and the settlements are legitimate Israeli outposts.

The settlers are not, however, a homogeneous group and can be roughly divided into two. The larger category comprises those who have moved to the settlements mainly for economic rather than ideological or political reasons: to take advantage of the subsidised housing, work opportunities and tax breaks that are provided by the Israeli state to encourage settlers. Connected by an increasing network of fast and exclusive highways, most of the larger and developed settlements are less than one hour's travel time from Tel Aviv, Jerusalem or the Mediterranean coast.[12] Many of them tend to be poorer Israelis, for most would prefer, if they could afford it, to live in the Israeli capital. The second group also benefits from all the subsidies and other incentives but is defined by its ideological commitment to Greater Israel (an Israel that stretches from Dan in Lebanon in the north down to Bersheeba in the south, and from the Mediterranean in the West to the Eastern Bank of the Jordanian river). These settlers cohere around biblical claims that they are God's chosen people who were granted the whole of what was mandated Palestine as their legitimate and rightful country.[13] For some, their commitment to Greater Israel means expanding their "re-occupation" to include parts of present-day Lebanon, Syria and Jordan.

For these settlers a settlement is the realisation of an ideological commitment to fulfil their destiny of colonising their god-given land, and although a minority among all settlers, they tend to be the most militant and violent. A particularly horrific example was Baruch Goldstein, a religious settler and a member of the ultra-nationalist sect called Kahk. He murdered 29 Palestinian worshippers in the Mosque of Abraham (also the Jewish Tomb of the Patriarchs) in Hebron in February 1994.

Yousef Ikhlayl, 17 years old, killed by settlers in Beit Umar, January 2011[7]

Over the period of our research, we heard more and more stories from young people about the violence and terrorism of the settlers. We never encountered or heard of a settlement which had reasonable relations with its Palestinian neighbours. Examples were numerous and various, including the general harassment of the Palestinians as they go about their daily business – going to school, minding their crops and animals, tending the olives – to the theft of water and land and the deliberate run-off of sewage onto Palestinian lands. In Hebron, the situation is particularly dire and is now internationally known for the extremism of the settlers who have, with almost total impunity, driven most of the Palestinians out of the centre of the old city. It has not gone unnoticed that no matter what outrages the settlers commit, and despite government claims that it will move the settlers, or at least control them, nothing has been done. Instead the settlers entrench themselves and flourish in Hebron, and throughout all the Occupied Territories protected by the IDF, sanctioned by the government and rarely protested by the West.

Arabs and Israelis

Of course, there are Israeli Jews who are not Zionists and who do not embrace the deeply-rooted racist views of Palestinians and other Arabs. Some actively intervene, such as the Women in Black who formed in Jerusalem in 1988 to protest against the violence of the IDF in the First Intifada by holding weekly vigils wearing black to mourn the dead. Others are to be found in a number of active human rights and solidarity groups opposing the construction of the Wall, monitoring checkpoints, fighting house demolitions and protesting against the growing discrimination against the Palestinian population living within Israel. Most of these groups believe Israel should withdraw to the 1967 Green Line, or perhaps even the borders of 1948, and their hostility is directed at the IDF and the settlers because they jeopardise the possibility of a "just peace".

There are a smaller number of young Jewish activists who have established links with Arabs within Israel itself and who are starting to pose larger questions about the very nature and presence of the Israeli state in the region – but they remain a tiny minority.

Many of the young people in the West Bank who we spoke to knew of the existence of such Israeli Jews and they were often cited as an illustration of why their problem was not with Jews but with Zionism. But in the main, the daily Palestinian experience of Israelis in the West Bank is that of a people who are overwhelmingly racist and cruel, who are committed to expansion and the colonisation of ever more land, and who are willing to use violence to achieve their end – the destruction of any vestige of Palestinian society.

Settlements and the Wall

As the barrier's [the Wall's] construction site nears their region, settlement councils have started applying as much political pressure as they can for the path to "loop around" and absorb them into the safer, western side they refer to as "Israel" even though it is in effect within the Occupied Territories... The logic behind the current frenzy in construction of outposts lies in the settlers' wish to influence the path of the barrier by seeding the terrain with "anchor points" around which the barrier should loop. Appearing to be wary of settlers' pressure, but actually using it as an excuse to perform what has been planned in advance, the government seeks to include as large a number of settlement points as possible and leave as few Palestinians as possible on the "Israeli" side of the barrier.

Against the Wall[9]

In so many ways the young people we met throughout the West Bank seem far in advance of their "leaders". Their utter disdain for the episodic "peace process" is just one example. Between 2006 and 2011 a number of "peace" initiatives were launched but came to be regarded with contempt, as round after round only deepened their losses. As such futile initiatives dragged on it was clear that the political and economic elites represented in the PA were drifting further and further away from the mass of the population. They were increasingly in quite different places both materially and ideologically.

We heard mounting criticism of the PA including, as we saw earlier, its failure to provide sufficient benefits to the poorest, its lack of vigour in protesting against the Wall, its involvement with some of the industrial zones, its failure to ensure that Palestinian workers did not have to resort to jobs in the settlements and, of course, its corruption. Outside of Ramallah many young people complained that the concentration of political power in that city had had adverse effects on the rest of the West Bank. In Nablus, Jenin, Tulkarm and Qalqilya we heard complaints of how the money stays in and around Ramallah with little getting elsewhere.

The depth of this chasm was also revealed in the PA's on-going commitment to a two-state solution; the vast majority of the young people we met were deeply sceptical about the viability of such an option despite the US and the EU continuing to assert that it was the only game in town. For those living in the West Bank such a strategy falls at every conceivable hurdle. Even if an Israeli government were willing and able to control the drive for further expansion from settlers, we met no one who believed that Israel would dismantle its massive colonial infrastructure and presence in the West Bank and no amount of tunnelling or bridge building can make a viable state out of fragmented cantons. No one

Hilltop youth

Groups of youngsters, some of them younger than 18, who have disengaged from the educational system and in most cases from their families, have settled on the hills on the margins of Jewish settlements and have created for themselves a closed, alternative subculture of violence, harassment of Palestinian neighbours, and confrontation with representatives of the state which they perceive as "foreign rule"… These young people see the state and its institutions as a nuisance at best and in many cases as an enemy…these hilltop youth perceive themselves as soldiers in the unending struggle that bends every other value not only to another dunam and another hill but to the establishment of their own state, which as far as they are concerned has not yet arisen.

Lords of the Land[10]

we met felt that Israel would negotiate away its control over the increasingly significant water resources located in the West Bank (and also the Golan Heights) given the country's dire shortage of water. And the reasons were simple. Israel was under no pressure and not only continues to break international law and conventions at will but is always rewarded and never punished.

The West Bank's greatest riches are its people. This is especially true of the young who make up the majority of the population. It is one of the most highly educated populations in the region. Alongside formal schooling there is the education of the people in resistance to the occupation. It is a powerful combination which gives rise to a young population that is astute, self-confident and able. Moreover it is a population that wants to do something, to serve its people and their cause. We heard so many young people tell us that their choice of university course was determined by what they thought would be useful to the country. But it was in the youth centres in the refugee camps that we witnessed most clearly what could be achieved and sustained by young people with virtually no income or resources other than a building commonly funded by an NGO. Art, drama, dance, film, sports, trips, parties and classes of many kinds catering for hundreds of children and young people were taking place day in and day out over years (and often in the face of IDF incursions and destruction) with young people in the lead.

The PA, on the contrary, seems more concerned with containing and constraining this energy and commitment and rarely initiates activity which seeks to mobilise or engage the mass of young people. It seemed a terrible waste to us that more wasn't being done to engage young people in the West Bank – not least because under the intolerable conditions of the occupation, a sense of common humanity and solidarity has emerged which is enormously precious and inspiring and provides an extraordinary base from which to plan and act; to consider both the possible and the impossible.

**Settlers and Israel:
The view from *Ha'aretz***

A state within a state has arisen in the territories; it is standing up to the country that created it and is overcoming it.

"The state today is the enemy of the people of Israel," some people defiantly said on Thursday in Hebron.

The government therefore has to decide who it fears most – the judges or the settlers. By default, it has actually decided. On Sunday the ministers will once again pound the cabinet table: We will under no circumstances come to terms with this, they will say as usual. We have decided to uproot the wild weeds [settlers in Hebron]. All who hear will laugh, or cry.

Not only did they not evacuate the disputed house, they did not even dream of evacuating it.[14]

Ha'aretz, 29 November 2008

The growing significance of the Palestinian Boycott Disinvestment and Sanctions (BDS) movement[15] and the actions against the Wall in Bil'in are but two recent examples of popular initiatives which have been treated with suspicion by the PA. Their anxiety over any popular gatherings which they don't directly control was demonstrated by the PA's break-up of attempts to show West Bank solidarity for the Egyptian people's uprising against the Mubarak regime during February 2011. In Ramallah the French-trained Special Palestine Police Force, which is one of the best trained and funded sections of the many-faceted PA security network, was used to break up the crowd. According to Dr Mamdouh al-Aker, the general commissioner of the Palestinian Independent Commission for Human Rights, there are two reasons for the PA's actions. The first is that, "due to the close relations with the Mubarak regime, the leadership is perplexed by expressions of support for the opponents of a friend. The second reason – when a regime is insufficiently democratic, it fears that popular demonstrations might spin out of control".[16]

And so it goes on…

While none we spoke to talked of a police state in the West Bank, the extraordinary number of people in the uniform of the various PA security services and their increasing interventions in daily life was troubling to many. It didn't feel as if they were being protected by these security services as the PA insists, but instead stifled and controlled. The range of security forces operating in the West Bank include the Presidential Guard, Preventive Security, Special Police Services, the National Security Force, Internal Security and General Intelligence. The security services of the PA consume over 30 percent of its budget and at 1:80 give the West Bank one of the world's highest security to civilian ratios. Their presence is everywhere in the West Bank, including in 2011 the operation of new Palestinian checkpoints into major cities such as Nablus. The almost entirely Western-funded Palestinian security system is also set to include 52 new prisons and new security and detention centres in eight of the main West Bank cities.[18] It is largely these growing resources from the West that account for the recent growth in the West Bank economy, so much lauded from afar as signs of hope.

The recently leaked Palestinian Papers (2011)[19] confirm what many already know concerning the deep involvement of Western governments and corporations in the training, funding and creation of the PA's security services. For the West it is one of the success stories of their intervention that the PA now has a security system that can increasingly police and manage their

Police state in the West Bank

All through the ten years I spent as a student in the US, I dreamed of returning to Palestine and contributing to a future Palestinian state. Coming from a modest background in Hebron and having had the privilege of an education at some of the best universities in America, I felt an obligation to help my people, always mindful that I had been more fortunate than friends and siblings who stayed behind.

Yet, from the moment I returned last September, I found a wall higher than the Israeli separation barrier blocking me from helping my Palestinian brothers and sisters. That wall was made up of America's Palestinian horses: Palestinian Authority Prime Minister Salaam Fayyad and President Mahmoud Abbas.

The moment I began publicly raising objections to the police state being formed in the West Bank, and the fear instilled in people who might dare to criticise the government, Fayyad's intelligence services started harassing me, to the point where I no longer felt safe in the West Bank. Even now that I have returned to the US, I still receive threatening phone calls for my criticism of Fayyad and Abbas. Several friends back home were arrested or called in for questioning by Palestinian intelligence officials over Facebook and Twitter activities that criticise Fayyad and Abbas.

Fadi Elsalameen, Al Jazeera[17]

own population at the behest of Israel. The Papers note the Israelis' growing satisfaction with these developments.[20]

The security services are now at the very core of the PA. They provide a much needed source of employment and hence patronage directly in the hands of PA leaders. But above all, as the Papers clearly tell, they have become the PA's principal tool for smashing its only political rival, Hamas, both in the West Bank and elsewhere. As one Hamas legislator noted, "The PA has succeeded more than the Israelis in crushing Hamas in the West Bank".[22] It has been estimated that up to 10,000 Hamas supporters have been arrested by the PA since 2007.

This is not to say that the PA does not present itself as the democratic representative of the Palestinian people. According to Jamal Zubeida, a council worker in Jenin:

We have more democracy than anywhere in the world. They use speakers to call us to come out to demonstrate; the Palestinian Authority even sends us buses to transport us to the protests. In Egypt, it's forbidden to demonstrate; here they send us buses. But they are not the right sort of protests.[23]

The right sort of protests are definitely discouraged for they would undoubtedly include a focus on the role and power of the PA as it increasingly takes over from the Israelis the day-to-day control and management of the Palestinian population.

We were in Nablus and Jenin during the last week of January 2011. Tunisia was in the throes of revolution, Cairo and Egypt were in the process of erupting and Al Jazeera was in the process of publishing the leaked Palestinian Papers. In both Nablus and Jenin the markets were open and busy and it seemed life was normal. But it was clear that our friends and the young workers in the market were following events in Tunisia and Egypt with great interest. Their sympathies were unconditionally with those fighting for freedom and justice.

The parallels with Egypt and Tunisia were not lost on Zubeida:

There were no demonstrations here in support of the Egyptian people, because our regime has ties to the Egyptian leadership, and it does not allow protests. But a new intifada could erupt here at any time. Voices are stifled in the West Bank, and they are stifled in Gaza; and the majority of the Palestinian people, the silent majority, know that what is happening in Egypt and Tunisia can happen here. Here, too, there are young people who studied in universities but have no work. There are many hungry people – we have that too. Here too there are people who are not allowed to speak out. Corrupt politicians – we have that too. And who opposes them? In Jenin there are 200,000 residents, and 500 policemen and soldiers. The ratio is the same in Hebron, Nablus and Ramallah. What would they do with hundreds of thousands of people rising up against them? The only question is when this will erupt.

Zubeida, Jenin, January 2011

Israel and the Security Services

The Dayton Battalion [so called after US General Dayton who until recently was responsible for the training of the PA's National Security Force] recruits have a single allegiance. Israel vets every recruit; the PA, the Jordanian government and a US database also approve each candidate. Israel notes the serial numbers of each and every weapon issued to Palestinian security forces – and maintains the right of veto on all equipment issued. Even the security forces' performance is determined by Israel: as one Western diplomat explained, the main criterion is Israeli satisfaction: "If the Israelis tell us that this is working well, we consider it a success".

Foreign Policy, January 2011[21]

The future is yet to be determined but a cause for optimism is that it looks increasingly likely that the overwhelming support for the rights of the Palestinians among the peoples throughout the region can no longer be ignored by their governments. Again, Zubeida represents the views of many Palestinians when he notes:

One of the reasons for our failure is the Arab regimes, which haven't helped us. We are not angry with the Arab people; our anger is aimed at its governments. These regimes never helped us. All they do is pressure Mahmoud Abbas to engage in another round of negotiations with Israel. They give him money, not to fight the occupation, but rather to pave roads. That will not take us anywhere. Now, after Tunisia and Egypt, we have hope regarding the Arab world. We always said: there is no war without Egypt, and there is no peace without Egypt. Perhaps Egypt and the Arab world will strengthen now, and begin to assist us. Iran has become stronger, as has Turkey, as well as China and India; it's only the Arab world that hasn't gotten stronger. Should it strengthen, should it become more democratic, it will help us.

Zubeida, Jenin, January 2011

We heard many voices telling us that the next intifada will not simply focus on Israel but will also confront the corruption and abuses of power that are embedded in the PA and the small but significant political and economic elite that currently prosper. The clamour of revolution spreading across the Arab world, fuelled by a passion for freedom, for justice and for dignity, has a deep resonance within the West Bank. This new great social movement of the second decade of the 21st century provides a vision of an alternative Middle East and, within that, of a future for Palestine. It is a vision that encapsulates the possibility that our friends the Amari family will be able to return to their land and their homes and live a life free from occupation.

Notes

1 "Real per capita income plunged from about $1,621 in 1999 to nearly $1,284 in 2008 while the per capita gross national product dived from nearly $1,959 to about $1,690. Real GNP per capita dipped from $1,707 to $1,108. 'Sector-wise, the agricultural sector which is a key component of the Palestinian economy and a major job provider has been severely hit because of the Israeli measures. In nominal terms, it recorded modest growth but real growth was negative mainly because of a sharp decline in olive production. Its contribution to the GDP shrank from about $294.5 million in 2007 to $235 million in 2008, depressing its share from 6.3 to 4.6 percent,' the [Arab League] report said. From 160,000 tonnes in 2007, olive output in the territories dived to only 34,000 tonnes in 2008 as Israel pushed ahead with its policy of land confiscation, uprooting of trees, devastation of farmlands, and closure of export outlets." N Kawach, 'Real per capita income of Palestine plunges', *Emirate Business*, 17 January 2010, www.business24-7.ae/Articles/2010/1/Pages/16012010/01172010_39da394d56624fcf9e617033e8d9d548.aspx (accessed 16 October 2010).

2 "All bypass roads have a 50-75m buffer zone on each side, where no construction is

allowed. These buffer zones have led to a great loss of agricultural and privately-owned Palestinian land. While illegally built on confiscated Palestinian land, these roads are forbidden for use by Palestinians. They consolidate Israel's creation of a system of Apartheid in the West Bank and fracture communities across Palestine. In August of 2008 there were 794 kilometers of bypass roads in the West Bank. To date it is unclear how many kilometers of road Israel is planning to build before it is finished." 'Israeli settlements', *Palestine Monitor* factsheet, updated 15 March 2010, www.palestinemonitor.org/spip/spip.php?article7 (accessed 19 September 2010).

3 "There are now more than 300,000 residents living in Jewish West Bank settlements, according to an Israel Defense Forces Civil Administration report covering the first half of 2009. As of June 30, the settlements had 304,569 residents, an increase of 2.3 percent since January. Most of the growth was in the most religious communities, including the ultra-Orthodox settlements. Modi'in Ilit gained 1,879 residents, a 4.5 percent increase. Beitar Ilit gained 1,074 residents, a 3.1 percent jump." C Levinson, 'Settlements', *Ha'aretz*, 27 July 2009, www.haaretz.com/hasen/spages/1103125.html (accessed 17 September 2010).

4 'Israeli settlements', *Palestine Monitor* factsheet, updated 15 March 2010, www.palestinemonitor.org/spip/spip.php?article7 (accessed 19 September 2010).

5 "Nablus – Ma'an – Israeli settlers set fire to 10 dunams of land in a Palestinian village near the West Bank city of Nablus on Monday evening, according to a Palestinian Authority official. Ghassan Doughus, the PA official charged with monitoring settler activity in the northern West Bank, said dozens of settlers from a settlement called Aliyah set fire to olive groves in the village of Labn. The official also said settlers assaulted farmers who were harvesting olives. It was unclear if anyone was significantly injured in the reported attack." This is typical. Rarely does a day pass in the West Bank when there are no such incidents. www.maannews.net/eng/ViewDetails.aspx?ID=233627 (accessed 30 Jan 2011).

6 Excellent data and accounts of settler violence can be found in Defence of Children International, Palestine Section, 'Under Attack: Settler Violence against Palestinian Children in the Occupied Palestinian Territory' (Ramallah, 2010); www.dci-pal.org/english/publ/research/Settler_violence_2010_report.pdf

7 From the website of Anarchists Against the Wall, 30 January 2011, www.awalls.org/ (accessed 5 February 2011).

8 I Zertal and K Eldar, *Lords of the Land* (Nation Books, 2007). See chapter 6 for more detail on the shifting relationships between settlers and the IDF. This book offers a fine analysis of the influential role of the settlers in the West Bank and on Israeli politics and their peculiar relationship to the Israeli state.

9 E Weizman, 'Hollow land: the barrier archipelago and the impossible politics of separation', in M Sorkin (ed), *Against The Wall* (New Press, 2005), p230.

10 I Zertal and K Eldar, as above, p44.

11 *Ha'aretz*, 'Army publication: Settlers heavily overrepresented among IDF commanders', 29 September 2010, www.haaretz.com/print-edition/news/army-publication-settlers-heavily-overrepresented-among-idf-commanders-1.316271 (accessed 30 September 2010).

12 As the following testimony illustrates, even for those who live on settlements primarily for material reasons, there is also an assumption that Palestinian land is

rightfully theirs: "at the settlement's large and unkempt trailer site, which is also built on private [Palestinian] land, a young newlywed couple is walking to the bus stop: 21 year old Aharon and his 19 year old wife, Elisheva. They speak nearly perfect Hebrew despite having grown up in the United States and having settled permanently in Israel just a few months ago, after Aharon completed his army service in the ultra-Orthodox Nahal unit. Now he is studying computers at Machon Lev in Jerusalem. Asked why they chose to live here of all places, they list three reasons: It's close to Jerusalem, it's cheap and it's in the territories. In that order. The couple pay their rent, NIS 550 a month, to the settlement secretariat. As new immigrants, they are still exempt from having to pay the arnona municipal tax. Aharon doesn't look upset when he hears that his trailer sits on private land. It doesn't really interest him. 'I don't care what the state says; the Torah says that the entire Land of Israel is ours'." Uri Blau, 'Secret Israeli database reveals full extent of illegal settlement', *Ha'aretz*, 30 January 2009, www.haaretz.com/hasen/spages/1060043.html (accessed 1 February 2010).

13 According to Yshar Beer among this ideologically driven group two-thirds are very religious, the rest traditionalist or even secular ultra-nationalists. All in all he says there are four subgroups: the most moderate "will not risk a major confrontation in the country to sustain their dream of a Greater Israel. Should there be a withdrawal from the West Bank, they'll kick up a fuss but submit to reasons of state. The pragmatists are more inclined to fight in order to preserve the maximum territory. These two groups are in the majority. Then there are the extremists, who find in *halakha* [religious law] the theological legitimation

for all acts of violence and take an active part in hunting down Arabs on the grounds of lawful self-defence. Finally, the lunatic fringe doesn't differentiate among the Palestinians, all of who are reduced to the status of Amaleck [the biblical archetype of the Hebrew's sworn enemy] who really has to be exterminated." Quoted in S Cypel, *Walled: Israeli Society at an Impasse* (Other Press, 2005), pp385-386.

14 Y Sarid, 'A state within a state has arisen in the territories', *Ha'aretz*, 29 November 2008.

15 For further details of the Global BDS movement see www.bdsmovement.net/

16 A Hass, 'Why isn't the PA supporting the Egypt uprising?', *Ha'aretz*, 3 February 2011.

17 F Elsalameen, 'US doubling down on Mid East horses', Al Jazeera (English), 7 February 2011, english.aljazeera.net/indepth/opinion/2011/02/20112710311546108.html (accessed 8 February 2011).

18 Details from the following: A Hass, 'Palestinian security suppressing West Bank fervor over Egypt protests; the European-trained Palestinian Special Police Force has become a leading security apparatus in the West Bank', *Ha'aretz* 7 February 2011; and A Byrne, 'Building a police state in Palestine', *Foreign Policy*, 18 January 2011, mideast.foreignpolicy.com/posts/2011/01/18/building_a_police_state_in_palestine (accessed 25 January 2011).

19 The Palestine Papers consist of nearly 1,700 files, thousands of pages of diplomatic correspondence detailing the inner workings of the Israeli-Palestinian peace process. These documents – memos, emails, maps, minutes from private meetings, accounts of high-level exchanges, strategy papers and even PowerPoint presentations – date from 1999 to 2010 and were leaked to Al Jazeera, which published them in January 2011. english.aljazeera.net/

Resources

We drew on a wide range of web-based resources which were generally much more informative than mainstream media channels, and most importantly included places where the voices of the Palestinians could be heard (in English). Below are listed just some of those which we found to be of value.

Furthermore, YouTube carries a number of clips of life in the West Bank, including from within the refugee camps. By typing in "Balata camp" for example, you can get to see many moving images.

Palestinian Voices

The Electronic Intifada: The Electronic Intifada (EI), found at electronicintifada.net, publishes news, commentary, analysis, and reference materials about the Israeli-Palestinian conflict from a Palestinian perspective. EI is the leading Palestinian portal for information about the Israeli-Palestinian conflict and its depiction in the media.

Palestine Monitor: The Palestine Monitor (palestinemonitor.org) has been recognised as a dynamic and independent voice of Palestinians living under occupation. Alongside rigorously researched news and updates, information, factsheets and regular political analysis, it also publishes first-hand eye-witness accounts of life in these occupied territories. These are the voices of ordinary Palestinians surviving under extraordinary circumstances.

The Palestine Information Centre: The Palestinian Information Centre (PIC) (www.palestine-info.co.uk) is an independent Palestinian organisation, established first in Arabic on 1 December 1997. The English language site was launched on 1 January 1998. PIC aims to promote awareness about Palestine, the Palestinians and the Palestinian issue and to balance the often distorted picture presented in the mainstream media.

Defence for Children International – Palestine Section: DCI-PS (www.dci-pal.org/english/) is an excellent source of material on Palestinian children and young people under occupation, including settler violence and imprisonment and torture.

BADIL: BADIL Resource Centre for Palestinian Residency and Refugee Rights is an independent, community-based non-profit organisation mandated to defend and promote the rights of Palestinian refugees (www.badil.org/en/about-badil). The website is full of useful information and reports.

Human rights and social justice

Addameer Prisoners Support and Human Rights Association is a Palestinian non-governmental civil institution which focuses on human rights issues (Addameer is Arabic for conscience). Established in 1992 by a group of activists interested in human rights, the centre's activities focus on offering support for Palestinian prisoners, advocating the rights of political prisoners, and working to end torture through monitoring, legal procedures and solidarity campaigns. Excellent website for information (www.addameer.org).

Machsom Watch: In existence since 2001, an organisation of peace activist Israeli women against the Israeli occupation of the territories and the systematic repression of the Palestinian nation. They call for Palestinian freedom of movement within their own territory and for an end to the occupation that destroys Palestinian society and inflicts grievous harm on Israeli society. Valuable reports on checkpoints and photographs. (www.machsomwatch.org/en).

B'Tselem The Israeli Information Centre for Human Rights in the Occupied Territories was established in 1989 by a group of academics, attorneys, journalists and Knesset members. It endeavours to document and educate the Israeli public and policymakers about human rights violations in the Occupied Territories, combat the phenomenon of denial prevalent among the Israeli public, and help create a human rights culture in Israel. It has published scores of reports covering most kinds of human rights violations that have occurred in the Occupied Territories. The reports have dealt, for example, with torture, fatal shootings by security forces, restrictions on movement, expropriation of land and discrimination in planning and building in East Jerusalem, administrative detention and settler violence. (www.btselem.org/English/About_BTselem/Index.asp).

If Americans Knew: This is an independent research and information-dissemination institute, with particular focus on the Israeli-Palestinian conflict, US foreign policy regarding the Middle East, and media coverage of this issue. Specifically, the organisation's objective is to provide information that is to a large degree missing from US press coverage of this critical region. (www.ifamericansknew.org/new.html).

Further reading

John Berger, *Holding Everything Dear: Dispatches on Resistance and Survival* (Verso, 2007).

Roane Carey (ed), *The New Intifada: Resisting Israel's Apartheid* (Verso, 2001).

Noam Chomsky, *The Fateful Triangle* (Pluto Press, 1999).

Jeff Halper, *An Israeli in Palestine* (Pluto Press, 2008).

Tikva Honig-Parnass and Toufic Haddad (eds), *Between the Lines* (Haymarket, 2007).

Saree Makdisi, *Palestine Inside Out* (W W Norton, 2008).

Ilan Pappé, *The Ethnic Cleansing of Palestine* (One World Publications, 2006).

John Rose, *Israel: The Hijack State* (Bookmarks, 1986).

Raja Shehadeh, *Palestinian Walks* (Profile Books, 2008).

Avi Shlaim, *The Iron Wall* (Penguin Books, 2000).

Eyal Weizman, *Hollow Land: Israel's Architecture of Occupation* (Verso, 2007).

Idith Zertal and Akiva Eldar, *Lords of the Land: The War over Israel's Settlements in the Occupied Territories 1967-2007* (Nation Books, 2007).